The Center for South and Southeast Asia Studies of the University of California is the unifying organization for faculty members and students interested in South and Southeast Asia Studies, bringing together scholars from numerous disciplines. The Center's major aims are the development and support of research and language study. As part of this program the Center sponsors a publication series of books concerned with South and Southeast Asia. Manuscripts are considered from all campuses of the University of California as well as from any other individuals and institutions doing research in these areas.

---

# Language Conflict
# and National Development

*This volume is sponsored by the
Center for South and Southeast Asia Studies,
University of California, Berkeley*

# Language Conflict and National Development

## GROUP POLITICS AND NATIONAL LANGUAGE POLICY IN INDIA

*Jyotirindra Das Gupta*

UNIVERSITY OF CALIFORNIA PRESS

BERKELEY, LOS ANGELES, AND LONDON 1970

*University of California Press*
*Berkeley and Los Angeles, California*
*University of California Press, Ltd.*
*London, England*
*Copyright © 1970 by*
*The Regents of the University of California*
*Library of Congress Catalog Card Number: 75-94992*

ISBN: 978-0-520-30111-5  (pbk. : alk. paper)

*To My Parents*

# *Preface*

Political analysis of language problems of the developing nations is often marked by a presumption that language politics belongs to the realm of "uncivil" politics, which is invariably opposed to the logic of modern national development. This work attempts to show that such a presumption prevents us from appreciating the complex nature of language politics and its contribution to the process of national development. The purpose of this work is first to separate the complex phenomenon of language politics into its constituent elements and then to relate these elements to the concrete processes of policy formulation and implementation that are relevant to political integration and national development.

The substantive materials are drawn from the scene of Indian language politics. The focus is on the national language question with special reference to the formulation and implementation of national language policy. The evolution of language loyalties, their political expression through the medium of organized associations, the role of these associations in the policy processes, and the intended, as well as unintended, consequences of associational language politics on national development are discussed in detail. The data presented in this work were collected mainly in north India. Field work for this project was done in 1964 and 1967, and it included interviews with the leading members of the language associations, language agencies in the administrative departments, and other relevant institutions.

Work leading to this book began in 1961 under the supervision of John Gumperz and Ralph Retzlaff, both of whom have been invaluable guides ever since. I am greatly indebted to Sheldon Wolin for his comments on an earlier version. I would also like to express my appreciation to Ramashray Roy, of the Center for the Study of Developing Societies in Delhi, for his cooperation. Many other persons in India and in the United States have contributed to this research project. I am grateful to the Institute of International Studies and the Institute of Governmental Studies of the University of California, Berkeley, for their financial support of this project. I alone, of course, am responsible for any errors of fact or analysis. In my field work and in the preparation of this manuscript, I have exploited the labor, patience and training in political science of my wife, Rupasree.

Jyotirindra Das Gupta

*Berkeley, California*

# Contents

# *Tables*

# I

# *Language Conflict and National Development*

The high incidence of group conflict generated by segmental social divisions in some transitional political systems has given rise to a deep sense of despair in many quarters. These conflicts are usually related to the competing demands made on the national political authority on the basis of ethnic, religious, and linguistic loyalties. The tendency to treat these loyalties as inherently antinational is widespread. The stubborn persistence of these particularist loyalties has even persuaded many perceptive observers to point out that the destructive impact of such loyalties may drive the drama of development toward a tragic end.[1] Such an ominous overtone is especially noticeable in the scholarly works and popular commentaries devoted to the analysis of the Indian scene.

The implications of such trends of thought need some elaboration. Political development requires a rational ordering of goals and a conscious direction of the instruments fashioned for their achievement. A properly constituted national political authority is essential for the ordering, promotion, and achievement of such goals. The stronger the foundation of the national political

[1] For example, see Gunnar Myrdal, *Asian Drama*, vol. 1, chap. 3, esp. pp. 83–122 (paperback). Myrdal refers to the general uncertainty of outcome but his particular study is tilted in the dismal direction.

community the greater will be the effectiveness of the directing authority. The strength of the nation, according to this way of thinking, is supposed to vary inversely with the degree of conflict generated by subnational loyalties. If the strength of the nation is to be assured, the subnational loyalties must be dispensed with. The process of elimination may involve authoritarian suppression or democratic persuasion. The nature of the subnational loyalties is such that democratic methods and measures are likely to encourage them. Only strong-handed authoritarian measures seem to be capable of discouraging them. To that extent, a democratic system, according to this kind of reasoning, is inconsistent with national integration and orderly political development.

The generality of these implications and their particular applicability to the concrete Indian situation raises grave doubts about the prospects of achieving national and political development through democratic institutions and processes. It is surprising that many of the Western observers who believe in democratic principles have, nevertheless, readily conceded the futility of democratic operations for political development in transitional societies. They have been saying in effect that it is not possible to derive a valid theory of development from democratic principles and practice. In other words, according to this logic of despair, democracy does not admit of a theory of development.

The burden of this study is that the type of reasoning noted above is neither logically warranted nor empirically justified. In the first place, there is no reason to assume that subnational loyalties are necessarily inconsistent with national loyalty. Social divisions are not automatically translated into political cleavages. Even when some of them are politically translated, there may be a wide variation in their direction, momentum, and consequences. Not all political cleavages are translated into open conflicts, and when they are, such conflicts may promote integration rather than disintegration. The extent to which political groups and group conflicts may be channeled into integrative behavior will depend on, among other things, the nature of the general decision-system in which they are made to operate. For example, if the political system in which they operate is based on a pluralist decision-system rather than an authoritarian decision-system, the probability of political integration will be higher. Integrative consequences of group conflict are likely to be greater in a political system where the distribution of cleavages is crosscutting and mutually offsetting, and where plural divisions are likely to be accommodated in aggregative social and political organizations. Finally, certain positive factors of cohesion may achieve an overarching dimension such that the scale of damaging conflict may not substantially disturb the foundations of the national community.

These points will be elaborated later. At this stage, it should be added that the empirical material required for the discussion of these points is derived from a study of language politics in India. The focus of this particular study is on the evolution of language loyalty in India and its political expression through voluntary associations devoted to the promotion of the interests of the respective language groups. The role of such language associations in the formulation and implementation of national language policy is described in detail for the purpose of analyzing a concrete decision-area and the nature of the decision-system involved. The linkage points between the language groups and other groups, their mutual interaction and selective aggregation in the pluralist framework, are described and analyzed. An attempt is made to trace the actual political consequences of such behavior on the national political community. Finally, an effort is made to relate the findings of the empirical investigation to the wider questions of democratic political development.

Before we discuss the substantive details of our investigation, we should explain some of the basic concepts and conceptual arrangements in particular theoretical contexts which we have utilized in the course of our study. This will enable us to define our terms precisely and to place them in the context of the particular framework of analysis which we propose to use.

## Political Modernization

Most definitions of modernization are essentially enumerative. They indicate a selective list of conditions derived from model societies as the basic components of modernization. Usually included in such lists are literacy, urbanization, per capita income, areal mobility, exposure to communication, industrialization, political participation, and so forth.[2] In many studies, the dimensions of modernization specifically related to the social, economic, and political areas are delineated separately. For our purpose such a separation is important to the extent that it enables us to stress the impact of political factors on the general processes of modernization. The importance of the role of a general, directive authority in designing and guiding the processes of modernization is commonly acknowledged—especially in the newly modernizing societies, where the forces of modernization are more externally induced than internally generated. Compared to these, there was less drama in the classical cases of modernization in the advanced Western societies, since the pace of change was slow, gradual, relatively unplanned, and generally free from high-pressure tensions.[3] Being pioneers, these societies were able to program the innovations in such a way that the strain generated by the sequence of changes could be adequately handled by the respective national authorities in society and politics. The evolutionary transition was also aided by the fact that the political consciousness and the institutional representation of the masses in such societies were substantially limited.

Modernization in new nations, while attempting to emulate the patterns of modern societies, is not historically favored by the possibility of following the sequences mentioned above. Contemporary modernization processes have their roots in exogen-

[2] See, for instance, Robert E. Ward and Dankwart A. Rustow, *Political Modernization in Japan and Turkey* (Princeton, N.J.: Princeton University Press, 1964), pp. 6–7, and Gabriel A. Almond and James S. Coleman, eds., *The Politics of Developing Areas*, pp. 52 ff.

[3] A good comparative account is presented in C. E. Black, *The Dynamics of Modernization* (New York: Harper and Row, 1966), chap. 4.

ous influences. These processes involve comprehensive attacks on traditional structures and follow a program of rapid transition, with sudden thrusts and dramatic reconstructions. Several dimensions of modernization are attempted simultaneously and rapid results are sought by cutting short a number of stages. At the same time the contemporary modernizers have to take into account the pressures of mass politics on the decisions of the national authorities. This implies that the production of values can no longer be separated from the pattern of distribution preferred by the politicized masses. Contemporary modernization, therefore, is much more complex and confronts problems of far greater magnitude than its counterpart processes of the classical European and American cases.[4]

The distinguishing feature of contemporary modernization is its attempt to achieve too many things in a short span of time. Such an enterprise can succeed only when there is adequate planning to coordinate all sectors of modernization into an integrated program. Planning at this level can be successfully undertaken only by the authority attending to the general needs of the society. This indicates the critical role that the national political authority is expected to play in assuring the success of modernization in our time. However, the existence of a competent national political authority cannot be taken for granted. Most new nations are based on fragile political communities, which in their turn cannot be expected to sustain strong political authorities. This raises the crucial question of how the task of building the nation can be synchronized with the task of using the national authority to accomplish modernization.

But how does one build a nation? The idea of nation-building as an architectural enterprise appears to overemphasize the role of deliberate design and the freedom of the political architects in impressing this design on social materials. It neglects the contributions of organismic evolution to the formation and growth of nations. The development of nations invariably depends on

[4] For details, see Samuel P. Huntington, *Political Order in Changing Societies*, pp. 93 ff.

various combinations of the architectural and the organismic processes.[5] A proper concept of national development, therefore, should emphasize the interaction between the act of deliberate building and the evolutionary growth of the social units leading to the successive stages of the integration of a nation. Such a concept of national development puts a premium on the treatment of the nation as a dynamic process of integrating a plurality of social groups into a common framework of identity and loyalty structured in a political community.

## Cohesion and Community

The use of the concept of community in the analysis of national development is not free from semantic ambiguities. Historically, it has been used to refer to a wide range of cohesive arrangements, including, for example, the classical notions of polis and cosmopolis, the Hebrew and the Christian notions of the community of believers, and a variety of idealistic, utopian, romantic, totalitarian, and pluralistic variations on this theme.[6] Such wide variations in the range of referents have made it difficult to use this term in contemporary discussions without specifying the particular meaning intended. In modern political science, the concept of the political community has been used in some cases as a "practical concept," and in others as an "analytical concept."[7] As a practical concept, its primary function is to guide action, to direct attitudes, and to state commitments. As an analytical concept, it is used to describe various possible cohesive arrangements. One popular analysis tends to identify the concept of political community with that of political system.[8] A care-

[5] This is elaborated by Karl Deutsch in *Nation-Building*, ed. Karl W. Deutsch and William J. Foltz, p. 3.

[6] For a discussion of the evolution of the notions of community, see Sheldon S. Wolin, *Politics and Vision*, and Robert A. Nisbet, *Community and Power* (New York: Oxford University Press, 1962).

[7] See J. Ladd, "The Concept of Community: A Logical Analysis," in *Community*, ed. Carl J. Friedrich (New York: Liberal Arts Press, 1959), p. 270. See also G. W. Blackwell, "Community Analysis," in *Approaches to the Study of Politics*, ed. R. Young (Evanston, Ill.: Northwestern University Press, 1958), pp. 305–317.

[8] In Karl Deutsch's works the central focus is on the way in which groups

ful attempt to separate these two concepts can be seen in the works of David Easton, who reserves the concept of political community "for the special purpose of identifying one particular aspect of a political system, as one of a number of basic political objects toward which support may be extended, or from which it may be withdrawn."[9] In Easton's use of the term political community, the focus is on a group of persons who, for one reason or another, are joined together in a common enterprise. Easton implies that the way in which a common enterprise is conducted may vary with regard to the degree and the kind of cohesion that is brought to bear on the working of the community. The political community is bound by the primary tie of a political division of labor. Apart from this primary tie there is always the possibility of various degrees of affective solidarity sustaining the political community. But the degree of the affective ties "will only be a possible characteristic of a political community, not an essential part of the meaning of the term."[10]

Though Easton's usage does not tie the concept of political community exclusively to national political communities, his analysis has an important bearing on the understanding of national development in heterogeneous societies.[11] It is worth noting that his usage is based on a clear distinction between the sociological concept of the social community and the political concept of political community. The sociological idea of community is based on a paired set of ideal types introduced by Ferdinand Tonnies.[12] These types refer to two fundamental

of people gradually form units for the peaceful solution of their problems. See his *Political Community at the International Level* (Garden City, N.Y.: Doubleday, 1954), p. 16. In E. B. Haas the focus is on the loyalty of the specific groups and individuals to their central political institutions. See *The Uniting of Europe* (Stanford: Stanford University Press, 1958), p. 5.

[9] David Easton, *A Systems Analysis of Political Life*, p. 176.

[10] *Ibid.*, p. 177.

[11] Easton identifies political systems at different levels of inclusiveness from parapolitical systems to international systems. See his *A Framework for Political Analysis*, pp. 23–58.

[12] See his *Gemeinschaft and Gesellschaft*, translated by C. P. Loomis under the title *Community and Society* (East Lansing, Michigan: Michigan State University Press, 1957). For a critical discussion, see Marion J. Levy, Jr.'s

forms of human will that underlie two forms of social relationship. These types of wills are characterized as natural and as rational wills. A social collectivity is characterized as a community insofar as its members think of the grouping as a gift of nature. This natural community is distinguished from the social collectivity that is based on rational will, in the sense that the individuals involved wish to attain through it a definite end and are willing to join hands for this purpose. Such a social collectivity is referred to as a society, in the special sense of the term envisaged by Tonnies. In fact, the paired terms community and society refer to two forms of social relationship which in reality are often found to coexist in various proportions.[18] Their analytical separation is intended to bring out sharply the instrumental and the affective ties governing social relations.

By separating the concept of political community from the sociological sense of community, we can keep the question of the character of cohesion relatively open. In this way we can conceive of a political community independent of the question of natural solidarity of the members of the common political enterprise. This is especially important in analyzing national development in the new states based on various kinds of segmentary diversity. Moreover, by postulating this conceptual framework, it is possible to arrive at a better understanding of the sequential development of various kinds of cohesion. Thus it is important to remember Easton's suggestion that "it is quite possible, . . . that in the formation of new societies and associated political systems, a sense of belonging together politically may normally follow rather than precede the emergence of a political community. If this is so, there could be little doubt that a political community is phenomenally independent, at least in its initiation, from the

analysis in H. Eckstein, ed., *Internal War* (New York: Free Press, 1964), pp. 233–266.

[18] The use of paired concepts to comprehend "natural" and "rational" forms of social relationship is not limited to the pair suggested by Tonnies. Witness, for example, the dualistic constructions suggested by Henry Maine in the form of status and contract societies, Durkheim's mechanical and organic solidarities, Howard Becker's sacred and secular societies, and Robert Redfield's folk and urban societies.

feelings of solidarity that are usually considered to be a major pre-condition."[14]

This implies that the political integration of a nation can be considered separately from social, cultural, and other forms of integration that are subsumed under the general category of national integration. This is not to deny that these questions are related, but rather to suggest that an analytical separation of these dimensions of integration may yield a better insight into their mutual relations.

*Political Integration*

In discussing the concrete processes of political integration, most studies have concentrated on the problems of reducing cleavage, discord, and parochial loyalties facing the new states. The burden of these studies is that the way to integration lies through forcible subordination of the parochial groups under authoritarian rule. For example, Rupert Emerson suggests that the achievement of ordered societies in the West "was in good part the product of the firm authoritarian rule which bridged the transition from the Middle Ages to the contemporary world."[15] Accordingly, he states that the prime requirement of the new states is not for more freedoms, but for discipline; not for opposition, but for a national consolidation; and in countries with tribal, racial, or religious hostilities, he claims, "the essential need is strong and unified management."[16] For further evidence of this mood among social scientists, one can turn to the analysis of David Apter, who singles out the effect of cultural strain as one of the most important determinants of the future of new nations.[17] According to him, this creates a problem for the leadership groups of the new nations. Their political leaders are rebels against tradition. Their goals of progress require social mobilization, which in turn requires an organizational revolution that offends the natural conservatism of the public. He con-

[14] David Easton, *Systems Analysis*, p. 188.
[15] Rupert Emerson, *From Empire to Nation*, p. 289.
[16] *Ibid.*, p. 290.
[17] See David E. Apter in *Comparative Politics*, ed. Harry Eckstein and David E. Apter, p. 649.

cludes that "autocracy is thus intrinsic to a development situation in which political entrepreneurship is the source of change and government its director."[18] Similarly, turning more specifically to national development in India, commentators, both Indian and Western, have stated that the cost of the survival of the nation may very well result in a succession of stresses and strains, leading to a situation which is "certain to overwhelm free institutions."[19]

What is the basic source of these stresses and strains besetting national development in the new states? This source has usually been identified as the natural ties of the segmental groups to their own given order of existence. One study draws a sharp distinction between the natural ties and the civil ties, or as they have been called, the primordial order and the civil order,[20] partially reminiscent of the distinction made by some in political theory between the public realm and the realm of private and parochial attachments.[21] Specifically, primordial attachment has been described as

one that stems from the "givens"—or more precisely . . . the assumed "givens"—of social existence; immediate contiguity and kin connection mainly, but beyond them the givenness that stems from being born into a particular religious community, speaking a particular language, or even a particular dialect of a language, and following particular social practices. These congruities of blood, speech, custom and so on are seen to have an ineffable and, at times, overpowering cohesiveness in and of themselves.[22]

In contrast, the civil loyalties are revealed in classes, parties, and

---

[18] *Ibid.*, p. 654.

[19] Selig S. Harrison, *India: The Most Dangerous Decades*, p. 338.

[20] See, for example, Edward Shils, "Primordial, Personal, Sacred and Civil Ties," *British Journal of Sociology*, June 1957, pp. 130–145.

[21] For a discussion of the distinction between the private, the social, and the public realms, see Hannah Arendt, *The Human Condition* (Garden City, N.Y.: Doubleday, 1958), p. 24 ff. (paper). Also S. S. Wolin, *Politics and Vision*, p. 429.

[22] Clifford Geertz, "The Integrative Revolution, Primordial Sentiments and Civil Politics in the New States," in *Old Societies and New States*, ed. Clifford Geertz, p. 109.

so forth. The range and intensity of the threats posed by the civil loyalties are supposed to be considerably less than their primordial counterparts. As Geertz puts it, civil loyalties rarely threaten to undermine the nation itself, though they may challenge existing forms of government, whereas the primordial loyalties threaten partition, irredentism, or merger, and hence pose a new definition of the national domain.[23] This, as we shall see later, is a tenuous assumption.

Like all paired concepts, the primordial-civil dualism is only partially useful. It does not sensitize us to the complexity of these factors in reality. By looking at the origin of the social cleavage rather than examining it in the dynamic context of the social and political transformation, such a dualistic notion often tends to oversimplify the primordial in national development. So far as national development is concerned, the static distribution of the multiplicity of primordial groups is of less consequence than the dynamic processes of the political transformation of these groups through the existing political channels of negotiation, adjustment, and resolution of conflict.[24] Given this perspective of dynamic interaction, it may be more useful to assume that the political role of the multiple social groups cannot be automatically derived from their given bases of social existence.

In the transitional politics of national development of the new states, the social bases of the primordial groups themselves tend to change in significant ways. The source of such changes may be found in the political factors. The political impact of a primordial group depends to a large extent on how a hitherto unpoliticized group has transformed itself into a significant politicized group. In other words, social segmentation by itself does not tell us much about the patterning of the social groups' participation in politics and its consequences on political integration. The mode of participation depends on the definition of political interest of such groups, the style of their leadership, the nature of the political system in which the leaders act, and the methods of

[23] *Ibid.*, p. 111.
[24] See Karl W. Deutsch in *Nation-Building*, ed. Karl W. Deutsch and William J. Foltz, p. 6.

action which have been found in practice to gratify the demands of the conflict groups. There is no reason to assume in advance that primordial groups, because of their natural origin, would stick to naturally defined rigid interests. On the contrary, it is conceivable that political prudence of the leaders of the primordial groups may very well make their definition of group interest flexible and amenable to adjustment. This is more likely to be the case when in the distribution of segmental groups no single group can overwhelm others and many of the groups may cut across each other.[25]

In general, it may be said that social divisions are of consequence to the study of national development to the extent that they are manifested as political divisions.[26] It is possible to distinguish among various kinds and characteristics of political divisions.[27] Thus, political divisions may mean simply concrete policy disagreements. Or, political divisions may be related to cultural divergence of the social groups in a political community. A third type of political division may be related to segmental cleavage. In this case the divisions are not merely due to the different cultural orientations of the actors involved; they are in addition related to the actors' attachments to their segmental groups. In studying the political divisions of a country one has to know the extensiveness of the salient divisions. It is not enough to know how many types of divisions exist in a country. One has to find out the nature of the divisive issues and the target of divisive politics. For example, a simple disagreement on a specific governmental policy reflects a less extensive division than does an uncompromising political division, which may in certain

[25] For a specific account of the complexity of conflict arising from segmented group structure, see Richard D. Lambert, "Some Consequences of Segmentation in India," *Economic Development and Cultural Change* 12, no. 4 (July 1964): 416–424.

[26] It is important to note here that not all social divisions attain the form of political divisions.

[27] The following distinction of political divisions is treated in detail in Harry Eckstein, *Division and Cohesion in Democracy: a study of Norway*, pp. 33–36.

cases threaten the existence of the political community itself. The intensity of political division must also be taken into account. Political division in a country may be extensive, but it may not develop great intensity, owing to less affective involvement of the actors, to lesser degree of organization, or to many other factors. But in certain cases, the extensiveness and the intensity of division may coincide, and this cumulative effect when reinforced by violence may pose a greater threat to political community.

Thus it is important to recognize the complex variety of divisions, their variable characteristics, and the alternative possibilities of alignment of conflict-groups in order to assess their impact on political integration. Moreover, the divisions themselves have to be balanced against the factors of cohesion. Political cohesion is often thought to be the result of a relative lack of political divisions. Or it is sometimes suggested that political cohesion can exist despite divisions, if not because of political divisions.[28] In order to study contemporary problems of political integration the first of the possibilities of cohesion suggested above may not be very important, especially because of the nature of divisive materials involved in heterogeneous new states. But the two other possibilities of cohesion will be of great importance because of our assumption that political divisions do not necessarily hinder political integration. We are also assuming that even when these divisions take the form of concrete political conflicts, these conflicts may prove to be a factor of positive sociation leading to a possibility of integration.[29] But even if the conflicts are not moderated by their mutually crosscutting nature and even if they are not mutually balanced, there may be parallel

---

[28] See *ibid.*, p. 69.

[29] For a detailed treatment of conflict as a process of sociation, see Georg Simmel, *Conflict and the Web of Group Affiliations*, part 1, chap. 1 (paperback); Lewis Coser, *The Functions of Social Conflict*, esp. chap. 7 and 8 (paperback). See also Ralf Dahrendorf, *Class and Class Conflict in Industrial Society* (paperback), and Robert C. Angell, "The Sociology of Human Conflict," in *The Nature of Human Conflict*, ed. Elton B. McNeil, (Englewood Cliffs, N.J.: Prentice-Hall, 1965), pp. 91–115.

cohesive norms and institutions which may contribute to political integration.[30] It is in this context that the positive role of the political institutions of the community and a normative legitimation of certain overarching values may be important for political integration.[31]

At this stage, it is necessary to clarify what we mean by political integration. We have already pointed out that for us the concepts of political integration and national integration refer to two analytically separable categories. Political integration, for the purpose of this work, will be defined as the minimal cohesion necessary for the coordination of the political groups through the institutionalized procedures of the political community.[32] This minimal cohesion does not simply mean a lack of violence in the resolution of group conflict.[33] The institutionalization of group coordination through a pluralist decision-making system is of primary importance to the process of political integration that we will study.

*Language and National Development*

The impact that social divisions based on language have on political integration in multilingual new states may be appreciated better in the context noted above. Patterns of language division in multilingual societies vary widely. In order to comprehend a specific pattern, it is important to consider, among other things, the number of language groups, their relative size,

[30] See Lewis A. Coser, *Functions of Social Conflict,* pp. 72–80, and E. A. Ross, *Principles of Sociology* (New York: Century, 1920), pp. 164–165. See also S. M. Lipset, *Political Man,* pp. 76–82 (paperback).

[31] For one view concerning this point, see Gabriel A. Almond and Sidney Verba, *The Civic Culture,* pp. 490–493.

[32] For a detailed discussion of cohesion, see P. E. Jacob and H. Teune, in *The Integration of Political Communities,* ed. P. E. Jacob and J. V. Toscano (Philadelphia: Lippincott, 1964), p. 4 (paperback).

[33] For a positive evaluation of the role of nonviolence in this respect, see K. W. Deutsch et al., *Political Community in the North Atlantic Area* (Princeton: Princeton University Press, 1957), p. 5; and E. B. Haas, *Uniting of Europe* (n. 8 above), p. xv. For a negative view, see Herbert J. Spiro, "Comparative Politics: A Comprehensive Approach," *American Political Science Review* 56, no. 3 (September 1962): 589.

the degree of relatedness and distinction among them, variation in the standard languages and dialects, the differential literary tradition of the languages, the relation of language division to other social divisions, and the importance attributed to the language factor by the speech communities concerned.[34]

Language has been defined as the totality of utterances that can be made in a speech community.[35] In Bloomfield's analysis, language as a complex of communicative symbols is inextricably related to social activity. Of the media of communication, language is the most versatile. In analyzing linguistic phenomena within the wider context of politics and society, the role of language in the speech communities and the relationships among these communities in the social and political environments are usually emphasized. By a speech community we mean "any human aggregate characterized by regular and frequent interaction, by means of a shared body of verbal signs and set off from similar aggregates by significant differences in language use."[36] For social and political analysis, it may be convenient to distinguish the different elements that are subsumed under the category of language. Thus, one may speak of different standard *codes* (e.g., English, Chinese), *regional variants* within a single code (e.g., the casual conversational English of Boston), *social class variants* of a particular regional variant, *stylistic variants* related to levels of formality and so forth.[37] Most major languages have such internal variations revealed in the standard form and the dialectal divisions, and stratifying as well as stylistic variants. It is there-

[34] For an attempt to construct typologies of multilingual societies, see Heinz Kloss, "Types of Multilingual Communities: A Discussion of Ten Variables," *Sociological Inquiry* 36, no. 2 (Spring 1966): 135–145.

[35] See Leonard Bloomfield, "A Set of Postulates for the Science of Language," in *Language* 2 (1926): 153–156; this definition stresses the point that the sounds and grammatical patterns are always abstracted from social activity.

[36] John J. Gumperz, "The Speech Community," in *International Encyclopedia of the Social Sciences* (New York: Macmillan, 1968), 9:381. See also Leonard Bloomfield, *Language* (New York: Holt, 1933), for an early discussion of some of these points.

[37] See Introduction to *Readings in the Sociology of Language*, ed. J. A. Fishman, (The Hague: Mouton, 1968), p. 5.

fore important to locate the language centers and the leading groups which set the standard language and act as leading agents in relating the linguistic factors with the political community.[38]

People's love for their own language is as old as recorded history. But the political affirmation of language loyalty and the political manifestation of language rivalry have assumed salience in a relatively recent period of history. The invention of printing, the spread of education to the middle and lower classes, Humanism and the Reformation, and the increasing participation of the general population in national politics have been some of the decisive factors in the placing of a premium on language loyalty and its expression in the politics of nationalism.[39] These developments in the European scene gradually persuaded some Romantic thinkers to believe that language is the most important identifying characteristic of peoples and therefore it should be the obvious criterion of national political boundaries.[40] Modern scholars prefer to discount such simplistic notions, and they take into account the vast complexities in the relationship between language and political community.

Language is not a static factor. Although language loyalty has often been characterized as a primordial loyalty, when the dynamic development of language is considered, it will be found that language loyalty is a variable, dependent at times on important political factors. One author has aptly pointed out:

The linguistic divisions among the Romance languages today reflect the dynastic boundaries of the tenth to eighteenth centuries. The revival of Gaelic was the consequence, not the cause of Irish discontent with British rule. The Landsmaal movement in Norway emphasized the non-Danish elements of the vernacular to reinforce the earlier political separation from Denmark, and the attempt to "purify" Turkish from Arabic elements became official policy after military defeat had severed the Arab parts from the Turkish state.[41]

[38] See K. W. Deutsch, *Nationalism and Social Communication*, p. 43 (paperback).

[39] See Frederick Hertz, *Nationality in History and Politics* (London: Routledge, 1951), pp. 81–85.

[40] See *ibid.*, pp. 86–87, 353–361.

[41] D. A. Rustow, *Leadership in the Emerging Nations* (Washington, D.C.; Brookings Institution, 1964), pp. 20–21 (mimeo). For a detailed treatment,

The idea of a natural speech of a people occasionally proves to be extremely tenuous. Many of the ancestors of the people using French as their native tongue once spoke Latin or one of the Celtic or Teutonic languages, and many an ancestor of those who now speak English on both sides of the Atlantic once spoke very different languages. All modern languages can be traced to their respective origins, but as Boyd Shafer remarks, none sprang into being all at once, and in some ways all are medleys built upon older languages, which in turn are derived from still older languages.[42] The myth of a natural tongue is also undermined by the fact that often various conquerors and rulers have relied on force or threat of violence or material sanctions to impose languages upon peoples.

Both in Europe and elsewhere the transformation of traditional societies into modern political communities has been accompanied by corresponding linguistic modernization. Many political scholars have tended to overlook the phenomenon of linguistic modernization and have preferred to describe the linguistic scene primarily in terms of intergroup phenomena, neglecting at the same time the intragroup interactions and transformations. One important feature of the traditional societies is that they show extremes of internal linguistic diversity in the sense that, in such societies, administration, religious affairs, literary activity, and ordinary communication tend to be carried on in different languages. Thus, in a traditional society, classical or foreign languages may be employed for administration and religious affairs, whereas the local populations generally speak a variety of unofficial and sometimes unwritten languages or local dialects. Low literacy and the considerable efforts needed for language training tend to favor polarization of power in a small elite, and internal linguistic diversity symbolizes extremes of social and political stratification.[43] With the advancement

see his *A World of Nations* (Washington, D.C.: Brookings Institution, 1967), p. 48.

[42] Boyd C. Shafer, *Nationalism, Myth and Reality*, p. 49. See also Leon Dominian, *The Frontiers of Language and Nationality in Europe.*

[43] Cf. John J. Gumperz, "Linguistic Indices in the Study of Modernization," Berkeley: University of California, May 1964 (mimeo).

toward modernity, the gap between the literary languages and the popular native tongues tends to be reduced. Standardization of language advances, and with increasing literacy such standard languages become more accessible and the distance between the variants within the language gradually diminishes.

In Europe, the processes of linguistic modernization followed from about the eleventh to the nineteenth century, and similar processes can be detected in the contemporary modernizing stages of Asia and Africa. Karl Deutsch shows that, by the end of the eighteenth century, the classical languages of Europe had been replaced by thirty modern standard languages.[44] He detects two trends in such developments: the creation of new standard languages from a locally current dialect or from that of a neighboring city or from a commonly employed trade language, and the assimilation of other existing dialects or tribal languages and their replacement by the newly rising standard languages. Such processes were evidently facilitated and expedited by social mobilization and political transformation.[45] As more and more people broke away from the old ways of their relatively isolated existence and restructured themselves in new economic patterns, in dynamic status systems, and in participative political frameworks, they needed more efficient media of communication. Thus was the ground prepared for the emergence of standard languages and a decrease in the distance between the variants of the same language.

The exact process of the standardization of the vernacular languages differed widely depending on political situations, intel-

---

[44] K. W. Deutsch, "The Trend of European Nationalism—The Language Aspect," *American Political Science Review* 36, no. 3 (June 1942): 533–541.

[45] Social mobilization has been defined by Karl Deutsch as "the process in which major clusters of old social, economic, and psychological commitments are eroded or broken and people become available for new patterns of socialization and behavior." Karl W. Deutsch, "Social Mobilization and Political Development," *American Political Science Review* 55, no. 3 (September 1961): 494. See the comparable notion of fundamental democratization in Karl Mannheim, *Man and Society in an Age of Reconstruction* (New York: Harcourt, Brace, 1941), pp. 44 ff. The political dimensions of mobilization are discussed in J. P. Nettl, *Political Mobilization*; see especially chap. 5.

lectual initiatives, forms of national consciousness, and language loyalty in different parts of Europe. But one common feature that stands out is the positive role played by developing nationalism, which consciously promoted the standardization of the major vernacular languages in Europe.[46] The new standard languages destroyed the dominance of the classical languages, and in this process the linguistic unity of the European elite was sacrificed in favor of building a bridge of communication between the elite and the masses within each national political community.

## Language in the Developing Areas

If political factors have played an important role in the development of national languages in many areas of Europe—and with an extraordinary intensity between 1900 and 1937—they have assumed a still greater importance in the multilingual new states of Asia and Africa since the Second World War. The importance of language for the people of these states can be ascertained from the fact that language often serves as one of the most important symbols of identification and distinction.[47] However, the political importance of language varies to a certain extent with the differences in the multilingual pattern that can be discerned in these states. Roughly, the multilingual situation of these states can be classified into several broad patterns.[48] In the first place,

[46] See Einar Haugen, *Language Conflict and Language Planning*, esp. pp. 5–14. In this process, at times, leading individuals like Machiavelli and Luther played prominent roles. But their chief importance lay in the fact that they gave a necessary impetus to what was already moving. See Otto Jesperson, *Mankind, Nation and Individual from a Linguistic Point of View*, pp. 44–45 (paperback). Also, C. J. H. Hayes, *Essays on Nationalism*, pp. 31 ff; and Stanley Rundle, *Language as a Social and Political Factor in Europe*, pp. 13–16 and 47–50.

[47] It has been said that in these states language distinguishes one person from his neighbor, gives him access to his own cultural tradition, and often serves as the canonical representation of his religion. See W. H. Wriggins, "Impediments to Unity in New Nations: The Case of Ceylon," *American Political Science Review* 55, no. 2 (June 1961): 313–320.

[48] Our classification follows the one elaborated by D. A. Rustow in his *World of Nations*, pp. 51–55, cited above (n. 41). It is possible to have many other classificatory schemes. On the general problem of classifying multi-

a variety of closely related languages may coexist, with one of them being accorded the status of a lingua franca. This type of situation can be found in Indonesia. Or there may exist a number of languages not closely related, of which only one has a long literary tradition, such as can be found in Morocco, for example. Or there may be a variety of unrelated languages, no one of which can claim a long literary tradition. This is the situation in many parts of tropical Africa. Finally, there are situations where a variety of languages may exist, each with its substantial literary tradition. This situation can be found in India, Pakistan, Ceylon, and Malaysia. In the first and second types of situation, the multiplicity of languages is not likely to pose major political problems. In the third and fourth types, the lack of an assured dominance of a single language tends to generate language rivalry expressed in political forms.

Though language diversity has existed in these areas for a long time, only after the rise of political mobilization has it given rise to a political problem. In many of these areas, open language conflict became acute immediately following national independence. Under colonial regimes, the imposition of the colonial language as the dominant language often helped to keep these language rivalries latent, at least temporarily.[49] But after independence, the question of the replacement of colonial language by indigenous languages tended to bring language rivalries into the open, especially where the indigenous languages were claimed to be competent to replace colonial languages.[50] The question of replacing the alien language by a national language invariably became a matter of prestige, related as it is to the wider question of removing the symbols of former alien domination. But once the alien rulers were gone, it was important for the new rulers to balance the matter of prestige with

lingual situations, see William A. Stuart, "An Outline of Linguistic Typology for Describing Multilingualism" in *Study of the Role of Second Languages in Asia, Africa, and Latin America*, ed. Frank A. Rice, pp. 15–25.

[49] For a detailed discussion, see S. S. Harrison, *The Most Dangerous Decades*, p. 3.

[50] See Rupert Emerson, *From Empire to Nation*, p. 136.

the substantial interests of the major language groups within the multilingual new states.

The problem was further complicated by the fact that the national language question had to be considered in the perspective of the growth of literacy, the expansion of education, and the extension of communication that accompanied modernization. Once massive educational expansion is planned, it becomes almost impossible for these new states to educate vast numbers of people through the medium of one or more colonial languages. At this stage, it may seem to be inevitable to conduct the extension of education in the language of the people concerned.[51] In this context, the recommendation of a meeting of experts of UNESCO is worth noting. It points out that "the use of the mother tongue be extended to as late a stage in education as possible. In particular pupils should begin their schooling through the medium of the mother tongue, because they understand it best and because to begin their school life in the mother tongue will make the break between home and school as small as possible."[52]

It is true that the task of replacing the former colonial languages by national languages is not easy. In most cases, the latter have been generally too unprepared to allow an easy changeover. Moreover, in a multilingual new state the choice of one national language tends to generate intense language rivalry, especially in those situations where it is difficult to assess the dominance—qualitative and quantitative—of one single language. The choice of a national language involves so many political problems that convenience, rationality, and efficiency are not necessarily the decisive criteria. In this sense, the problems of language policy have to be considered more from the political perspective than from a predominantly technical viewpoint. The complexity of the political problems of national language policy may be indicated by a brief consideration of some concrete cases.

[51] See *ibid.*, p. 136.

[52] *The Use of Vernacular Languages in Education*, Paris, UNESCO, 1953, pp. 47–48. For a critique of the report, see W. E. Bull's review in *International Journal of American Linguistics* 21 no. 3 (July 1955): 288–294.

*Variations in National Language Policy*

The role of deliberate political efforts in shaping a national language and promoting its development becomes clear when one considers the evolution of the national language policy in Indonesia. Some two hundred and fifty languages and dialects grew up in Indonesia over the past centuries. Out of a population of nearly a hundred million, Javanese is spoken as the mother tongue by some forty million people.[53] Other languages, like Sudanese, Madurese, and Balinese, are spoken by numbers which do not effectively challenge the dominant position of Javanese. Yet, confronted by a question of choosing a national language, the Indonesian political elite created Bahasa Indonesia as the new national language and imposed it effectively on the heterogeneous population. This language is based on Malay, which is the native tongue of a small minority of the population (roughly six million). Several factors contributed to the choice of this new language and the success of its acceptance—some of which are unique to the Indonesian situation. Being an easy language to learn and containing few implications of social superiority—unlike Javanese—the case for Malay was a strong one. Since no competing regional language of major strength was elevated to a favored position, the ground for language rivalry was weakened. And when the Japanese landed in Indonesia in 1942, they immediately attempted to suppress the Dutch language—until then the official language—and for necessary communication they were obliged to use Malay only.[54] In this way Malay became the language of official use, public law, and educational establishments. This paved the way for the rising consciousness that Malay, or "the Indonesian language," was the symbol of national unity. Although as early as 1926 some nationalist leaders had been propagating the case for such a language as a symbol of

[53] See S. Takdir Alisjahbana, "The Indonesian Language—By-Product of Nationalism," *Pacific Affairs* 12 (1949): 388–392, and Ben Anderson, "The Languages of Indonesian Politics," *Indonesia*, no. 1 (April 1966): 89–116.
[54] See Takdir Alisjahbana, *Indonesian Language and Literature: Two Essays*, p. 29.

national integration, it was the brief Japanese occupation which gave it a unique impetus, and when the provisional constitution during the revolution raised "Indonesian" to the rank of official language, they were no longer announcing an objective—they were confirming a fact. Since the consolidation of new Indonesia the same official language has continued and has already made its mark as an interesting experiment in language planning carried out through political initiative and authority.

A contrasting picture of extreme linguistic variety and the consequent difficulty in replacing the colonial languages can be seen in Africa, south of the Sahara. In this part of Africa there are nearly eight hundred distinct tongues and innumerable dialects.[55] None of these is spoken by a significant majority in any political community. Where Swahili and Hausa are used widely, no more than 8 percent of the population is involved. Most of these languages have no written form, and only a few, like Swahili, Hausa, Yoruba, Luganda, may claim a limited literary tradition. Political deliberations at the parliamentary level are mostly conducted in foreign languages, whereas political dialogue away from the center is conducted in the indigenous languages. When in Northern Rhodesia indigenous languages had to be used in the parliamentary elections in 1962, six languages were used in the polling. Not even all the candidates understood the linguistic difficulties arising out of three different electoral rolls and the mass of linguistic hurdles inherent in such a situation.[56] In Ghana alone, for nearly six and a half million people, there are about a hundred tongues, of which, excepting Twi, Dagari, Ewe, and a few others, none is used by sizeable groups. Hausa is current as a lingua franca in some areas only. The only common language of expression used by the educated minority is English. Nearly the same situation prevails elsewhere in tropi-

[55] For general discussions on various aspects of language policy in Africa, see *Language in Africa*, ed. John Spencer, esp. chaps. 3, 8, and 12. See also the essays of William J. Samarin and Ruth E. Sutherlin in *Study of Second Languages*, ed. Frank A. Rice, pp. 54–78, and J. A. Fishman, C. A. Ferguson, and J. Das Gupta, eds., *Language Problems of Developing Nations, passim*.
[56] See Jacob Ornstein, "African Seeks a Common Language," *Review of Politics* 26, no. 2 (April 1964): 205–214.

cal Africa. As a result, the former colonial languages are still dominant in the sphere of politics.[57] However, the logic of national authenticity is likely to impel the leaders of the coming generations to elevate some of the vernaculars to literary and political status.

A more complicated and potentially more explosive linguistic situation can be observed in South Asia. The choice of a national language in India is complicated by the fact that no one language can claim an overwhelming dominance over the others. In addition, about ten languages that are regionally salient and numerically important have distinct literary heritages. This situation has some parallels in Pakistan, Ceylon, and, to take a case from another part of Asia, Malaysia. Linguistic and religious divisions, however, tend to coincide in the cases of Ceylon and Malaysia, while in India and Pakistan this is not always so—here liguistic allegiance very often cuts across religious groups. In Ceylon before independence, nearly 61 percent of the population spoke Sinhalese, while the nearest rival linguistic group was the Tamil-speaking group covering about 23 percent of the population. The majority of the former are Buddhists while that of the latter are Hindus. The Official Language Act of 1956 proclaimed Sinhalese to be the official language of Ceylon. The status of Sinhalese as the sole official language was resented by the supporters of English and more particularly by the Tamil speakers. The latter demanded special official recognition for their language, and this demand was sponsored by their own political party, the Federal party. The problem of language politics in Ceylon was complicated by the fact that around 1956, the linguistic, the religious, and the party cleavages were found to coincide. The party of composite nationalism, the United National party, was at that time extremely weakened by the bipolar crystallization of these cumulated cleavages. In 1958, the confrontation of these bipolar forces exploded into massive violence. It should be noted, however, that the cumulation of the cleavages did not prove to be permanent. Thus, in 1965 the United National party

[57] See Jacob Ornstein, "Patterns of Language Planning in the New States," *World Politics* 17, no. 1 (October 1964): 40–49.

was able to reassert its power by forming a coalition of interests cutting across the bipolar cleavages. It has since tried to reverse the extremes of Buddhist and Sinhalese policies and has found a workable measure of accommodation among the Sinhalese and the Tamil language interests.[58]

A complicating factor in the Ceylonese language rivalry lies in the fact that the Tamil speech community is culturally linked with its counterpart in South India. This linkage gives rise to a political suspicion on the part of the Sinhalese community concerning the political implications of extraterritorial cultural loyalty. A similar factor complicates the language politics in Malaysia. The population of the Federation of Malaya, according to the 1957 census report, was composed of Malays with a share of 50 percent, the Chinese with 37 percent, and the Indians with 12 percent. These communities are predominantly Malay, Chinese, and Tamil speaking. Each of these communities has its own distinctive culture and tradition. With a marginal majority, Malay nationalists are constantly haunted by a feeling that the allegiance of the Chinese and the Indians to a composite Malayan nationalism is not too strong. The cultural linkage of the Chinese and the Indians with China and India is perceived by the Malayas as being detrimental to the growth of Malaysian nationalism.[59]

[58] See Robert N. Kearney, *Communalism and Language in the Politics of Ceylon* (Durham, N. C.: Duke University Press, 1967) for a detailed analysis. For a general background of the problems of official language in Ceylon, see Howard Wriggins, *Ceylon: Dilemmas of a New Nation*, pp. 228–270, and his "Impediments to Unity in New Nations: The Case of Ceylon," pp. 313–320; for a historical account see B. H. Farmer, *Ceylon, A Divided Nation*, and E. F. C. Ludowyk, *The Modern History of Ceylon* (London: Widenfeld and Nicolson, 1966), esp. pp. 245ff. For language diversity, see W. A. Coates, "The Languages of Ceylon in 1946 and 1953," *University of Ceylon Review* 19, no. 1 (April 1961). For a perceptive account of violence connected with linguistic particularism, see Tarzie Vittachi, *Emergency '58* (London: Andre Deutsch, 1958). For a leading politician's account from the Sinhalese viewpoint see S. W. R. D. Bandarnaike, *Towards a New Era* (Colombo: Department of Information, Government of Ceylon, 1961), esp. pp. 359ff. For comparison, see S. J. Tambiah, "The Politics of Language in India and Ceylon," *Modern Asian Studies* 1, no. 3: 215–240.

[59] For a perceptive discussion of the origin and development of nationalism in Malaysia, see William R. Roff, *The Origins of Malaya Nationalism*

In 1957 the Constitution of the Federation of Malaya declared Malaya to be the national language and allowed the concurrent use of English in official transactions for ten years. In 1967 the Malaysian Parliament passed the National Language Act with the intention of implementing the changeover. The demand for Malay as the sole official language has always evoked strong resentment from the well-organized Chinese community. But language rivalry in Malaysia has been tempered considerably by the compromising attitudes of the leaders of the coalition—the Alliance party—who were more interested in putting up a joint front against Indonesia than in hardening language conflict at home. It is this external challenge joined with the internal politics of compromise that has taken the violent edge out of Malaysian language rivalry. The National Language Act of 1967 signifies an attempted symbolic gratification of the Malay language demands more than a frantic hardening of the official stand on language. In general, the official attitude to the non-Malay languages including English has been one more of persuasive adjustment than of deliberate suppression.[60]

Both in Ceylon and Malaysia, religious and language divisions generally tend to coincide. But in Pakistan language divisions cut across religious affiliations. Before the formation of Pakistan the leaders of the Pakistan movement used Urdu as a symbol of Muslim separatism. But the symbolic capability of Urdu as a factor of Muslim unity began to decline after the formation of Pakistan. However, the leaders of the new government of Pakistan failed to recognize the fact that linguistic division was in-

(New Haven: Yale University Press, 1967), esp. chap. 5 for the linguistic aspect of this development.

[60] For details up to 1960, see K. J. Ratnam, *Communalism and The Political Process in Malaya* (Kuala Lumpur: University of Malaya Press, 1965), pp. 126–141. For later developments, see Margaret Roff, "The Politics of Language in Malaya," *Asian Survey* 7, no. 5 (May 1967): 316–329. See also, R. B. Le Page, *The National Language Question*, esp. pp. 63–76; R. S. Milne, *Government and Politics in Malaysia* (Boston: Houghton Mifflin, 1967), pp. 239–242; C. Enloe, "Issues and Integration in Malaysia," *Pacific Affairs*, Fall 1968, 372–385; and Richard Noss, *Higher Education and Development in South-East Asia*, chap. 9. Comparable discussion on Indonesia is in chap. 7.

creasingly cutting into the religious cohesion of the Muslims of Pakistan. For instance, the symbolic capability of the Bengali and Pushto languages to unite the Bengalis and the Pathans respectively and to confer a sense of identity on them was not appreciated by these leaders during the earlier years of Pakistan's formation.[61] These leaders accordingly declared that Urdu alone would be the official language of Pakistan.[62] It should be noted that Bengali is spoken by the largest number of Pakistanis, whereas Urdu is the native speech of only about 4 percent of the total Pakistani population.[63]

Even in West Pakistan, Urdu cannot claim to be a major regional language. The greatest challenge to the Urdu policy of the central leadership came from the Bengali speakers. They initiated large-scale popular agitations in February 1952 in favor of making Bengali an official language in addition to Urdu. The result was violent suppression, which in its turn led to a wave of protest and indignation from all over East Pakistan.[64] Ultimately, the Bengali movement succeeded in its aim, and the Constituent Assembly of Pakistan recognized both Urdu and Bengali as official languages.

[61] For the leaders' attitudes, see Chaudhri Muhammad Ali, *The Emergence of Pakistan* (New York: Columbia University Press, 1967), pp. 364ff. For linguistic regionalism in Pakistan, see A. Tayyeb, *Pakistan: A Political Geography* (London: Oxford University Press, 1966), esp. pp. 175–187; and Khalid B. Sayeed, "Pathan Regionalism," *South Atlantic Quarterly* 63, no. 4 (Autumn 1964): 478–506.

[62] M. A. Jinnah, the founder of Pakistan, told an East Bengal audience in 1948: "Let me make it very clear to you that the State Language of Pakistan is going to be URDU and no other language. Anyone who tries to mislead you is really the enemy of Pakistan." Quoted in Keith Callard, *Pakistan*, p. 182. See also pp. 180ff. for a general background of the language debate in Pakistan.

[63] The percentage breakdown of population in 1961 in terms of language was Bengali (55.5), Punjabi (29.0), Urdu (3.7), Sindhi (5.5), Pushto (3.7); see *Census of Pakistan*, 1961, vol. 1. Pakistan, pp. iv–31. For a general discussion of the language composition of Pakistan, see Donald N. Wilber, *Pakistan, Its People, Its Society, Its Culture* (New Haven: HRAF Press, 1964), pp. 71–83.

[64] For a detailed background and history of the Bengali language agitation, see Hasan Hafizur Rahman, ed., *Ekushe February* (Decca: Punthipatra, 1965), esp. pp. 15–30, 209–232 (in Bengali).

Despite a series of changes in the constitutional and political arrangements in Pakistan, the decision regarding the official parity of two languages has continued without any change. Meanwhile, the leaders of East Pakistan, who had accepted the unique status of Urdu before the formation of Pakistan, have not shown any eagerness to popularize Urdu in East Pakistan. Various non-Urdu language communities in West Pakistan have shown a willingness to learn Urdu as a second language.[65] But the East Pakistanis have not reconciled themselves to such a policy. The linguistic distance between East and West Pakistan has therefore tended to increase.[66] However, all the leaders of Pakistan have shown a tendency to continue to use English as the operative language of official transaction. The first constitution of Pakistan (1956) had declared that English should be used for official purposes for twenty years. Subsequent changes in the regime have not disturbed the status of English. Because of the general reluctance of the leaders of Pakistan to dislodge English from official communications, the mutual linguistic incomprehensibility between Urdu and Bengali has not substantially affected national transactions.

In comparison with the language situations and the related political problems that we have discussed above, the corresponding Indian situation seems to be much more complex. In our discussion of the Indian language situation in subsequent chapters we will analyze in greater detail the pattern of language division, its extensiveness and intensity, and its relation to other social divisions in India. We will try to analyze the evolution of politicized language rivalry in the context of the general processes of modernization. In studying this evolution, the role of the organized language associations will be emphasized. At the same time, these associations will be studied in the general context of the development of interest-group politics in India. The na-

[65] The degree of willingness has varied, with the Pushto speakers as perhaps relatively the least willing.

[66] For a general discussion of the East-West conflict in Pakistan, see Khalid B. Sayeed, *The Political System of Pakistan*, chap. 8.

tional language policies of the nationalist and the separatist movements before independence will also engage our attention. The major emphasis of this study will be on the role of language associations in the formulation and implementation of the official language policies in independent India.

The problems of language planning and the impact of such planning on the national political life as well as on the social structure of the language communities will be analyzed. Language politics has usually been considered mainly at the level of intergroup rivalry. We will try to bring out the intragroup as well as the intergroup consequences of language planning and development. Finally, our purpose will be to relate the role of language politics to the broader questions of political integration and political development.[67] We will specifically consider the impact of associational language politics on the democratic modes of political integration. This will involve a study of the contribution of associational language politics to the institutionalization of the pluralistic decision-making system sustaining the political community.

It should be made clear that we will discuss primarily the language politics related to the national language policy-making processes. The questions of regional language politics will be

[67] For a general discussion of national integration, see for example, Karl W. Deutsch, "The Growth of Nations: Some Recurrent Patterns of Politican and Social Integration," *World Politics* 5, no. 2 (January 1953): 168–195; and Leonard Binder, "National Integration and Political Development," *American Political Science Review* 58, no. 3 (September 1964); 622–631. On the question of political integration, see Myron Weiner, "Political Integration and Political Development" in *Political Development and Social Change*, ed. J. L. Finkle and R. W. Gable, pp. 551–562. For a consistent defense of political integration by authoritarian means, see Claude Ake, "Political Integration and Political Stability," *World Politics* 19, no. 3 (April 1967): 486–499. For distinction between political development and modernization see S. P. Huntington, *Political Order in Changing Societies*, chap. 1; and F. W. Riggs, "The Theory of Political Development," in *Contemporary Political Analysis*, ed. J. G. Charlesworth, pp. 317–349. Huntington seems to measure political development in terms of institutionalization, which he would define by the adaptability, complexity, autonomy, and coherence of the organizations and procedures of the political system (p. 12). This notion is useful for our analysis of political development in India.

brought in only insofar as they are related to our primary concern. Hence, the problems of the linguistic reorganization of states will generally be left out of our account.[68] Because of the obvious importance of the politics of Hindi language policy, the major part of our materials will be drawn from North India, and in our discussion of the language associations the North Indian associations will occupy our major attention. In the course of analyzing our materials, this study will utilize the appropriate theoretical works developed in several fields, including comparative politics, political sociology, political theory, and sociolinguistics. The primary theoretical perspective of this study will be drawn from the corpus of contemporary political science.

[68] These have been discussed in Joan V. Bondurant, *Regionalism Versus Provincialism: A Study in the Problems of Indian National Unity* (Berkeley: Institute of International Studies, University of California, 1958). For a detailed case study of regional language politics in one area, see G. S. Singh, *Maratha Geo-Politics and the Indian Nation* (Bombay: Manaktalas, 1966).

# II

# *The Language Situation in India*

Scholarly interest in language in India is reflected in ancient literary and philosophical writings. Many such works have been credited with detailed linguistic observation, classification, and analysis in philological and philosophical terms.[1] None of these works, however, throws any light on the social consequences of the linguistic diversity in India. It is perhaps natural that the Indian literati have been traditionally more concerned with their ingroup communication than with intergroup communication.[2] For information about linguistic diversity in India one finds it more profitable to turn to early Muslim commentators.[3] Such information dates back to the fourteenth century. These observations were by no means systematic studies of the linguistic diversity existing at that time. They were mostly impression-

---

[1] For some contemporary Western evaluations of such works, see Otto Jespersen, *Language* (London: Allen and Unwin, 1922), p. 20, for a linguist's approach; A. L. Basham, *The Wonder That Was India*, rev. ed., (New York: Hawthorne Books, 1963), pp. 389 ff., for a historian's approach; and for a philosopher's approach, H. Nakamura, *Ways of Thinking of Eastern Peoples*, rev. trans. (Honolulu: East-West Center Press, 1964), pp. 60 ff. and *passim*.

[2] For a perceptive comment on the limited field of communication in which the traditional literati of India performed their function in ancient times, see Max Weber, *The Religion of India*, trans. H. H. Gerth and D. Martindale (Glencoe, Ill.: Free Press, 1960), pp. 137 ff.

[3] For instance, in Amir Khusrau and Abul Fazl. See G. A. Grierson, *Linguistic Survey of India*, vol. 1, part 1 (Calcutta: Government of India, Central Publication Branch, 1927), p. 1.

istic accounts of the multiplicity of speeches prevalent in India. Thus the accounts left by such commentaries give us little more than a rough, and often confusing, listing of the names of diverse languages.

A better inventory of information tends to emerge from the European commentators' efforts in the seventeenth century and later. In part this enterprise was due to the early European travelers' curiosity about communications. But to a large extent it was due to the commercial and religious needs of a new breed of men intent on exploring an exotic land of multiple speech-communities. A more systematic inquiry began when William Jones introduced Sanskrit as a serious object of comparative linguistic study. The efforts of William Jones and Franz Bopp opened up new channels of inquiry into Indian languages, their connection with the languages of Europe, and the relationship between the literary and the popular languages of India. Scholars working through the Asian Society, missionary organizations, and administrative institutions carried on this kind of inquiry to further success. During the nineteenth century linguistic controversies related to educational modernization produced useful information about the development of the Indian languages. The work which the defenders of classical languages, vernaculars, and English directed toward the question of the medium of instruction was of a high order, and it proved to be of considerable value for an understanding of some of the crucial aspects of the language situation in India.[4]

Systematic studies of the language situation in India, however, date back to 1881 when the recording of the mother tongue of individuals was undertaken by the Indian census of 1881. This was followed by the most detailed account of Indian languages and their sophisticated analysis, prepared by George Grierson in his monumental study published in nineteen volumes from 1903

[4] For a brief summary of these debates see S. N. Mukerji, *History of Education in India* (Baroda: Acharya Book Depot, 1966), pp. 30 ff. For documents relating to these debates see *Selections from Educational Records* (Calcutta: Superintendent Government Printing), part 1, 1781–1839, ed. H. Sharp (1920); part 2, 1840–1859, ed. J. A. Richey (1922); *Selections from Educational Records of the Government of India* (Delhi: National Archives), vol. 1 (1960), vol. 2 (1963).

to 1928.[5] The impact of this work is reflected in almost all subsequent studies on the language situation in India, including the first detailed tabulation of language data produced after independence by the Census of India in 1961.

Grierson's study discovered the existence of 179 languages and 544 dialects in undivided India. According to the Census of India in 1951, there were a total of 845 languages or dialects spoken in India. The 1961 Census of India mentions 1,652 "mother tongues," of which 103 were foreign mother-tongues. These are spoken by 439 million people inhabiting a country roughly the size of Europe without Russia, with an area of approximately 1,178,995 square miles. Of these 1,652 mother tongues, the 1961 census authorities found it difficult to classify 527 of them. The number of speakers involved in some cases is as small as two or even one.[6] In fact, 87 percent of the total Indian population has been classified by the census of 1961 as speakers of the fourteen major languages specified in the original Eighth Schedule of the Constitution of India, and English. The major literary languages in India are Assamese, Bengali, Gujarati, Hindi, Kannada, Kashmiri, Malayalam, Marathi, Nepali, Oriya, Punjabi, Sindhi, Tamil, Telugu, and Urdu, together with English and Sanskrit, which have a special place. Of these, English, Sindhi, and Nepali were not included in the original Eighth Schedule. Sindhi was included in 1967. The most numerous linguistic family in India is the Indo-Aryan, with 574 mother tongues and accounting for about 73 percent of the total population.[7] Then follows the Dravidian family, accounting for more than 24 percent of the Indian population and including 153 mother tongues, covering the four literary languages of South India.[8] Numerically less significant are the Tibeto-Chinese family and the Austric family of lan-

---

[5] G. A. Grierson *Linguistic Survey of India*, vol. 1, part 1.

[6] *Census of India, 1961*, vol. 1, India, part II-c(ii), Language Tables (Delhi: Manager of Publications, 1964), p. clxiii.

[7] The major languages in this category are: Assamese, Bengali, Oriya, Hindi, Urdu, Punjabi, Kashmiri, Gujarati, and Marathi. These cover the dominant literary languages of North, West, and East India.

[8] These four, dominant in South India, are Tamil, Telugu, Malayalam, and Kannada, which cover more than 95 percent of the entire population specified as belonging to the Dravidian linguistic family.

guages—the former covers 226 and the latter 65 mother tongues, as returned in the 1961 census.[9] Tables 1 and 2, on pages 46 and 47, provide breakdowns of the major tongues in 1961 and 1951.[10]

Before we attempt to analyze the linguistic diversity that is apparent from the data presented above, we should note some complexities in the very notion of linguistic diversity itself. Most political studies of multilingual politics have taken into account the number of speakers of particular languages as the basic datum. The percentages of the population referring to mother tongue, though important, do not reveal very much about the language situation and its effect on social communication. Detailed data regarding the number of bilinguals in the population, the degree of control over languages used in addition to the mother tongue, the relationship between such languages, and other such specifications are important markers of the language situation. It is more important, however, to gather materials on "when and under what circumstances each language is used and what the attitudes of the people are toward the two languages."[11] When we have such materials, it will be possible for us to evaluate the significance of the languages used in a multilingual situation.

The available data on bilingualism in India does not allow us to take into account all such dimensions of inquiry. The data we have, however, reveals some important features. One such feature is that although India is commonly referred to as multilingual because of the great diversity of languages—which is a fact—the people of India, in one important sense, are mostly monolingual. Thus, out of 439 million people, only 30 million, as revealed in the 1961 census, can be said to be bilingual, with the reservation that the actual number of persons having the ability to read, write, and speak two languages with fluency and efficiency is

[9] For classification by families, see *Census of India, 1961*, pp. clxv ff.

[10] The figure cited in table 2 for Hindi is not comparable to that of table 1. The same difficulty arises in the cases of Urdu, Punjabi, Kashmiri, and Hindustani.

[11] Charles A. Ferguson, "Background to Second Language Problems" in Frank A. Rice, ed., *Study of the Role of Second Languages in Asia, Africa and Latin America*, p. 2.

even less.[12] The definition of bilingualism adopted by the 1961 census authorities is based on the knowledge a person has of any language, Indian or foreign, in addition to his mother tongue. In recording the second language, care was taken to exclude dialects of the same mother tongue.[13] The census procedure was obviously too simplified, for it does not enable us to inquire into the switching of codes between the literary language and the everyday spoken dialect that seems to be a universal feature in most sectors of Indian communication.[14] It is therefore worth noting that the various ranges of bilingualism within monolingual communities, and also the complexities of the social use of bilingualism, cannot be determined from the elementary data presented in the 1961 census.

Granting the limited nature of the census data, it is important to note that fewer than 7 percent of the total population know an Indian language other than their mother tongue. The choice of a second language reveals interesting patterns. Thus, although nearly 223,000 returned English as their mother tongue, more than eleven million people returned as knowing English. In fact, English is the most widely known second language in India, followed by Hindi, covering a little more than nine million second-language speakers. The comparison in terms of numbers is not an adequate indication of the relative importance of these two second languages in the social and political life in India. In most cases, Hindi or any other regional language in India is acquired and used as a second language only when facile communication is desirable in business or social transactions wherever such languages are predominant.[15] Since these languages are predominant only in certain areas in India, to that extent the use of Hindi as a second language, for example, tends to be regionally and transactionally limited. The use of English as a second language

[12] For data on bilingualism see *Census of India, 1961*, pp. 437–517.

[13] *Ibid.*, p. 437.

[14] See John J. Gumperz, "Language Problems in the Rural Development of North India," in *Journal of Asian Studies* 16, no. 2 (February 1957): 251–259.

[15] See Gerald Kelley, "The Status of Hindi as a Lingua Franca," in *Sociolinguistics*, ed. W. Bright, pp. 299–308.

is, in comparison, areally and transactionally much more extensive. Being the most important link language coordinating all the regions of India, the most important language of academic communication at higher levels, the language of national administration, and a window to the wider world, English as a second language provides a much wider range in area and transaction, as well as opportunity. In this sense, the circumstances in which English as a second language is used, and the popular attitudes to it, differ very widely from those governing the use of Hindi or any other second language in India.

## National and Official Language

Given the facts of the language situation in India, it appears that the principal languages to be reckoned with in a discussion of the political consequences of the language problem are some twelve regional languages which cover fairly specific areas of the country. Though most of these languages have affinity in varying degrees among themselves, a conspicuous rivalry for recognition at various levels of political and social life has characterized their interrelations in recent Indian history. In addition, their relationship to English poses another dimension of language rivalry in India. The framers of the Indian constitution, in their eagerness to have one official language for the entire nation, provided fresh grounds for intense rivalry among the language groups when they chose Hindi as the official language of India. This is not to say that language rivalry had its beginning in independent India. As we will see later, this rivalry is much older. The framing of the Indian constitution and the politics of its implementation provided, rather, a new framework for the organization of the old rivalry in new channels.

If the framers of the Constitution of India took care to choose one single "official language," the status of this category has not always come out clearly in the political and social deliberations in India. A good deal of semantic confusion has persisted from the very first demands for national language during the early phase of nationalist struggle. It is not surprising that such demands were basically related to nationalist aspirations colored by a simplicity of conviction characteristic of nationalist politics before independence. A lack of appreciation of the complexity governing the question of a national language in a multilingual society can be discerned in the speeches and writings of the leaders and intellectuals during this phase of Indian nationalism. These leaders rarely drew a distinction between the categories of common language, national language, and official language. They tended to use these as interchangeable categories. Gandhi, the most ardent proponent of a national language policy during the national movement, advocated the acceptance of Hindustani as the "common language." For Nehru, the same language appeared as the "all-India language." For C. Rajagopalachari, it became the "national language." For Gandhi the basic concern was to find a common symbol for India as a single nation. Nehru, however, perceived the all-India language as approximating an official language, as well as an interregional link language.[16] Though the distinction between these demands was significant, there was no attempt to clarify this significance. Perhaps this was of relatively less consequence as long as the political excitement of the negative phase of the national movement dominated the scene.

With the assumption of the responsiblity for formulating an official language of an independent nation, it became imperative to use such categories with a greater sense of caution. For analytical convenience, it may be suggested, then, an official language should imply an accepted language of administration as well as a means of communication between the government and the governed.[17] Such an official language may or may not be the same as the diplomatic language used for external relations. It is necessary to interpret the notion of a common language in a much wider sense than what is implied in the narrower category of official language. Common language should stand for a generally

[16] For the views of Gandhi, Nehru, Rajagopalachari, and others during the national movement, see Z. A. Ahmad, ed., *National Language for India*, pp. 34, 71, 201, and *passim*.

[17] This is how the UNESCO experts reporting on vernacular languages have defined official language. See *The Use of Vernacular Languages in Education*, p. 46.

comprehensible code of communication used throughout the nation. It is conceivable that the common language may not be co-extensive with the national language. In fact, in a multilingual society there may be a plurality of national languages. The criterion of a national language may lie in its being the natural speech of a major linguistic community for which the members of the group nurture a primordial affection.[18] Given these analytical distinctions,[19] it is possible to describe a political community where the official language may not be a common language, just as several national languages can exist and be recognized within such a political community without all or most of them being designated as official languages. In Switzerland, for example, German, French, Italian, and Romanche have been designated as national languages. Only the first three have the status of official languages of the federal system, and none of them can claim to be the common language of Switzerland. It is of course possible to create deliberately or to accept a common language in a multilingual society by means of a conscious language policy. Hebrew in Israel and Bahasa Indonesia in Indonesia are examples of such deliberate efforts to create a common language.

The provisions of the Indian constitution regarding language explicitly avoided the notion of common or national language. But the pronouncements of the Indian leaders have not avoided the terms. Many ministers have referred to Hindi as "the national language."[20] The official report of the Committee on Emotional Integration refers to all the fourteen languages listed in the original Eighth Schedule of the Constitution as having the "status of national languages,"[21] although the report of the Offi-

[18] Here the term primordial is used in the sense in which Edward Shils and Clifford Geertz distinguish between civil and primordial ties. See for instance, Clifford Geertz's essay in his *Old Societies and New States*, p. 109.

[19] I am assuming that these distinctions are useful for my analytical purpose.

[20] This is cited in the *Report of the Official Language Commission 1956* (New Delhi: Government of India Press, 1957), p. 22 (hereafter cited as *R.O.L.C.*).

[21] India, Ministry of Education, *Report of the Committee on Emotional Integration* (Delhi: Manager of Publications, 1962), p. 51.

cial Language Commission refers to those languages (excepting Sanskrit) as "regional languages."[22] Even as late as in 1963, Nehru, addressing the Indian Parliament, said that all the "thirteen or fourteen" languages of the Eighth Schedule of the Constitution are "national languages."[23] The confusion increases when the writers in Hindi normally refer to it as the "state language" (Rashtrabhasha), for the term state language may signify any or all of the following (a) merely a language used by a state on formal or ceremonial occasions; (b) a synonym for official language; (c) and, like state religion, a state language with a unique status.[24] Usually, the leaders of the Hindi areas mean by a state language the last two categories.

This confusion in terminology indicates an important feature of the language problem in India. From the very beginning of the spread of modern education in India the nationally oriented intellectuals have been groping for a means of communication among the various regions and language communities in India. Many of them looked to the past for a possible answer. The revival of interest in Sanskrit convinced some intellectuals in the nineteenth century that Sanskrit might be the answer. Most of these intellectuals, however, were persuaded of the limited usefulness of Sanskrit as a common medium of modern communication. They were aware that Sanskrit was historically the language of one section of the Hindu literati. The status of Sanskrit was mostly confined to higher literature and some of the religious practices of the Hindus. By the time of the Buddha the masses spoke languages that were referred to as Prakrits, which were supposed to be "low" forms.[25] The story of the development of

---

[22] *R.O.L.C.*, p. 22.

[23] See *Jawaharlal Nehru's Speeches*, 4:65. Also note the report of a speech of Sri K. B. Sahay, the then chief minister of Bihar, "Hindi, . . . spoken by a very large number of people in the country was and could alone be the national language" (*Amrita Bazar Patrika*, March 14, 1965).

[24] See A. S. Ayyub, "The National, State, Link and Official Language of India," *Mainstream* 3, 31 (April 3, 1965): 11.

[25] For a historical account, see P. J. Ruparel, "Historical Survey" in *Seminar*, no. 11 (July 1960), pp. 14–18. See also A. L. Basham, *Wonder that Was India*, pp. 393 ff.

the Indian languages from the early Prakrits to the developed form of the modern vernaculars is one of widespread regional variety. In addition, southern India developed its own languages of the Dravidian family. Except for the language of the literati, confined to a very small proportion of the population, there was no common language of the people, who were politically divided and culturally fragmented as well as socially confined to very restricted frontiers of communication. During the Muslim rule the official status of Persian failed to attain the status of a common language. During the British rule, for the first time in Indian history, one single language provided a medium of communication across the entire subcontinent. Thus, English "gradually came to supersede the Indian languages in the work, activities and thought processes of the higher intelligentsia of all the linguistic regions,"[26] and served as a link among all the educated people of the country.

## Introduction and Limitations of English

The history of the introduction of English dates back to the earlier decades of the nineteenth century. Initially it was associated with the evangelical zeal of the missionaries of various Christian denominations. The East India Company furthered this process in association with the British Parliament by trying to maintain schools for Indians.[27] The introduction of English as the medium of instruction was also facilitated by the conscious efforts of some Indian leaders who were eager to utilize English education in modernizing their countrymen.[28] The Charter Act of 1813 signified the beginning of the East India Company's re-

---

[26] *R.O.L.C.*, p. 31.

[27] See B. D. Basu, *History of Education in India Under the East India Company* (Calcutta: Modern Review, n.d.); N. N. Law, *Promotion of Learning in India by Early European Settlers* (London: Longmans, 1915); and especially G. B. Kanungo, *The Language Controversy in Indian Education* (Chicago: Comparative Education Center, University of Chicago, 1962), chap. 3.

[28] For a discussion of nonofficial Indian attempts to introduce English education, see R. C. Majumdar, *Glimpses of Bengal in the Nineteenth Century* (Calcutta: Firma K. L. Mukhopadhyay, 1961), pp. 31 ff. See also Ram Gopal, *Linguistic Affairs of India*, p. 7.

sponsibility for educating Indians. But the stated objectives of education at this point were vague. There was no planning for the realization of these objectives, and as a result the policy-making processes were marked by ad hoc measures and amateurish adjustments. This was expected, since the administrators of this time had neither the expertise nor the experience necessary to plan the role of the state in promoting education. State planning in education did not exist in England at this time, and the lack of a precedent at home evidently puzzled the officials in India.

During this confusing period of transition, the question of the medium of instruction raised intense controversies among the officials. One school of thought among the officials, with a strong base in Bengal, advocated the encouragement of oriental languages like Sanskrit and Arabic.[29] A second school, mainly based in Bombay, wanted to promote the modern Indian languages as the media of education.[30] The strongest group, however, was in favor of English as the language of instruction.[31] Indians themselves were undecided about these proposed alternatives. Conservative Indians were, of course, on the side of the classical oriental languages. The few modernized leaders emerging about this time were divided in their relative emphasis on English and the vernacular languages.

In Bengal, Rammohun Roy opposed the investment of state funds in oriental education. He wanted to see the state funds

[29] See, for example, H. T. Prinsep's notes in *Selections from Educational Records*, part 1, pp. 117–138 (n.4 above). For a general background, see David Kopf, "Orientalism and the Genesis of the Bengal Renaissance" (Ph.D. dissertation, University of Chicago, 1964).

[30] The minutes by Jervis and Shankarset are good samples. See *Selections from Educational Records*, part 2, pp. 11–14, 16–17 (n.4 above). Jagannath Shankarset wrote : "If our object is to diffuse knowledge and improve the minds of the natives of India as a people, it is my opinion that it must be done by imparting that knowledge to them in their own language. . . . I am far from wishing to discourage the study of English, but I believe it to be beyond the reach of the masses of people" (p. 17).

[31] The opinion of this group was embodied in its sharpest form in Macaulay's Minute of February 2, 1835 reproduced in *Selections from Educational Records*, part 1, pp. 107–117.

that were allocated for education used mainly in the promotion of modern higher education.[32] He formulated plans to establish educational institutions for the instruction of the youth in the science and literature of Europe.[33] This was the basis for the foundation of the Hindu College, later known as the Presidency College of Calcutta. Rammohun Roy himself started an English school in 1816 for the free instruction of students and collected funds for its maintenance. In a letter to Lord Amherst in 1823, Rammohun Roy pointed out that the Sanskrit system of education would keep the country in darkness. This letter was not the only reflection of the growing demand for Western education in English language. In 1833 a prominent newspaper of Calcutta regretted that the British government paid no heed to the views of the newspapers that demanded English education.[34] In principle, the demand for English education was not opposed to vernacular education. Rammohun Roy, for example, believed that English education would be an important step toward the modernization of Indian languages. His own work is impressive evidence for this point; in addition to being the pioneer of social reform, he is regarded as the father of modern Bengali prose.[35]

The language debate in the Presidency of Bombay followed another direction.[36] Here the predominant emphasis was on vernacular education. During Montstuart Elphinstone's administration (1819–1827), the investment of public funds for vernacular education in schools had shown encouraging results. The

[32] See S. C. Chakravarti, ed., *The Father of Modern India* (Calcutta; Rammohun Roy Centenary Committee, 1935), part 2, p. 44. For Roy's urge for English education, see S. D. Collet, *Life and Letters of Raja Rammohun Roy* (London: Mercury Press, 1900).

[33] See Nirmal Kumar Bose, *Modern Bengal* (Calcutta: Vidyodaya Library, 1959), pp. 47 ff.

[34] See *Sambad Sudhakar*, Calcutta, September 7, 1823 (in Bengali).

[35] For his contribution to the modernization of Bengali language, see Sisir Kumar Das, *Early Bengali Prose* (Calcutta: Bookland, 1966).

[36] This direction is traced in detail in Kenneth Ballhatchet, *Social Policy and Social Change in Western India, 1817–1830* (London: Oxford University Press, 1961), chap. 10, and John D. Windhausen, "The Vernaculars, 1835–1839: A Third Medium for Indian Education," in *Sociology of Education* 37, no. 3: 254–270.

efforts of the Bombay Native Education Society till 1840 lent an impressive support to the future prospect of vernacular education. It was this record which inspired a strong group of officials from different parts of India to defend vernacular media for mass education against classical oriental languages and English.

The logic of mass education, however, was of secondary importance to the rulers of the time. Macaulay's Minute of 1835—advocating English education and giving as the reason colonial superiority and moral authority—was closer to their limited perception of immediate political-administrative interest than anything else. His Minute, no wonder, was immediately accepted by Lord Bentinck. Protests from the vernacularists and the orientalists lingered on for a few years. The issue was apparently settled by Lord Auckland's Minute of 1839 in favor of English.[37] Auckland, to be sure, confirmed Macaulay's convictions, but at the same time he was careful to concede the need to maintain the existing facilities for oriental and vernacular instruction. Essentially, his policy was to clear the road to higher education through the medium of English. He believed in the theory of downward filtration of education from the upper to the lower classes, with the responsibility of the administration confined to elite education alone.[38] This simplistic notion failed to satisfy those who cared more for mass education. But they did not give up. In fact, the use of vernacular languages for school education continued to expand. The Woods Dispatch of 1854 could not afford to ignore this trend, and it recognized the role of English as well as vernacular media for schools. With the extension of education in general, the expansion of the use of Indian languages could no longer be resisted.

In 1837 English and Indian languages had already replaced Persian in the proceedings of the law courts—English in the higher and vernacular languages in the lower courts. Thus in both education and the law courts, language became a marker of

[37] For the text, see *Selections from Educational Records*, Part I, pp. 147–170.

[38] For a brief discussion of this notion, see S. Nurullah and J. P. Naik, *A Student's History of Education in India*, pp. 84–88.

two separate levels of social operation—the upper level reserved for English, the lower for the vernaculars. The policy of the administrators consciously promoted this association of English with status of privilege. At the same time many social reformers and nationalist leaders associated English with a promise of modernization and liberation. Both these trends converged to make English the most important medium of communication in the upper sector of national life.

The range of communication in English was always restricted to the educated people, and among them, too, for some specific occasions and purposes. During the initial stages of the introduction of English, the urge to accept English education was relatively higher among the Hindus than the Muslims. Even among those Indians who had accepted English education, the use of English was—and still is—confined to certain behavioral situations. In fact, for them, English provided only one code in what some linguists refer to as the "code matrix" in a specific community. The center of the individual's life, comprising home, family, and kindred, rarely saw the use of the English code for communication. English, therefore, was reserved for official, academic, and other relatively cosmopolitan behavioral situations. In addition, the type of English that was used in India also deserves notice. In the past, as well as today, the constant alternation between English and Indian codes by an Indian-educated speaker has resulted in the creation of an Indian English with its characteristic features. It has been said:

An Indian may speak English with near-native control; he may read it, write it, and lecture in it with great success. But when he uses English in India his speech will share many of the features of the other Indian codes, with which English alternates in the daily round of activities. Indian English will thus deviate considerably from the norms current among native speakers of English in the American Midwest. This kind of deviation represents not a failure to control English but a natural consequence of the social conditions in the immediate environment in which Indian English is spoken.[39]

[39] J. J. Gumperz, "Hindu-Punjabi Code-switching in Delhi," in *Proceed-*

To be sure, the limited range and depth of the acceptance of English in India made it a language of elite communication rather than a medium of mass communication. In the second decade of the twentieth century, the gradual entry of the masses into the national movement turned the leaders' attention to the question of finding a language that could serve as the symbol of the national movement. In 1934 the constitution of the Indian National Congress, for the first time, gave official recognition to Hindustani—a compromise between Hindi and Urdu—and installed it as the language of the proceedings of the Congress and its committees.[40] During the early decades of the twentieth century and later, however, Hindi, Hindustani, and Urdu struggled with each other to gain acceptance as national languages. During the deliberations of the Constituent Assembly of India, the conflict was narrowed to a choice between Hindi and Hindustani, with Hindi ultimately winning constitutional recognition as the official language of the Indian Union.

### The Cases for and against Hindi

The position of Hindi in the linguistic map of India has been compared to "the place of the German component in the Hapsburg Monarchy, which totalled 23 percent, largest single block in the Empire, but faced powerful Magyar, Slav and Rumanian rivals."[41] The 1951 census did not publish a separate figure for Hindi. Instead, it published a combined figure—for Hindi, Hindustani, Punjabi, and Urdu speakers—of 149 millions (42 percent of the Indian population). On most occasions this was publicized as the figure for Hindi.[42] The 1961 census puts the Hindi-speaking population at 133 millions (30 percent of the Indian population). Ranged against Hindi are such important Indian languages as Telugu (8.6 percent), Bengali (7.7 percent), Ma-

---

*ings of the Ninth International Congress of Linguists* (The Hague: Mouton, 1964), pp. 1116–1117.

[40] See N. V. Rajkumar, *Development of the Congress Constitution* (New Delhi: All India Congress Committee, 1949), pp. 70–85.

[41] Selig S. Harrison, *India: The Most Dangerous Decades*, p. 305.

[42] Even the *Report of the Official Language Commission* mentions Hindi as the mother tongue of 42 percent of the Indian population (p. 37).

TABLE I
MAJOR LANGUAGES IN INDIA, 1961

| Languages | Number of speakers | % of total population* |
|---|---|---|
| Hindi | 133,435,360 | 30.37 |
| Telugu | 37,668,132 | 8.57 |
| Bengali | 33,888,939 | 7.71 |
| Marathi | 33,286,771 | 7.57 |
| Tamil | 30,562,698 | 6.95 |
| Urdu | 23,323,518 | 5.31 |
| Gujarati | 20,314,464 | 4.62 |
| Kannada | 17,415,827 | 3.96 |
| Malayalam | 17,015,782 | 3.87 |
| Oriya | 15,719,398 | 3.57 |
| Punjabi | 10,950,826 | 2.49 |
| Assamese | 6,803,465 | 1.54 |
| Kashmiri | 1,956,115 | 0.44 |
| English | 222,781 | 0.05 |

SOURCE: *Census of India, 1961*, vol. 1, part II-c (ii), p. 106 for English and pp. 1–29 for others.
NOTE: Sanskrit was returned by 2,544 people only.
*Total population in 1961: 439,235,082. See *Census of India, Paper No. 1 of 1962*, 1961 Census (Delhi: Manager of Publications, 1962), p. v.

rathi (7.6 percent), and Tamil (7 percent) (see tables 1 and 2). Numerically, therefore, Hindi cannot expect to achieve an overwhelming dominance. A delicate balance of linguistic strength exists in India, with nine major regional languages pitted against Hindi. Technically, Hindi is both the official language and a regional language. As for status, it has been said that "Hindi falls short of the mark as a standard national language because it lacks sufficient prestige. . . . 'Hindi' . . . includes a plethora of . . . dialects, mostly spoken by illiterate peasants and often having less affinity with one another than with the neighboring dialects of other languages."[43] The speakers of many non-Hindi languages in India tend to rank Hindi, in terms of its literary value, comparatively lower than two or three other Indian languages.[44]

[43] Paul Friedrich, "Language and Politics in India," in *Daedalus*, Summer 1962, p. 550.
[44] Paul Friedrich reflects such opinions when he says: "Objective and weighty criteria tend to rank it [Hindi] below at least Sanskrit, Tamil and

TABLE 2
MAJOR LANGUAGES IN INDIA, 1951

| Languages | Number of speakers | % of total population* |
|---|---|---|
| Hindi, Urdu, Hindustani, Punjabi | 149,944,311 | 42.01 |
| Telugu | 32,999,916 | 9.24 |
| Bengali | 25,121,674 | 7.03 |
| Marathi | 27,049,522 | 7.57 |
| Tamil | 26,546,764 | 7.43 |
| Gujarati | 16,310,771 | 4.57 |
| Kannada | 14,471,764 | 4.05 |
| Malayalam | 13,380,109 | 3.69 |
| Oriya | 13,153,909 | 3.68 |
| Assamese | 4,988,226 | 1.39 |

SOURCE: Computed from *Census of India, Paper No. 1 of 1954* (Delhi: Manager of Publications, 1954).
NOTE: English was returned by 171,742 and Sanskrit by 555 persons only. Comparable figures for Kashmiri were not available. Separate figures for Hindi, Urdu, Hindustani and Punjabi were not issued, partly for the reason that the returns in some states were incorrect due to deliberate falsification of the replies to the language questions. Such difficulties were experienced mostly in the Punjab, Himachal Pradesh, Delhi, Pepsu, and Bilaspur areas where language rivalry became extremely intense and sometimes violent during census operations.
  * Total population in 1951: 356,879,394 (up to March 1, 1951, excluding Jammu and Kashmir and the tribal areas of Assam).

The defenders of Hindi argue that the "status of the official language is not an award for literary merit in a language." They point out that Hindi has been

adopted as the official language for the official business of the Union and for purposes of interstate communication, *not* because it is better developed than the other regional languages are; not because a greater or more varied wealth of literary output is available in it; nor because it has presently a large availability of books in the sciences and in different other branches of modern knowledge. It is chosen for performing the job of the official language medium on

Bengali. Certainly, most Indians having non-Hindi mother tongues would rank Hindi beneath at least one other Indian language as well as English" (*ibid.*, p. 552). Selig Harrison suggests that Hindi "cannot compare in literary development to at least three of its rivals, Bengali, Tamil, and Marathi" (*India: The Most Dangerous Decades*, p. 305).

pan-Indian levels because it happens to be understood and spoken, amongst the regional languages, by the largest number of people. . . . We are concerned merely with the prevalence of knowldge of the language in relation to the appropriate sectors of activity and the conclusive guidance relevant is the one to be obtained from the census figures.[45]

The report of the Official Language Commission makes it clear that for the advocates of Hindi as the official language, the reason of relative numbers, the sense of urgency about replacing English, and the feeling that only one language—"obviously Hindi" —can be the official language, have been the conclusively persuasive points of defense.[46]

During the national movement and through the initial years of independent India, the opponents of Hindi appeared to have generally agreed with the defenders of Hindi that in the interest of the increasing entry of the masses into the educational and the public fields of national life, the role of English had to be revised. More and more grounds were to be left open to the Indian languages. But many leaders of the non-Hindi groups were not prepared to tolerate the imposition of Hindi on them as the single official language of the Union. Some of them failed to see the reason for having only one language as the official language. If, it was argued, "Switzerland did not attempt . . . to force one of the languages as the official language upon the whole nation, though German holds a much greater proportionate position in Switzerland, than Hindi does in India,"[47] India too could afford to have more than one language declared official.

These critics also refer to Spain, Mexico, Belgium, Canada, the Union of South Africa, and other such states as feasible examples of states that did not need the imposition of one single

---

[45] *R.O.L.C.*, p. 37 (emphasis in the original).

[46] *Ibid.*, pp. 31–37, 401.

[47] Hans Kohn, "Language as a Political Issue," in *The Most Dangerous Decades: An Introduction* . . . , ed. S. S. Harrison, p. 74. For details about the Swiss experience, see Hans Kohn, *Nationalism and Liberty: The Swiss Example* (New York: Macmillan, 1956).

language.[48] Such critics were not in a great hurry to remove English from its official status or as the medium of advanced academic communication. For them the idea of English as the symbol of foreign domination had lost its relevance after independence, and they suggested that since India had accepted so many foreign elements in different aspects of her national life, she could also accept English. It is interesting that for some of them the increasing intensity of language rivalry has contributed to an increasing attachment for English.[49] It was further argued that the question of the stage of development of a language that aspires to be the official language is not an irrelevant one. Moreover, since Hindi is primarily a regional language, its official status is likely to favor the political, economic, social, cultural, and educational power of the Hindi elite. And, the question of a link language brings with it the question of whose link it is going to be. At the level of the relatively immobile rural life, the regional languages are expected to be adequate. At the urban level in South India this is also likely to be true.

Despite some popularity of a corrupt form of Hindi in the Indian urban life outside of South India, the need for a link language in the form of standard Hindi is not generally appreciated. For the educated community, English has served as the effective link language, with Sanskrit sometimes serving in very limited areas of ritual and academic communication. In none of these cases, the critics urge, can the role of Hindi be very significant in the near future.[50]

Neither English in elite communication nor the regional languages in mass communication are easy to displace. Finally, many in South India view Hindi as the symbol of North Indian domi-

---

[48] See, for example, Suniti Kumar Chatterjee, *Languages and Literatures of Modern India*, pp. 5–7.

[49] For example, see the changes in the attitudes of leaders like C. Rajagopalachari, who in 1928 tried his best to popularize Hindi as the future official language of India, suggested in 1956 that English and/or Hindi should be the official language, now advocates the case for English alone as the official language of the Union. See his "English for Unity," *Seminar*, no. 68 (April 1965); 18–26.

[50] See A. S. Ayyub, *op. cit.* (n.24 above), p. 12.

nation, just as the opponents of Hindi in all parts of India view the attempt to impose Hindi as an effort to facilitate the rise of five Hindi states as a "new Prussia" within the Indian Union.[51] Thus, the opponents of Hindi appear to build their case on the following grounds: a general suspicion regarding Hindi's present and future capability and its potential for being nationally accepted; fear about the dominance of the Hindi elite over the national life; reluctance to dislodge English from its role as a link language; and a concern for equal opportunities for the regional languages.

### Hindi as a Language

At this stage it may be useful to describe the various uses of the term Hindi. Standard literary Hindi is a relatively recent speech, barely a century and a half old. In Hindi literature, however, one encounters a mass of compositions in a variety of speeches: (1) the modern Hindi literature dating back to the middle of the nineteenth century; (2) literature in Braj-bhasha and Bundeli; (3) the Awadhi speech, with the related Bagheli and Chattisgarhi dialects; (4) a variety of Rajasthani dialects; (5) the lyrics and ballads in the Pahari speeches; (6) the Bihari speeches, Bhojpuri, Magahi, and Maithili; (7) sometimes a mixture of Punjabi and Western Hindi literature of devotional poetry; (8) Urdu literature is also claimed by the Hindi elite as a part of Hindi literature on the ground that Urdu is simply a style of Hindi; and (9) contemporary Hindi scholars claim the literature in Dakhni of South India composed in the various Western Hindi dialects, as part of Hindi literature.[52]

---

[51] See Hector Abhayavardhana, "Political Implications," *Seminar*, no. 11 (July 1960): 34.

[52] For details regarding such components, see Suniti Kumar Chatterjee, *Languages and Literatures of Modern India*, pp. 109–111. The author remarks: "If in Europe we could conceive of Portugese, Spanish, and Catalan ceasing to produce literature . . . and the speakers of all these accepting French as their main literary language, studying only French at school and reading and writing only French, and if on that basis we were to lump together the earlier (and even modern) literatures in all these languages and dialects as 'French' literature, then we would be in an analogous situation for 'Hindi' " (p. 111).

The emergence of Hindi is usually traced from the *Apabhramsa* works appearing between the eighth and twelfth centuries A.D.[53] The earliest examples of generic Hindi are usually confined to various North Indian languages written in Devanagari script. About the twelfth century A.D. Muslim settlers in North India tried to adopt this Hindi for some of their commercial and social communications. Some Muslim poets occasionally turned to Hindi dialects and incorporated them in their works for various reasons. Modern historians of Hindi sometimes claim Amir Khusrau to be the first eminent writer in emerging Hindi.[54] This view is challenged by some historians of Muslim culture, who tend to believe that Amir Khusrau, like some other Muslim poets, occasionally wrote Hindi verses for amusement and not for any serious purpose.[55] During the fifteenth century the poems of Kabir presented a mixed Hindi which reflected a combination of Braj, Kosali, and even Bhojpuri forms. Subsequently, the advent of Delhi "Hindustani" in the seventeenth century led to a conflict of dialects—especially in the Deccan where Dakhni style had flourished—and ultimately Delhi Hindustani won.[56]

Conscious attempts to write literature in Persianized Delhi Hindustani—"the speech of the exalted Court"—led to the emergence of Rekhta, which may be said to be the earliest form of the present-day Urdu-Hindustani poetical speech. In the beginning the Hindus of North India, satisfied with their Braj and Awadhi, remained indifferent to the "Muslimization" of the language, while the Muslim rulers patronized the latter. Gradually, however, the Hindus were also attracted to Urdu, and its influence spread significantly. The impact of Urdu was relatively stronger

[53] See B. N. Prasad in V. K. Narasimhan et al., *The Languages of India*, pp. 35 ff.

[54] Amir Khusrau (1253–1325), though of Turkish descent, was perhaps one of the first Indian Muslims who was proud of his Indian origin. See Aziz Ahmad, *Studies in Islamic Culture in the Indian Environment*, p. 115.

[55] For such a view, see *ibid.*, pp. 116–117, 241. According to him a great deal of Hindi poetry attributed to Amir Khusrau is spurious and written in dialect forms of much later periods.

[56] See Suniti Kumar Chatterji, *Indo-Aryan and Hindi*, pp. 202–208.

on those segments of Hindi population which came closer to the Muslim administration. By the end of the eighteenth century the standard Court speech gained more support. It became known as Khadi Boli, or the "standing language," while Braj, Awadhi, and other dialects came to be known as Padi Boli or the "fallen languages."

The ascendance of Urdu was due largely to the political patronage accorded to it by the Muslim rulers, dictated by their political, military, and administrative needs. In addition, the status of the Muslim writers and officials facilitated the spread of Urdu among some sections of the Hindus. The decline of the Muslim rule in India and the advent of British rule were accompanied by a corresponding decline of Persianized Urdu. During the early years of the foundation of British rule, Dr. J. B. Gilchrist of Fort William at Calcutta engaged a group of writers to write Hindustani prose.[57] This form of prose was channeled into two distinctly different styles: Hindi, purged as far as possible of Persian words, and Urdu, remaining as close as possible to a Persianized style. From this time onward, the difference between Hindi and Urdu became increasingly sharper. And yet the affinity between Hindi and Urdu cannot be overemphasized. It is now widely accepted that literary Hindi and Urdu are "two styles of the same language . . . both have the same inflectional system and a common core of basic vocabulary; they differ in the learned or abstract words used and in word order."[58] However, during the late nineteenth and the twentieth centuries many among the Hindi and Urdu elite have tended to exaggerate the difference between Hindi and Urdu because of the different scripts employed by these languages. Deliberate policies of Sanskritizing

[57] For J. B. Gilchrist's important role, see M. Atique Siddiqi, *Origins of Modern Hindustani Literature, Source Material: Gilchrist Letters* (Aligarh: Naya Kitab Ghar, 1963), especially pp. 17–42.

[58] J. J. Gumperz, "Language Problems in the Rural Development of North India" (n. 14 above) p. 252. On the evolution of the Hindi-Urdu differences, see for example, G. A. Grierson, *Linguistic Survey of India* (n.3 above), vol. 1, part 1, pp. 166 ff.; Suniti Kumar Chatterji, *Languages and the Linguistic Problem*; Ram Babu Saxena, *A History of Urdu Literature*; and S. S. Narula, *Scientific History of the Hindi Literature*.

Hindi and Persianizing Urdu have also tended to accentuate this difference.[59]

One interesting point, usually forgotten during the Hindi-Urdu controversy, is that Hindus of every class in the Hindi areas are now apt to refer to their own speech as Hindi, whether they speak a village dialect or the standard language, just as Muslims refer to their speech as Urdu, although to the listener there might be little difference between their speech and that of their Hindu neighbors. According to a linguist, a "formal analysis of at least one village dialect has shown that the differences between the speech of touchable and untouchable caste are much greater than those between that of Muslims and Hindus."[60] As current in the urban areas, the standard spoken Hindi is relatively uniform. The literary Hindi idiom is increasingly replacing the older literary idioms based on Braj, Awadhi, and Maithili, for instance. In the field of spoken language, however, those dialects are still very important and may be said to occupy "a somewhat intermediate stage between standard spoken Hindi and the local village speech, since they are spoken in relatively uniform form over a large area."[61] Even after improvement of communications, increasing mobility, education, and the impact of the media of mass communication, it is mostly the standard spoken Hindi, and not the literary idiom, that is spreading.

## The Hindi Region

In analyzing Indian politics many writers have used the notion of regionalism as an explanatory category. The Indian politicians themselves have found this term to be convenient for a variety of purposes. As a political notion, regionalism suffers from am-

[59] For examples of such controversies, see Yashpal, "Urdu: Hindi Writer's View," *National Herald*, January 2, 1952, and Raghupati Sahay Firaq, "Urdu Without Prejudice," *Hindustan Times Weekly*, October 11 and 18, 1959, and his "Friends and Not Foes Harming Hindi," *ibid.*, December 6, 1959. Also "Kya Hindi Bolechal Ko Bhasha Nahin Hai?" *Saptahik Hindustan*, (editorial), June 24, 1962, p. 3 (in Hindi).

[60] J. J. Gumperz, "Language Problems in the Rural Development of North India" (n.14 above), p. 253.

[61] *Ibid.*, pp. 253–254.

biguity. Broadly, regionalism refers to the tendency to assign
primacy to the region as a value in comparison with the nation
as a value. This tendency may be concretely expressed in cultural, linguistic, economic, political, and administrative terms.
These specific components may be combined in various proportions. The interests in each of these components may be com-
plementary or conflicting. There is no automatic harmony
among the specific components subsumed under the category
of regionalism.

Given these general considerations, the specific question of
Hindi regionalism assumes a clearer perspective. The primary
component of Hindi regionalism seems to be linguistic. Unlike
most states in the Indian federation, the political and the linguistic boundaries of the Hindi states do not concide, for the
Hindi area is divided among several states. The major Hindi
states are Uttar Pradesh, Madhya Pradesh, Bihar, Rajasthan, and
Haryana. All of them are situated in North and Central India.
Together they give the impression of being the largest single
bloc of states with Hindi as a common concern. When it comes
to political, economic, and administrative interests, they do not
necessarily present a common front. However, as long as the linguistic dimension of politics remains salient in India, the linguistic bond of such a large bloc of states will tend to give the
impression that the Hindi area represents the heartland of India.
The significance of this area in terms of physical area and population is immense. The largest states in India in terms of area and
population are included in the Hindi area, as shown in table 3.[62]

Uttar Pradesh, with 73 million people, is not only the most
populous Hindi state but also the major intellectual and political
center of Hindi, Urdu, and Hindustani. The contributions of
Uttar Pradesh to the development of the Indian National Congress, the Muslim League, and various other political movements have made it one of the most important centers of political
action in India. After independence and until the fourth general

---

[62] In this as well as in the subsequent tables, the bifurcation of Punjab
into Punjab and Haryana has not been taken into account because it took
place in 1966, long after the 1961 census.

TABLE 3
RANKING OF INDIAN STATES IN TERMS OF POPULATION AND AREA, 1961

| State | Rank in population | % of Union's population | % of Union's area | Rank in area |
|---|---|---|---|---|
| Uttar Pradesh* | 1 | 16.81 | 9.65 | 4 |
| Bihar* | 2 | 10.59 | 5.71 | 8 |
| Maharashtra | 3 | 9.02 | 10.08 | 3 |
| Andhra Pradesh | 4 | 8.20 | 9.03 | 5 |
| West Bengal | 5 | 7.96 | 2.87 | 13 |
| Madras | 6 | 7.68 | 4.27 | 10 |
| Madhya Pradesh* | 7 | 7.38 | 14.54 | 1 |
| Mysore | 8 | 5.38 | 6.30 | 6 |
| Gujarat | 9 | 4.70 | 6.14 | 7 |
| Punjab | 10 | 4.63 | 4.01 | 11 |
| Rajasthan* | 11 | 4.60 | 11.22 | 2 |
| Orissa | 12 | 4.00 | 5.11 | 9 |
| Kerala | 13 | 3.85 | 1.27 | 15 |
| Assam | 14 | 2.71 | 4.00 | 12 |
| Jammu, Kashmir | 15 | 0.81 | † | † |

SOURCE: *Census of India, Paper No. 1 of 1962*, 1961 Census, p. xi.
NOTE: Figures for Delhi and Himachal Pradesh and other Union Territories and Areas have not been included in this table.
  * Hindi-speaking states
  † Not available in the Census statement

elections, it served as one of the greatest sources of support for the Congress party as well as for the Union government. The continued political importance of Uttar Pradesh, its size, and its relation with the other Hindi areas have occasionally generated an apprehension that this state has exercised a unique measure of control over the affairs of India. This apprehension has been reinforced by the fact that the most important political office, the prime-ministership of the Indian Union, has gone consistently to leaders drawn from Uttar Pradesh. Some authors have gone to the extent of claiming that the Indian constitution vests control in the Hindus of the North,[63] and that "the sons of U. P. do, in fact, guide the country's destiny."[64] The States Reorganization Commission reports that many states had expressed the view that

[63] Ivor Jennings, *Some Characteristics of the Indian Constitution* (Madras: Oxford University Press, 1953), p. 58.
[64] S. S. Harrison, *India: The Most Dangerous Decades*, p. 307.

the structure of government in India led to the dominance of Uttar Pradesh in national political affairs.

One of the grounds for fear was that the Indian constitution contains no deliberate measure to diminish the disparity of representation or to offset the predominance of one unit, since parliamentary representation is accorded on the basis of population. In his note on Uttar Pradesh appended to the report of the States Reorganization Commission, K. M. Panikkar explicitly recognized this problem and advocated a partition of the state into two parts: "Since the normal constitutional device for equalizing grave disparities between the units in a federation, that is the provision of equal or at least heavily weighted representation in the House representing the federal principle, is not now possible in our case, and even if it were possible, would not now be a satisfactory solution, in view of the dominant position of the House of the People, the only remedy open to us is to reconstitute the overgrown state in such a manner as to lessen the differences—in short to partition the state."[65] There is a certain degree of exaggeration as well as oversimplification in the apprehensions concerning the actual measure of threat posed by the size and influence of Uttar Pradesh or of the Hindi area in general. But the fact remains that in the political groups outside this state and especially outside the Hindi region, a great deal of apprehension exists concerning the role of Uttar Pradesh. It is not surprising that most people, when they think of Hindi areas, focus their attention on Uttar Pradesh.

If Uttar Pradesh leads the Hindi area, it is by no means a leading state in India in terms of the commonly acknowledged major indexes of development. The Hindi area as a whole, taking into account the major Hindi-speaking states, is substantially less developed in comparison with the major non-Hindi states like Maharashtra, West Bengal, Gujarat, Madras, Kerala, and Andhra Pradesh. In the first place, literacy rates in the major Hindi

[65] *Report of the States Reorganization Commission* (Delhi: Manager of Publications, 1955), p. 245. The entire note, pp. 244–252, contains a wealth of details supporting this idea.

TABLE 4
LITERACY RATES IN THE STATES OF INDIA, 1961

| States | % of literacy |
|---|---|
| Hindi States | |
| Bihar | 18.4 |
| Uttar Pradesh | 17.6 |
| Madhya Pradesh | 17.1  Mean 17.7% |
| Rajasthan | 15.2 |
| Non-Hindi States | |
| Kerala | 46.8 |
| Madras | 31.4 |
| Gujarat | 30.5 |
| Maharashtra | 29.8 |
| West Bengal | 29.3 |
| Assam | 27.4  Mean 27.1% |
| Mysore | 25.4 |
| Punjab | 24.2 |
| Orissa | 21.7 |
| Andhra Pradesh | 21.2 |
| Jammu, Kashmir | 11.0 |

SOURCE: Computed from *Census of India, Paper No. 1 of 1962*, p. xxxii.

states are significantly lower than those of the major non-Hindi states. In fact, leaving aside Jammu and Kashmir, literacy rates in the Hindi states are the lowest in the Indian scale. (See table 4.)

In the second place, educational development at the popular level in the Hindi states is much lower in comparison with that of the major non-Hindi states. In a report prepared on a perspective plan for the development of elementary education in India, it has been pointed out that the problem of providing free and compulsory education in India centers primarily on providing universal education in the six educationally most backward states. Uttar Pradesh, Madhya Pradesh, Rajasthan, and Bihar are included in this list. In the age group 6–11, out of the total number of non-school-attending children in India as a whole, more than 60 percent belong to the six less developed states containing about 45 percent of the Indian population.[66]

[66] J. P. Naik, "A Perspective Plan for the Development of Elementary Education in India," in *Indian Yearbook of Education, 1964* (New Delhi: National Council of Educational Research and Training, 1964), p. 613. The

The same report also indicates that the proportion of non-school-attending children in these six states to the total number of their counterparts in the entire country increased from 60 percent in 1960–1961 to 67 percent in 1965–1966. This lag in educational development is not limited to the elementary stage of education, since similar trends can be observed in middle-school education as well.[67] The ranking remains unfavorable at almost all the levels of education. It is only at the level of nontechnical university degrees that three Hindi states attain an improved ranking. (See tables 5 and 6.) It may be noted also that in respect of investment in educational development, per capita expenditure of the Hindi states is close to the lowest rank in the national order. (See table 7.)

The score of the Hindi states in terms of other indexes of development also tends to be substantially low in comparison with the major non-Hindi states. The comparatively low percentage of the urban population associated with the Hindi speakers is evident from table 8. A ranking of states according to per capita income for 1960–1961 reveals that the Hindi states remained close to the bottom of the national scale. According to one calculation, taking the all-India average as 100, the per capita income score of the Hindi states ranges between 89 and 66, whereas the respective score of the major non-Hindi states reveals 140 for Maharashtra, 139 for West Bengal, 118 for Gujarat, 100 for Madras, and 94 for Kerala.[68] A more detailed estimate for 1950–1961 is presented in table 9. The relative backwardness of the Hindi states can be understood more clearly if one considers the level of development of states in terms of a composite index based on ecological, economic, demographic, and social features.

author was an important adviser to the Ministry of Education, Government of India.

[67] *Ibid.*, pp. 615–617.

[68] These are based on the calculations made by the National Council of Applied Economic Research. The exact index scores of the Hindi states are as follows: Uttar Pradesh (88.9), Madhya Pradesh (85.3), Rajasthan (79.9) and Bihar (66.0). For details, see *Distribution of National Income by States, 1960–61* (New Delhi: National Council of Applied Economic Research, 1965), pp. 8–9.

## TABLE 5
### LEVELS OF EDUCATION, STATES OF INDIA, 1961

| | Literate without education | | Primary or Junior basic education | | | | Matriculation and above | | | |
|---|---|---|---|---|---|---|---|---|---|---|
| | % population | % total literate | % population | Rank | % total literate | Rank | % population | Rank | % total literate | Rank |
| Andhra | 12.6 | 59.5 | 7.0 | 6 | 33.0 | 4 | 1.6 | 7 | 7.42 | 8 |
| Assam | 19.4 | 70.8 | 6.8 | 7 | 24.9 | 7 | 1.2 | 10 | 4.37 | 14 |
| Bihar | 13.6 | 74.0 | 3.5 | 11 | 19.2 | 12 | 1.3 | 9 | 6.77 | 10 |
| Gujarat | 9.8 | 32.1 | 19.2 | 1 | 63.1 | 1 | 1.5 | 8 | 4.83 | 13 |
| Jammu & Kashmir | 6.8 | 61.7 | 2.7 | 12 | 24.6 | 8 | 1.5 | 8 | 13.62 | 1 |
| Kerala | 31.9 | 68.0 | 2.0 | 13 | 25.6 | 6 | 2.9 | 2 | 6.33 | 11 |
| Madhya Pradesh | 12.3 | 71.9 | 3.7 | 10 | 21.9 | 11 | 1.1 | 11 | 6.20 | 12 |
| Madras | 21.5 | 68.3 | 7.6 | 5 | 24.3 | 10 | 2.3 | 5 | 7.37 | 9 |
| Maharashtra | 14.7 | 49.2 | 12.7 | 2 | 42.8 | 2 | 2.4 | 4 | 7.96 | 5 |
| Mysore | 19.3 | 76.0 | 4.2 | 9 | 16.5 | 13 | 1.9 | 6 | 7.49 | 7 |
| Orissa | 18.4 | 84.7 | 2.7 | 12 | 12.3 | 14 | 0.6 | 12 | 3.00 | 15 |
| Punjab | 10.9 | 44.9 | 10.2 | 3 | 42.4 | 3 | 3.1 | 1 | 12.74 | 2 |
| Rajasthan | 12.7 | 83.1 | 1.4 | 14 | 9.3 | 15 | 1.1 | 11 | 7.51 | 6 |
| Uttar Pradesh | 11.7 | 66.3 | 4.3 | 8 | 24.5 | 9 | 1.6 | 7 | 9.16 | 4 |
| West Bengal | 17.0 | 58.0 | 9.5 | 4 | 32.3 | 5 | 2.8 | 3 | 9.74 | 3 |

SOURCE: Computed from *Census of India, 1961*, vol. 1, part II-c (i) pp. 94–95, 108–173.

TABLE 6
HIGHER EDUCATION IN URBAN AREAS: STATES, 1961

| | University degree | | | | All technical degrees and diplomas | |
|---|---|---|---|---|---|---|
| | % literates | Rank | % matric | Rank | % literates | Rank |
| Andhra Pradesh | 0.74 | 8 | 10.08 | 7 | 0.25 | 5 |
| Assam | 0.40 | 13 | 9.20 | 10 | 0.05 | 12 |
| Bihar | 0.61 | 10 | 9.09 | 11 | 0.10 | 11 |
| Gujarat | 0.48 | 12 | 9.96 | 8 | 0.27 | 4 |
| Jammu & Kashmir | 1.60 | 1 | 11.80 | 5 | 0.33 | 3 |
| Kerala | 0.23 | 15 | 3.63 | 15 | 0.16 | 9 |
| Madhya Pradesh | 0.81 | 7 | 13.08 | 4 | 0.16 | 9 |
| Madras | 0.60 | 11 | 8.13 | 13 | 0.17 | 8 |
| Maharashtra | 0.86 | 6 | 10.91 | 6 | 0.51 | 1 |
| Mysore | 0.71 | 9 | 9.52 | 9 | 0.18 | 7 |
| Orissa | 0.27 | 14 | 8.99 | 12 | 0.10 | 11 |
| Punjab | 0.91 | 5 | 7.20 | 14 | 0.36 | 2 |
| Rajasthan | 1.05 | 4 | 13.98 | 2 | 0.12 | 10 |
| Uttar Pradesh | 1.09 | 3 | 11.98 | 3 | 0.12 | 10 |
| West Bengal | 1.42 | 2 | 14.65 | 2 | 0.20 | 6 |

SOURCE: Same as Table 5.

TABLE 7
EXPENDITURE ON EDUCATION BY STATES, 1961–1962

| | 1961–62 amount (rupees) | % increase over 1960–61 | Expenditure per capita (rupees) | Rank |
|---|---|---|---|---|
| Andhra Pradesh | 272,740,242 | 6.1 | 7.2 | 11 |
| Assam | 104,014,625 | 15.9 | 8.6 | 8 |
| Bihar | 249,564,791 | 10.5 | 5.2 | 14 |
| Gujarat | 214,318,140 | 13.0 | 10.1 | 6 |
| Jammu & Kashmir | 30,123,652 | 4.7 | 8.2 | 9 |
| Kerala | 220,306,170 | 13.7 | 12.7 | 2 |
| Madhya Pradesh | 248,935,595 | 23.2 | 7.5 | 10 |
| Madras | 386,679,097 | 21.7 | 11.2 | 3 |
| Maharashtra | 561,272,944 | 14.7 | 13.9 | 1 |
| Mysore | 217,726,619 | 23.2 | 9.0 | 7 |
| Orissa | 80,629,739 | 8.1 | 4.5 | 15 |
| Punjab | 215,313,981 | 14.3 | 10.4 | 5 |
| Rajasthan | 147,598,954 | 16.4 | 7.1 | 12 |
| Uttar Pradesh | 449,320,220 | 13.2 | 5.9 | 13 |
| West Bengal | 381,265,288 | 11.9 | 10.6 | 4 |

SOURCE: India, Ministry of Education, Report, *Education in India, 1961–62*, Vol. I (New Delhi, 1966), pp. 28–29.

TABLE 8
LANGUAGE SPEAKERS: URBAN AND RURAL, 1961 Census

| Language | % Rural | % Urban |
|---|---|---|
| Urdu | 59.66 | 40.33 |
| Gujarati | 72.40 | 27.59 |
| Tamil | 73.55 | 26.44 |
| Kashmiri | 78.53 | 21.46 |
| Marathi | 78.68 | 21.31 |
| Punjabi | 78.97 | 21.02 |
| Bengali | 79.26 | 20.63 |
| Telugu | 82.28 | 17.71 |
| Malayalam | 83.56 | 16.43 |
| Kannada | 83.75 | 16.24 |
| Hindi | 84.65 | 15.34 |
| Oriya | 93.65 | 6.34 |
| Assamese | 95.34 | 4.62 |

SOURCE: Computed from *Census of India, 1961*, vol. 1, part II-c (ii), pp. 31–67.
NOTE: For Sanskrit speakers the rural percentage is 21.93 and the urban percentage is 78.06.

TABLE 9
COMPARATIVE PER CAPITA INCOME: STATES, 1950–1961
(at 1960–1961 prices)

| | 1950–51 per capita income (rupees) | Rank | 1955–56 per capita income (rupees) | Rank | 1960–61 per capita income (rupees) | Rank |
|---|---|---|---|---|---|---|
| Andhra Pradesh | 257.5 | 9 | 278.0 | 10 | 289.1 | 11 |
| Assam | 334.6 | 5 | 336.6 | 5 | 328.4 | 6 |
| Bihar | 180.6 | 14 | 193.3 | 14 | 222.0 | 14 |
| Gujarat | 381.0 | 3 | 378.9 | 4 | 402.8 | 4 |
| Kerala | 303.9 | 6 | 312.9 | 6 | 326.2 | 7 |
| Madhya Pradesh | 235.8 | 13 | 278.0 | 9 | 293.4 | 9 |
| Madras | 244.7 | 12 | 292.0 | 8 | 343.8 | 5 |
| Maharashtra | 373.3 | 4 | 403.8 | 2 | 479.4 | 1 |
| Mysore | 286.8 | 7 | 307.9 | 7 | 313.2 | 8 |
| Orissa | 251.8 | 11 | 249.0 | 13 | 267.9 | 13 |
| Punjab | 404.4 | 2 | 389.4 | 3 | 441.3 | 3 |
| Rajasthan | 256.3 | 10 | 275.0 | 11 | 272.0 | 12 |
| Uttar Pradesh | 270.5 | 8 | 261.6 | 12 | 391.7 | 10 |
| West Bengal | 471.4 | 1 | 449.3 | 1 | 461.9 | 2 |
| All-India | 295.8 | | 307.6 | | 336.3 | |

SOURCE: *Estimates of State Income* (New Delhi: National Council of Applied Economic Research, 1967), p. 57.

One such index constructed by the Census of India shows that the distribution of total population among levels of development in the Hindi states tends to cluster substantially more around the poorer levels (table 10).

Given the importance of language in mass communication, the comparative performance of the Hindi area deserves careful attention. The 1967 report of the Press Registrar indicates that the performance of the Hindi press lags far behind the English press and the major non-Hindi press of India. In terms of readership, the circulation figure of Hindi daily newspapers per thousand persons was surpassed by seven other Indian languages. Thus, the revelant figures for 1966 are Hindi 5.4, Kannada 11.1, Urdu 11.4, Bengali 12.8, Marathi 15.6, Gujarati 20.6, Tamil 20.9, and Malayalam 36.9 (table 11).

Although English was understood by only 2.5 percent of the Indian population, daily newspapers in this language consistently commanded the largest share in the total circulation of all

TABLE 10

DISTRIBUTION OF TOTAL POPULATION AMONG LEVELS OF DEVELOPMENT: STATES, 1961

| | % Low level | % Lower middle | % Upper middle | % High level |
|---|---|---|---|---|
| Andhra Pradesh | 7.83 | 36.46 | 44.21 | 11.50 |
| Assam | 4.83 | 37.17 | 40.94 | 17.06 |
| Bihar | 32.55 | 45.35 | 8.84 | 13.26 |
| Gujarat | .. | 12.30 | 45.04 | 42.66 |
| Jammu & Kashmir | 67.50 | 17.98 | .. | 14.52 |
| Kerala | .. | 10.51 | 79.24 | 10.25 |
| Madhya Pradesh | 25.77 | 41.27 | 16.68 | 16.28 |
| Madras | .. | .. | 38.59 | 61.41 |
| Maharashtra | 4.62 | 22.37 | 20.39 | 52.62 |
| Mysore | 4.67 | 29.99 | 41.87 | 23.47 |
| Orissa | 53.64 | 42.04 | .. | .. |
| Punjab | 5.33 | 8.77 | 7.57 | 78.33 |
| Rajasthan | 15.21 | 40.01 | 20.58 | 24.20 |
| Uttar Pradesh | 50.12 | 9.16 | 20.12 | 20.60 |
| West Bengal | 3.90 | 33.96 | 4.14 | 58.00 |
| India | 19.66 | 25.02 | 24.60 | 30.72 |

SOURCE: *Census of India, 1961*, vol. 1, part I-a (i), p. 19.

dailies. From 1964 to 1966 the share of English dailies increased from 24.9 to 25.3 percent. Hindi on the other hand, despite its 30 percent share of national population, revealed a decline of its percentage of total circulation from 14.1 to 13. Compared to Hindi's share, the percentage of circulation enjoyed by Malayalam was 11.3 (population share, 3.8 percent), Tamil 11 (6.9), Marathi 9.4 (7.6), Gujarati 7.9 (4.6) , and Bengali 7.9 (7.7) . If in addition to the daily newspapers all the other newspapers and periodicals are taken into account, English again stands out, with the largest share of the total circulation. (See table 12.)

The comparatively poor performance of Hindi in the field of circulation, especially when measured in proportion to population, is matched by a significantly low rate of increase in circulation. For example, in 1966 the percentage rate of increase for Hindi was recorded as 2.4 while the corresponding figure for Bengali was 10.1. In this respect, the score for Hindi fell behind several other languages including English (table 12) . Again, among the fourteen daily newspapers exceeding a circulation of one hundred thousand, five are in English, three in Bengali, in-

TABLE 11

READERSHIP BY LANGUAGE GROUPS: CIRCULATION PER THOUSAND
MOTHER-TONGUE SPEAKERS

| | All Newspapers | | | | Daily Newspapers | | | |
|---|---|---|---|---|---|---|---|---|
| | 1964 | 1965 | 1966 | Rank/ 1966 | 1964 | 1965 | 1966 | Rank/ 1966 |
| Hindi | 31.6 | 31.9 | 26.0 | 8 | 5.8 | 6.5 | 5.4 | 8 |
| Assamese | 17.2 | 18.6 | 8.2 | 10 | 0.9 | 2.0 | 1.9 | 11 |
| Bengali | 35.0 | 34.5 | 32.6 | 6 | 8.7 | 10.9 | 12.8 | 5 |
| Gujarati | 67.6 | 71.0 | 63.2 | 3 | 20.3 | 22.9 | 20.6 | 3 |
| Kannada | 37.5 | 35.9 | 30.8 | 7 | 12.2 | 12.3 | 11.1 | 7 |
| Malayalam | 94.9 | 99.2 | 88.6 | 1 | 38.2 | 41.2 | 36.9 | 1 |
| Marathi | 42.6 | 44.4 | 36.3 | 4 | 15.9 | 18.0 | 15.6 | 4 |
| Oriya | 10.4 | 11.0 | 7.2 | 11 | 4.1 | 4.5 | 3.7 | 10 |
| Tamil | 87.6 | 83.2 | 78.6 | 2 | 21.5 | 21.6 | 20.9 | 2 |
| Telugu | 21.8 | 22.2 | 22.3 | 9 | 4.3 | 4.3 | 4.5 | 9 |
| Urdu | 53.9 | 48.3 | 35.4 | 5 | 12.3 | 13.7 | 11.4 | 6 |

SOURCE: India, Ministry of Information and Broadcasting, *Press in India, 1967* (New Delhi, 1967), part 1, pp. 49 and 103.

TABLE 12
COMPARATIVE NEWSPAPER CIRCULATION IN INDIA

| | 1966 circulation ('000) | | % share in national circulation: dailies | | | % change in comparable circulation* |
|---|---|---|---|---|---|---|
| | Dailies | Total | 1964 | 1965 | 1966 | 1965 to 1966 |
| English | 1,651 | 5,559 | 24.9 | 24.4 | 25.3 | +3.4 |
| Hindi | 813 | 3,913 | 14.1 | 14.6 | 13.0 | +2.4 |
| Assamese | 15 | 63 | 0.3 | 0.4 | 0.3 | −16.4 |
| Bengali | 496 | 1,243 | 5.4 | 6.3 | 7.9 | +10.1 |
| Gujarati | 498 | 1,447 | 7.6 | 7.8 | 7.9 | +2.9 |
| Kannada | 221 | 604 | 3.8 | 3.6 | 3.5 | +6.9 |
| Malayalam | 708 | 1,698 | 11.4 | 11.3 | 11.3 | +4.3 |
| Marathi | 589 | 1,361 | 9.5 | 9.8 | 9.4 | −1.7 |
| Oriya | 66 | 128 | 1.1 | 1.1 | 1.0 | +5.4 |
| Tamil | 688 | 2,707 | 11.6 | 10.1 | 11.0 | +1.6 |
| Telugu | 189 | 945 | 3.0 | 3.1 | 3.0 | +1.1 |
| Urdu | 308 | 931 | 5.1 | 5.4 | 5.0 | +0.9 |

SOURCE: *Press in India, 1967*, pp. 5, 39, and 47.
* Includes circulation data of newspapers and periodicals common to 1965 and 1966.

cluding one with the largest circulation in the country, two in Malayalam, and only one in Hindi. The latter gained access to this group as late as 1965 and 1966 remained in twelfth position.[69] Another index of the low exposure of the Hindi area to printed communication may be derived from the comparatively low consumption of newsprint in the Hindi states (table 13). The continuing backwardness of the Hindi press seems all the more glaring when one considers its vast market and the status and patronage resources that follow from the position of Hindi as the official language of the Union and five states.

It is true that in a country of widespread illiteracy, the circulation of the daily or the periodical press is not a reliable indicator of efficient communication of the people. However, with a very low percentage of the population possessing radio sets, and with the lack of popularity of most of the other media of mass communication having direct relevance to political exposure, the

[69] India, Ministry of Information and Broadcasting, *Press in India, 1967* (New Delhi, 1967), part 1, p. 98.

TABLE 13
CONSUMPTION OF NEWSPRINT: STATEWISE ALLOCATION, 1966
(in metric tons)

| | Quantity allocation for newspapers | Allocation per hundred thousand population | Rank |
|---|---|---|---|
| Andhra Pradesh | 4,999.00 | 12.53 | 8 |
| Assam | 916.04 | 6.59 | 10 |
| Bihar | 3,369.95 | 6.42 | 11 |
| Gujarat | 8,485.25 | 35.62 | 5 |
| Kerala | 12,894.27 | 66.81 | 3 |
| Jammu & Kashmir | 124.50 | 3.29 | 15 |
| Madhya Pradesh | 2,293.47 | 6.21 | 13 |
| Madras | 28,809.90 | 78.28 | 1 |
| Maharashtra | 33,656.70 | 74.29 | 2 |
| Mysore | 5,667.86 | 21.23 | 6 |
| Orissa | 1,226.42 | 6.22 | 12 |
| Punjab | 3,360.25 | 14.14 | 7 |
| Rajasthan | 778.69 | 3.31 | 14 |
| Uttar Pradesh | 5,627.58 | 6.78 | 9 |
| West Bengal | 20,122.16 | 49.93 | 4 |

SOURCE: *Press in India, 1967*, pp. 289 and 290.

circulation of the daily press seems to provide a realistic index of what is the efficient medium of communication for the literate people. Many non-Hindi speakers of India point to the growing popularity of the English press and the press in their own languages as an indication that Hindi has not yet made its mark at the national level. When the proponents of Hindi attempt to explain that the relatively low place occupied by the Hindi press is due to the widespread illiteracy of the Hindi areas, their critics answer that "the language issue concerns only the literates, not those who cannot read any language."[70]

Again, in that area of exposure to mass communication where literacy is not a requisite, the record is equally unfavorable as far as the Hindi area is concerned. Thus when one considers the exposure of the people to radio broadcasting, one finds that judging by the number of broadcasting receiver licenses in force, the Hindi-speaking states have far less access to radio listening than most of the major non-Hindi-speaking states. (See table 14.)

[70] C. Rajagopalachari, *The Question of English*, p. 53.

TABLE 14
BROADCAST RECEIVER LICENSES: STATES
(as of December 31, 1966)

|  | Total | Persons per receiver | Rank |
|---|---|---|---|
| Andhra Pradesh | 447,375 | 80.43 | 8 |
| Assam* | 95,244 | 128.19 | 13 |
| Bihar | 238,486 | 194.79 | 15 |
| Gujarat | 547,036 | 37.71 | 2 |
| Jammu & Kashmir | 61,178 | 58.20 | 6 |
| Kerala | 159,333 | 106.09 | 9 |
| Madras | 608,632 | 117.09 | 12 |
| Mysore | 313,397 | 55.34 | 5 |
| Maharashtra | 938,045 | 42.16 | 4 |
| Madhya Pradesh | 276,472 | 75.26 | 7 |
| Orissa | 95,998 | 182.80 | 14 |
| Punjab* | 599,718 | 33.86 | 1 |
| Rajasthan | 183,361 | 109.92 | 10 |
| Uttar Pradesh | 639,388 | 115.33 | 11 |
| West Bengal | 882,360 | 39.58 | 3 |

SOURCE: Computed from *India, 1967* (New Delhi: Ministry of Information and Broadcasting, 1967), p. 129.
NOTE: In this case postal circles, mostly identical with states.
* Assam circle covers Assam, Manipur, Tripura, Nagaland, and NEFA. Punjab circle comprises Punjab, Haryana, and Himachal Pradesh.

Again, if we consider the comparative number of language speakers who have some facility in using and understanding another language current in India, we will find that the speakers of Hindi are less interested in a second language than are the speakers of other major Indian languages. (See table 15.) If learning a second language is taken as an indication of additional facility in communication, the Hindi speakers' low score on this point is a sign of their comparatively lower exposure to communication.

The picture of contrast that emerges has provoked the political leaders of the non-Hindi regions to claim that the major defense of Hindi in the linguistic landscape of India lies more in the weight of population numbers than in qualitative criteria. Thus one critic has argued, on the basis of the 1951 census figures, that while "15.5 million are literates in Hindi . . . 42.8 million are literates in the other languages. Now it is clear that the adoption

TABLE 15
PERSONS SPEAKING A LANGUAGE SUBSIDIARY TO
THE MOTHER TONGUE, 1961

| Mother tongue | Number of* persons bilingual | % Bilingual |
|---|---|---|
| Hindi | 6,280,974 | 5.10 |
| Oriya | 898,058 | 5.75 |
| Malayalam | 1,209,204 | 7.11 |
| Gujarati | 1,470,828 | 7.31 |
| Tamil | 2,470,850 | 8.11 |
| Bengali | 2,922,622 | 8.65 |
| Assamese | 610,241 | 8.96 |
| Marathi | 3,431,276 | 10.47 |
| Kashmiri | 204,763 | 10.69 |
| Telugu | 5,284,990 | 14.03 |
| Punjabi | 1,397,716 | 14.16 |
| Kannada | 2,498,351 | 14.43 |
| Urdu | 5,152,150 | 22.09 |

SOURCE: Compulte from *Census of India, 1961*, vol. 1, part II-c (ii), pp. 443–517.
* Note that the number of persons cited as speaking mother tongues in the "Bilingualism" section of this Census report is lower than that cited in our table 1. This is because of different definitions for these languages adopted for different tabulations in the Census. Thus, in table 1, we have cited the figure for Hindi speakers as 133,435,360, whereas in the section of the Census relevant for table 8, the corresponding figure has been cited as 123,025,489. The former figure refers to broad Hindi, the latter to Hindi without including some dialects that come under the "broad" category. Such variations, more or less, are found in respect of the other languages as well.

of Hindi as a federal language can only benefit these 15.5 million, while the 42.8 million literates in the other languages cannot derive any benefit from this change."[71] The situation in respect of comparative literacy had not changed in 1961 in favor of the Hindi states. In this respect the edge of attack of the non-Hindi critics has not lost its sharpness.

The choice of Hindi as the official language of India, and the language rivalry which is partly a result of this choice, can be studied meaningfully within the broader structure of the group politics that is characteristic of language politics in India. We

[71] D. D. Karve, "The Linguistic Problem in India," Berkeley: Center for South Asia Studies, University of California, 1960, pp. 13–14 (mimeo).

have analyzed the broader dimensions of the linguistic landscape in India and have presented the relative size of the major language groups and their social and political backgrounds. The great complexity of the language situation in India is apparent. However, neither the size of the language communities nor their relative social positions will serve to indicate their political roles and actions. What is more important is the organizational form in which the politics of language rivalry has been carried on. It will be our purpose to look into these organizational forms and processes in greater detail. We will attempt to discern the motives of the actors that are brought into the open arena of group conflict concerning language policy. In this connection we will first examine the relationships between the national movements and the organized language groups. The social, the historical, and other situational factors will be discussed in order to show the impact of the contextual factors on the actors, the groups, their performances, and their relation to the general political order. Perhaps the best way to begin such an analysis of group conflict is to consider the origin of organized group action in modern Indian political life. Any such account will have to begin with the emergence of voluntary associations in nineteenth century Indian society and politics and continue to the contemporary situation. Thus the emergence of organized political associations and their development, with special reference to those groups which were active and are still active in the language politics of India, as well as their impact on the general polity, will engage our attention in subsequent chapters.

# III

# *The Emergence of*
# *Modern Associations*

A landscape of language diversity in a multilingual society provides some basic information concerning the size of the language groups, the extension of their boundaries, their social characteristics, and their relative position in the language situation. Such information, however, does not offer a mapping of dynamic interaction of the language groups. Whatever may be the value of such static positions of the multiplicity of the language groups for social analysis, the students of politics have to go beyond these, and the objectives and the relevant methods of appropriate political analysis have to be spelled out in clear terms.

The purpose of this study is to relate the problem of language rivalry to the question of political integration. We are assuming that political integration must be studied in the context of the dynamic processes of social mobilization and organizational development. The reason for this assumption is that the dynamic interactions of the language groups are more significant in analyzing the expected outcome of the integrational processes than the static array of linguistic multiplicity.[1] Linguistic diversity has existed in India from the beginning of her recorded history. What is new and significant for political study is the mobilization

[1] See Karl W. Deutsch and William J. Foltz, eds., *Nation Building*, pp. 6–7.

of language groups for social and political objectives. These processes of mobilization invariably result in political restructuring of forces in the Indian society. Social groups are increasingly brought into the political arena. Such an entry into politics obviously involves an organizational transformation. New roles are evolved. These roles are structured in organizational media, which evolve modes of interaction as well as rules governing these interactions. They resort to mechanisms of adaptation to the wider political world. In short, organized political associations tend to emerge from the relatively diffuse categoric language communities and help create new modes of participation and development in a competitive field.

During the nineteenth century there arose in India a number of associations trying to promote linguistic identity and attempting to organize, as well as express the interests of, various language groups. Initially, such organizations were cast in the form of literary societies, but they were soon transformed into associations with distinct political roles. These associations attempted to formulate specific objectives of language politics, to mobilize people behind such objectives, to relate such mobilized resources to various segments of the wider political movements engaged in nationalist struggle, and to influence government at the national and regional levels. In this process these associations became involved in coalition, cooperation, and competition, as well as conflict, and assumed a great significance in modern Indian politics.

The role of voluntary political associations in the development of modern politics in India is admittedly not limited to the language sector of modern Indian political development. As we shall see later, such processes are of general importance in the emergence of many sectors of Indian political modernization. In fact, the Indian situation is not unique. The role of voluntary associations in political modernization has a general relevance with wide applicability. Perhaps what is unique in the Indian situation is the distinctive interrelation of political, social, and cultural forces that lends a particular color to Indian associational politics.

## Group Approaches to Politics

The obvious resemblance between associational politics as discussed above and interest-group politics may tempt one to apply generalized group theories of politics prevalent in modern political science toward an understanding of Indian language politics and its relation to Indian political development in general. The temptation is strong because it offers an alternative to the formal and legal descriptive studies that dominate Indian political analysis. It is true that group theories of politics emerged in the Western political tradition as a protest against descriptive formalism in comparative politics. It is also true that, on balance, the achievements of the group theories have been impressive. In fact, on general as well as particular grounds, the appeal of group theory to modern political scientists has proved to be almost irresistible.

The origin of such appeals is usually traced to Arthur Bentley, who wrote, "When the groups are adequately stated, everything else is stated. When I say everything I mean everything. The complete description will mean the complete science, in the study of social phenomena, as in any other field."[2] Bentley, writing in the first decade of this century, was seeking a way out from the descriptive formalism that prevailed in American political scholarship of his time. Initially, his work found poor reception. In was much later, especially after the Great Depression, that group analysis in politics became fashionable in the United States. However, the theoretical rediscovery of Bentley had to wait till 1951, when David Truman employed group theory with systematic care. The extension of group theory to systematic comparative politics began after Gabriel Almond and his associates spelled out a program for research in comparative politics with an emphasis on comparative study of interest groups. As Almond himself wrote, "The kinds of interest groups which are present in a society, the specificity or diffuseness of their demands, their conceptions of the political arena and of the 'rules

[2] Arthur F. Bentley, *The Process of Government*, pp. 208–209.

of the game,' the ethos which they bring with them into the political process—these are the 'raw materials' of politics—which
some set of mechanisms must transform into the political personnel and public policy."[3] Later, the concern for interest groups
was integrated into his general theory of comparative politics. It
should be noted that the relative importance assigned to group
analysis in the contemporary corpus of comparative politics tends
to vary in degree and intensity depending on the particular
writer's theoretical orientations.

Despite the popularity of group analysis, the expectation that
there is possibly an agreed formulation of a general theory emerging from group analysis itself is not likely to be fulfilled. If we
assume that general theories in comparative politics have to be
empirically meaningful and operationally feasible, the abstract
philosophical preoccupations of Bentley and his general formulations cannot be said to add up to such theory. Even the work of
Truman and many of his successors bears very little relation to
what Bentley had in his mind, and in any case, their own formulations neither claim nor have been accorded the status of such
general theory. The closest attempt to build such a theory was
offered by Charles Hagan when he proposed a descriptive system
trying to develop a unifying model based on what he calls the
"group concept." Hagan's starting point is provided by David
Easton's concept of politics as being concerned with the basic
problem of the authoritative allocation of values for a society.
For Hagan the significance of groups lies in the fact that such allocation processes operate through the conflict of groups.[4]

[3] Gabriel A. Almond, "A Comparative Study of Interest Groups and the
Political Process," in H. Eckstein and D. E. Apter, *Comparative Politics*,
p. 398. For similar attitudes in contemporary comparative politics, witness,
for example R. E. Scott, "It is the activities of . . . groups we wish to study,
for the study of politics is really the study of groups at work," in *Mexican
Government in Transition* (Urbana: University of Illinois Press, 1959), p. 18.
See also, G. I. Blanksten, who believes that the group emphasis offers the
way to a major contribution in comparative politics, including the underdeveloped areas. See his "Political Groups in Latin America," *American
Political Science Review*, March 1959, p. 124. And Myron Weiner, *The
Politics of Scarcity*.

[4] Charles B. Hagan, "The Group in a Political Science" in *Approaches to*

It should be recognized that both for Hagan and for Bentley the category of group does not denote anything like a clearly defined formal political association. For them the group is primarily an analytical construct. In their analysis, the group implies any mass of human activity tending in common direction.[5] This is far from the simplified concept of interest groups that has become popular in the literature of political science. Evidently, group theory operates on two broad levels. On one level all politics is perceived as group politics, and on another, group politics provides an important dimension of politics. Also on the latter level, usually an attempt is made to classify different kinds of groups in order to bring out the special character of the political interest groups. Given such a variety of conceptual usages of the category of group, it is doubtful if the claim of group theory to offer a general explanatory theory can be sustained. In fact, one perceptive author has suggested that group theory is not a theory at all, for it does not "relate any variables to one another, nor specify any possible relation between variables. . . . and the statements of 'group theory' are surely not falsifiable by any means whatever."[6]

If this is true about the claims of the generality of group theory, it does not necessarily mean that group analysis cannot yield valuable partial theories. Neither does it mean that the important empirical works produced by various writers on interest groups have been fruitless. Indeed, the question whether group analysis of politics is useful is independent of the more difficult

---

the *Study of Politics,* ed. Roland Young (Evanston, Ill.: Northwestern University Press, 1958), p. 40.

[5] See the critique of Hagan and Bentley by Harry Eckstein, "Group Theory and the Comparative Study of Pressure Groups," in H. Eckstein and D. E. Apter, *Comparative Politics,* pp. 389–397. In this essay, the author strips the group theory of "all non-essentials" and summarizes it as follows: "Politics is the process by which social values are authoritatively allocated; this is done by decisions; the decisions are produced by activities; each activity is not something separate from every other, but masses of activity have common tendencies in regard to decisions; these masses of activity are groups; so the struggle between groups (or interests) determines what decisions are taken" (p. 391).

[6] *Ibid.,* p. 392.

question whether group theory constitutes a general theory of politics. One can utilize group analysis by using "the concept of the interest group as an analytical tool, or as a system of describing some but not all aspects of the political process."[7] Such a consciously limited application of a group approach may offer a number of useful insights into the working of a political process, yet at the same time it will be free from simplistic notions of politics involving an explanation of all politics as being determined by organized pressure groups.[8] Once the limitations of the group approach is recognized, it may be possible to fit partial theories arising out of group approaches in with more general theories of politics.[9]

## Interest Groups in New Nations

In the tradition of political discourse the concepts of organized interest and organized groups have earned legitimate importance from the very beginning. From Greek political theory down to modern political analysis, these concepts have enjoyed great popularity. This is hardly surprising, because group formation on the basis of material and ideal interests has been a persistent social phenomenon which naturally had its effect on both political thought and actual political order. In this art of group formation, communal social relationship as well as associative social relationship has contributed different forms of integrative bonds. Max Weber draws a distinction between these two types of relationship, explaining that the first is based on sentiment and tradition, the second on belief in a reasoned value.[10] Perhaps the most effective instances of group formation affecting political orders in the early history of Europe may be found in the forma-

[7] Joseph La Palombara, *Interest Groups in Italian Politics*, p. 14. See also his "The Utility and Limitations of Interest Group Theory in Non-American Field Situations," *Journal of Politics* (February 1960), pp. 29–49.

[8] On the latter, see O. Garceau, "Interest Group Theory in Political Research," *Annals of the American Academy of Social and Political Science,* September 1958, pp. 104–112.

[9] This is being increasingly done, as for example, in the general theories of political development spelled out by Gabriel Almond in his introduction to G. A. Almond and J. S. Coleman, eds., *The Politics of Developing Areas.*

[10] For a discussion of these aspects, see Reinhard Bendix, *Max Weber* (London: Heinemann, 1960), pp. 291 ff.

tion of religious and occupational groups in medieval history. However, the significance of organized associations based on reasoned defense of political values markedly increased in Western Europe as a result of the process of modernization generated by the forces of industrialization.

In the history of the political evolution of Western Europe the decisions on the right to form associations and the right to receive a minimum formal education have been in a large way instrumental in preparing the ground for the participation of the masses in politics.[11] The relation between the growth of voluntary associations and the breakdown of the traditional order and of social inequality has been discussed by many social and political theorists. Perhaps one of the clearest statements regarding this question can be found in Georg Simmel's treatment of the dynamics of social organization. Simmel treats history as a story of successive detachments of the individual from his primordial attachments and personal dependency on his immediate social circles including kinship groups, villages, or guilds.[12] The grip of these circles on man, which in the past tended to be total, tends to loosen as modernization forces man to uproot himself from his diffuse natural setting. Modernization, in other words, disassociates man from all-embracing dependency, and prepares the ground for his voluntary relation to functionally specific associations. In this way man transforms himself into an individual, and as an individual he joins many circles, each of which commands only a part of his total involvement.[13] The basic factor involved in the modernization of associational life is functional differentiation whereby rational reflection and intelligent plan-

[11] See Reinhard Bendix, *Nation-Building and Citizenship*, pp. 79ff. See also, T. H. Marshall, *Class, Citizenship and Social Development* (Garden City, N.Y.: Doubleday, 1964).

[12] See Lewis A. Coser, ed., *Georg Simmel* (Englewood Cliffs, N.J.: Prentice-Hall, 1965), pp. 18–19.

[13] This is how Georg Simmel describes what he finds to be the "general trend" of the formation of groups in the context of modernization. See his *Conflict and the Web of Group-Affiliations*, pp. 137 ff. For an analysis of differentiation of functions, see Emile Durkheim, *The Division of Labour in Society*, (New York: Free Press, 1964), and its critique by Robert K. Merton, "Durkheim's Division of Labour in Society" in *Emile Durkheim*, ed. Robert A. Nisbet (Englewood Cliffs, N.J.: Prentice-Hall, 1965), pp. 105–

ning governs the definition and organization of interest. In addition, modernization provides a greater opportunity to develop organizational capability through wider communication, better education, and professional, routinized administration.

These general considerations on the impact of modernization on associational development do not throw much light, however, on the specific rate, direction, and pattern of group formation. It should be recognized that the relationship between social development and economic growth on the one hand and intellectual and political development on the other may not be the same in different historical and cultural contexts. For instance, in comparison with Western European history, in Eastern Europe and in many new nations, a relatively lesser economic growth and social development has been accompanied by a relatively more intense intellectual and political activity.[14] The suggestion here is that there is no way of automatically deriving intellectual and political roles as well as associational development from the rate of social change and economic development. The pattern of Western European development may be historically classic, but it is by no means typical of all patterns of modernization. In fact, recent literature suggests a great deal of divergence between the patterns of early modernization and the patterns of late modernization, just as within each such pattern there may be variations due to many intervening variables.[15] It is therefore expected that the institutional order developing in a new nation of our time may not follow the pattern of relationship with social change as it developed in the classic cases of the early modernizers.

Specifically, the pattern of educational changes in India in the

---

112 (paperback). See also, Talcott Parsons, "Durkheim's Contribution to the Theory of Integration of Social Systems" in *Emile Durkheim, 1858–1917*, ed. K. H. Wolff (Columbus: Ohio State University Press, 1960), especially pp. 129 ff. For a political theory of voluntary associations, see Alexis de Tocqueville, *Democracy in America, passim*. For an analysis of Tocqueville's approach on this point, see Jack Lively, *The Social and Political Thought of Alexis de Tocqueville* (London: Oxford University Press, 1962), esp. pp. 127–143.

14 See Reinhard Bendix, *Nation-Building and Citizenship*, p. 231.

15 For details, see *ibid., passim.* See also S. N. Eisenstadt, *Modernization: Protest and Change.*

nineteenth century seems to have been more effective in setting the pace and direction of the political and associational changes than what one would normally expect from economic and technological changes. When the political authority of the British rulers instituted a system of Western education, it prepared a crucial base for the rise of a new Indian elite. The social leadership of this elite came from the educated middle classes. Out of this leadership there arose a politically conscious fragment which in association with other educated people attempted to build a form of organization that would enable them to promote their own as well as what they believed to be the people's interests. In this sense, they behaved like intellectual notables who performed a function somewhat similar to that of the wealthy notables, especially of England, in initiating predemocratic representational processes.[16] Like the Russian intellectual notables during Tsarist Russia, well exposed to ideas from developed countries, who planned to go to the people in search of a base for a national renaissance, these Indian intellectuals tried to reach a wider audience in order to mobilize them for modernization.[17] They sought to reinforce their appeal by organizational efforts through the building of various secondary associations with specific programs. Their immediate perceived task was to create a new public in the modern sense of the term—a public that would be detached from the traditional sources of authority and would become a conscious instrument initiating social changes.

## Emerging Associations

The common denominator of such intellectual efforts along organizational lines could be discovered in a protest directed against the established order of things.[18] In their perception, the

[16] For the English case, see Max Weber in H. H. Gerth and C. W. Mills, *From Max Weber*, pp. 103 ff.

[17] For some points of difference, see Edward Shils, *The Intellectual Between Tradition and Modernity: The Indian Situation* (The Hague: Mouton, 1961), p. 15. For the Russian situation, see A. P. Mandel, *Dilemmas of Progress in Tsarist Russia* (Cambridge: Harvard University Press, 1961), pp. 66 ff.

[18] For a general discussion of the role of protest in modernization, see S. N. Eisenstadt, *Modernization*, chap. 2.

legitimacy of the traditional social order needed an urgent review and rational renovation. The confrontation with Western
learning with its rational mode of enquiry led to a questioning of
the very basis of the age-old norm that had been silently accepted
for centuries.[19] Since most of these intellectuals came initially
from the Hindu society, the protest was focused on the norms of
the Hindu social order. The organizational embodiment of this
challenge assumed the form of voluntary associations directed
toward social reform, educational change, and religious renovation. In the beginning most of these associations did not openly
discuss political issues—some were even too cautious to discuss
religion.[20] Gradually these two issues were increasingly included
in their legitimate order of business.

Most of such organizational efforts began on a very limited
scale. They were limited to small groups of like-minded reformers, educators, and students. In Bengal, Rammohun Roy's
experiments with the formation of the religious societies like the
Atmiya Society (1815) and the Brahmo Sabha (1828, later Brahmo Samaj), the conservative Hindu experiment with the Dharma
Sabha (1830), the "Young Bengal" group (1831) founded by a
group of rebel students—these were some of the earliest efforts in
the above direction.[21] These groups had either their own or
friends' newspapers to publicize their viewpoints and apparently
were fortunate enough to have the financial support of a few
upper-class persons. In respect of membership figures, newspaper

[19] See Bruce T. McCully, *English Education and the Origins of Indian
Nationalism*, chaps. 4 and especially 6.

[20] See N. S. Bose, *The Indian Awakening and Bengal* (Calcutta: Firma
K. L. Mukhopadhyay, 1960), pp. 219 ff. Also, C. H. Heimsath, *Indian Nationalism and Hindu Social Reform*, p. 57.

[21] See S. Natarajan, *A Century of Social Reform in India*, pp. 39 ff. Other
important societies arising in Bengal during this period were Gaudiya
Samaj (1828) for old and new generations, Academic Association (1828) for
the educated people, the Sarbatattadipik Sabha (1832), Sadharan Jnano-
parjika Sabha (1838), the Tattvabodhini Sabha (1839), etc. Valuable evidence about the operation of these societies can be found in a selection of
newspaper materials from 1800–1910 to be published in five volumes. Two
of them have been published so far. See B. Ghosh, ed., *Samayik Patre Banglar Samajchitra* (Calcutta: Bengal Publishers, 1962), 1:21–22; 2:9–15 and
*passim* (in Bengali).

circulation, or organizational support and finance, the operative scale was rather modest.[22] However, the influence exercised by these groups was much greater than data about their operative scale suggests. The leadership of these organizations was recruited from the educated middle classes. A study of the most important of such societies, the Brahmo Samaj, during its initial years shows that out of its most prominent founders and spokesmen, about 40 percent were government officials of relatively upper ranks and about 20 percent were lawyers.[23] Gradually, societies of similar type but often with a wider social base were established in India, notably in Poona, Bombay, Punjab, and other areas.[24]

In the course of a few decades, organizations with wider social support and political inclinations grew up in different parts of India. The earlier tendency of some of the Bengal groups to deviate dramatically from the traditional Hindu norms of religion and society gradually gave way to a pattern of organizations in North, West, and South India which tried to conduct reform activities without setting themselves apart from the Hindu so-

[22] The Tattvabodhini Sabha, though one of the most influential societies, started with only ten members. In three years membership rose to 138 persons and by 1858 to 800. See B. Ghosh, 2:14–15. About the year 1830 the monetary resources of the Brahmo Samaj was only a sum of eighty rupees contributed by Dwarkanath Tagore. The circulation figure for the *Tattvabodhini Patrika*, the organ of the Tattvabodhini Sabha, reached a figure of 700. See Ghosh, 2:28–31. The capacity to expand the organizational base of the Brahmo Samaj was reflected in the fact that from 1842–43 to 1859, apart from three in Calcutta, the Samaj had 11 branches in various districts of Bengal. From 1860 to 1869, there were 25 more branches in Bengal, 1 in Assam, 4 in Bihar, 3 in Orissa, 5 in North Western Province, 2 in Central India, 2 in Western India, 3 in Southern India, and 2 in Sind. See Ghosh, p. 31. After Keshub Chandra Sen joined the Samaj, in 1868, 72 units were added, while the Sadharan Brahmo Samaj added 125 more units. Some of such units, however, had different names. See A. C. Gupta, ed., *Studies in the Bengal Renaissance* (Calcutta: National Council of Education, 1958), pp. 475–480.

[23] Ghosh, p. 32.

[24] For information about such organizations in different parts of India, see S. Natarajan, *Century of Social Reform*; C. H. Heimsath, *Indian Nationalism*; N. S. Bose, Indian Awakening; and especially Anil Seal, *The Emergence of Indian Nationalism*, pp. 194–244.

ciety. The Satyashodhak Samaj (1873) of Poona, the Prarthana Samaj (1867) of Bombay, and the most significant reform association of the second half of the nineteenth century in North India, the Arya Samaj (1875), were some of the leading landmarks in associational development in the field of social reform drawing wider bases of social support than before. In the field of political reform, the Hindu educated classes were becoming equally organization-minded.[25] From the small beginning of the Zamindary Association of Bengal in 1837, the British Indian Association (1851), the Bombay Association (1852), and the Native Association of Madras (1850), to the larger all-India-based political associations, like the Indian League (1875) and later the Indian Association (1876), the strategy was one of gradually widening the support of the educated middle classes for organized activities.[26]

## Language Demands

Despite the wide divergences which separated some of these organizations, there was a common perception that their organizational success required wider communication with a potentially increasing audience. All of them recognized the utility of English education for social reform, but there was a difference of opinion

[25] For a detailed account, see B. B. Majumdar, *Indian Political Associations and Reform of Legislature (1818–1917)* (Calcutta: Firma K. L. Mukhopadhyay, 1965), especially chap. 2–5. We have included only a selected list of associations. See also R. C. Majumdar, *History of the Freedom Movement in India,* vol. 1, 1961; and Haridas and Uma Mukherjee, *The Growth of Nationalism in India (1857–1905).*

[26] While C. H. Heimsath restricts the use of the term middle class to westernized people, B. B. Misra has a much wider connotation. See C. H. Heimsath, *Indian Nationalism,* p. 63, and B. B. Misra, *Indian Middle Classes,* pp. 12–13. The increasing predominance of the middle classes among the educated people can be seen from the fact that during 1881 to 1882, out of 1,870 students of the Bengal colleges, 1,711 belonged to the middle-class groups, while 551 and 159 to the lower and the upper classes respectively. Bruce McCully classifies these students as lower class if their families had incomes around 700 rupees or less a year, as middle class with incomes between 700 rupees and 7,000 rupees, and as upper class with incomes exceeding 7,000 rupees a year. See Bruce McCully, *English Education,* p. 187.

concerning the utility of English as a medium to reach a larger audience. In fact, some of these organizations keenly felt that in order to generate support from their own people they must communicate in their own languages. The art of printing was becoming popular, and the use of the vernacular press from the beginning of the nineteenth century by the Christian missionaries as well as local institutions persuaded the organizational leaders of the vast communicational possibilities of the new medium.[27] It was therefore natural that the new organizational leaders should try to explore these possibilities through the medium of local languages. Thus, in order to popularize their objectives, they found it necessary to start various newspapers and periodicals. Many of these were published in the regional languages. It was not easy, however, to adapt the regional languages to the requirements of modern journalism. The early pioneers of the vernacular press had to modernize these languages for this purpose. This process started in Bengal and spread to other parts of India.

The network of periodicals founded by the leaders of various voluntary associations during the nineteenth century was in a large measure instrumental in communicating modern ideas in Indian languages. They thus created a new sense of pride in the regional languages. The enterprise of such communication of consciousness was directly related to the growth of modern prose styles and modern literature in general in the Indian languages. In their quest for new audiences, the organizational pioneers became linguistic reformers and creators of linguistic pride in different regions of India. It is not a mere coincidence that a man like Rammohun Roy was not only an organizational pioneer but also the founder of modern Bengali prose.

Together with the attempts to develop regional language and literature, there was a distinct trend in many quarters to support the idea of educating the people in regional languages. In spite of the enthusiasm for English education, many of the early re-

[27] For the missionary challenge and Indian response in this regard, see M. Mohar Ali, *Bengali Reaction to Christian Missionary Activities, 1833–1857* (Chittagong: Mehrub Publications, 1965).

formers thought that the general spread of education was possible mainly through the regional languages. In Bengal, newspapers started campaigning for the introduction of Bengali as the medium of school education.[28] In western India, Marathi and Gujarati were advocated as the media not only of school education but also of higher education.[29] Similar demands were expressed in North India.[30] The demands for vernacular education expressed by these leaders and their associations reflected only one dimension of the interest taken in the Indian languages.

Another important dimension can be discovered in the fact that many of the regional leaders were conscious of the need for popularizing one major Indian language to serve as a link language for interregional communication. Both the Brahmo Samaj and the Arya Samaj were in favor of popularizing Hindi for this purpose. Keshub Chandra Sen, a Bengali leader, and Dayananda Saraswati, a Gujarati leader, while working in different regions of India found Hindi to be a potential language of national communication. The expansion of the British administration to North India during the nineteenth century transplanted a series of Bengali communities outside the Bengali language area. These communities were the most vocal in advocating the cause of Hindi in North India. Working through the Brahmo Samaj and joined later on by the leaders of the Arya Samaj, they constantly campaigned for the adoption of Hindi for supraregional linguistic linkage.[31] Even within Bengal several intellectuals

[28] For an account of such concerns published in newspapers about 1843 and later, see statements in *Bengal Spectator*, August 1, 1843; *Sambad Prabhakar*, March 31, 1848, where an editorial claims that "the British attempts to popularize English by spending vast sums of money are likely to be in vain, because it is not easy to change the language of a people . . ." (in Bengali). See also, *ibid.*, April 9, 1848, where it criticized the neglect of the peoples' languages by the people themselves.

[29] See the case as argued by some leaders in 1847 reproduced in B. B. Majumdar, *Indian Political Associations*, pp. 11–13, and John D. Windhausen, "The Vernaculars, 1835–1839: A Third Medium for Indian Education," in *Sociology of Education* 37, no. 3; 254–270, for a general background.

[30] See C. H. Heimsath, *Indian Nationalism*, p. 105.

[31] See Kenneth W. Jones, "The Bengali Elite in Post-Annexation Punjab: An Example of Inter-Regional Influence in Nineteenth Century

worked actively to promote Hindi as a link language. The earliest Hindi newspapers were started in Bengal, and the eminent Bengali writer Bhudeb Mukhopadhyay was largely responsible for the introduction of Hindi in the law courts and the schools of Bihar.[32] An order issued by the lieutenant governor of Bengal in 1881 made such introduction compulsory and signaled the rise of an intense language rivalry in North India, the details of which will be discussed subsequently.[33]

Within the Hindi area, the most important organized movement devoted to the cause of the recognition of Hindi as a regional language emerged with the establishment of a language association at Benaras in 1893. The Nagari Pracharani Sabha, ostensibly a literary society, gradually developed into an association working for the literary and political promotion of Hindi written in Deva Nagari script.[34] The style of Hindi that the Sabha advocated was one that consciously sought to remove Persian and Arabic words and at the same time to borrow as much as possible from Sanskrit. From its very inception the Sabha succeeded in drawing support from various reformist and nationalist associations of North India. The growing popularity of the Arya Samaj was especially helpful for the Sabha.[35] The English-educated intellectuals contributed an important part to the

India" in *Indian Economic and Social History Review* 3, no. 4 (December 1966): 376–395.

[32] See Nirmal Kumar Bose, *Modern Bengal* (Calcutta: Vidyodaya, 1959), p. 81. The first Hindi newspapers in India were *Udant Martand* (1824) and *Bangdoot* (1826). See Madan Gopal, *This Hindi and Dev Nagri*, p. 106.

[33] According to one account this order "antagonised Muslims against the Hindus at whose instance Urdu had been misplaced. Angry representations were made to the government and the grievance was ventilated whenever an opportunity offered itself" (Ram Gopal, *Indian Muslims*, p. 41).

[34] The initial founders of this organization were Gopal Prasad Khatri, Ramnarayan Misra, and Shyam Sunder Das. For an account of the origin see *Hirak Jayanti Granth*, Banaras: Nagari Pracharani Sabha, Sambat 2011, p. 3 (in Hindi).

[35] The program of national education sponsored by Dayananda and followed by the educational institutions set up by the Arya Samaj in Lahore and Kangri had Hindi as the medium of education, with English compulsory in the higher classes and an insistence that Sanskrit should also be learned. See S. Natarajan, *Century of Social Reform*, pp. 74–75.

Sabha's promotional efforts.[36] The first important program of political action adopted by the Sabha was in the form of a deputation that was sent to William Muir, the then lieutenant governor of the North Western Provinces (later Uttar Pradesh) to plead for recognition of Hindi and Deva Nagari as the language and script respectively for use in the law courts in place of Urdu.[37] But the governor turned down the idea because he thought that Hindi was then not equal to Urdu as a language of culture. He was in favor of waiting till this language developed more. The Sabha's campaign bore some fruit, however, when on April 18, 1900, Hindi was recognized in the law courts, and the Deva Nagari script was accepted, along with Perso-Arabic and Kaithi, as a court script.[38] Meanwhile, from about 1850 onward, a distinct prose style was becoming established in Hindi, and by the 1880s under the influence of Bharatendu Haris Chandra and his circle of writers, together with the efforts of Dayananda and his Arya Samaj, Hindi was becoming increasingly established in the Hindu educated circles of North India.[39] The language thus developed was becoming increasingly Sanskritized, which the leaders of Hindi literature felt to be the best way to preserve the authenticity of the identity of Hindi.

It was this question of the authenticity of the identity of Hindi, or as it was called later, the genius of Hindi, that led to a major cleavage in the language politics of northern India. The leaders of the Hindi movement represented the new intellectuals of the Hindu segment of North India. In their effort to create a standardized form of Hindi and to substitute it for the established administrative language of Persianized Urdu, they gave the impression of identifying the case for Hindi with the cause of

[36] One of the earliest nationalist journals of North India, *The Reflector*, served as an English-medium vehicle for persuading the educated people of the merit of Hindi. It was started in 1868 by B. M. Bhattacharya and S. P. Sanyal.

[37] This deputation was led by Munshi Sadasukhlal, Gayaprasad, and Pyari Mohan Banerji.

[38] See Ram Gopal, *Indian Muslims*, pp. 83–84.

[39] For an account of the modernization of Hindi, see Suniti Kumar Chatterji, *Languages and Literatures of Modern India*, pp. 134 ff.

the rising Hindu intellectuals. In terms of administrative opportunity and cultural symbolism this policy was perceived by the Muslim elite as a threat to their status and culture. They saw the Hindi movement as essentially a Hindu movement self-consciously trying to discard all traces of Muslim influence that had accumulated over centuries of Muslim domination in North India.[40] The Muslim reaction to this perceived threat was reinforced by the feeling that throughout the greater part of the nineteenth century the Muslims had conspicuously lagged behind the Hindus in respect of utilizing English education and the benefits of westernization. A deliberate decision on the part of the Muslim elite to defer westernization after the consolidation of British rule largely accounted for this backwardness. In addition, the Muslims had little control over the commercial and financial resources of the country, even before the British rule. These resources were preponderantly controlled by the Hindus.

Despite these educational and economic handicaps, with regard to the public services in North India, the Muslims, as a legacy of former Muslim rule, retained a sizeable comparative advantage. The administrative system of North India did not have the integrated pattern that the established presidencies of Bengal, Bombay, and Madras had from the beginning of the nineteenth century. It was only in 1856 that Oudh was added to the North Western Provinces. The indigenous Muslim administration of Oudh was maintained till 1856. As a result, Muslim dominance in the administration of this area remained established long after it had ended in other parts of India. In fact, in the whole area of North Western Provinces and Oudh, the Muslims enjoyed a greater percentage of the judicial and executive jobs than their numbers warranted.[41] It was not surprising that

[40] For a statement of such perception, see the view of a major Pakistani scholar, I. H. Qureshi, in *The Struggle for Pakistan* (Karachi: University of Karachi, 1965), pp. 12–13. See also his *The Muslim Community of the Indo-Pakistan Sub-continent* (The Hague: Mouton, 1962).

[41] B. B. Misra, in *Indian Middle Classes* cites some interesting data. In spite of the fact that the percentage of Muslims "in the total population was 13.4 in 1886, for example, they held 45.1 per cent of the total number of posts in the judicial and executive service of the North Western Provinces

any threat to the status of Persian or Urdu as the language of administration would evoke a strong response from the Muslim elite, since this would be interpreted as a severe challenge to their last major stronghold in the middle-class status system.

### Muslim Associations

In North India some of the earliest responses to this perceived challenge were expressed by Sir Syed Ahmad Khan, who set up a series of associations for the westernization of the Muslims and to promote their social, political, and linguistic interests.[42] The immediate objective of Syed Ahmad Khan's was to popularize Western education among the Muslims in a way that would not prejudice their loyalty to Islam. He faced a strong challenge from the traditionalist Muslim elite. But he adopted the strategy of appealing directly to the growing apprehension of the Muslim middle classes concerning their declining status. He sounded a note of warning, saying: "If the Muslims do not take to the system of education introduced by the British, they will not only remain a backward community but will sink lower until there will be no hope of recovery left to them."[43] The expression of such an apprehension was not new. Already in Bengal the first

and Oudh. The Hindus held only 50.2 per cent of these posts, although they constituted 86.2 per cent of the total population" (p. 388). In other parts of India the Hindus far outnumbered Muslims in public service in a proportion that was not warranted by their numbers. For instance, in Madras, the percentage of Muslims in 1886 was 6.2, but they held 0.4 percent of the judicial and executive posts. In Bombay, with 18.8 percent of the population, they had 5.4 percent; in Bengal, Bihar, and Orissa, with 31.3 percent of the population, they had 8.5 percent; and in Assam, with 26.9 percent of the total population, they had 0.9 percent of the judicial and executive posts (cited from Census of India, 1901, by Misra, p. 388). See also Anil Seal, *Emergence of Indian Nationalism*, pp. 304 ff.

[42] Syed Ahmad Khan (1817–1898), educated in the traditional Muslim style, served the East India Company's government in a subordinate judicial post. During the mutiny of 1857, he was loyal to the British. He was an advocate of Western knowledge for the Muslims and was responsible for the rise of the new Muslim elite in India.

[43] Syed Ahmad Khan's letter to Mawtawi Tasadduq in W. M. Theodore de Bary, ed., *Sources of Indian Tradition* (New York: Columbia University Press, 1964), 2:192–193 (paperback). See also J. M. S. Baljon, *The Reforms and Religious Ideas of Sir Syed Ahmad Khan* (Lahore: Orientalia, 1958).

small group of English-educated Muslims had established the Mohammedan Association in 1856. This short-lived association was succeeded by the Mohammedan Literary Society. Abdul Lateef, the founder of this association, urged the acceptance of English education by what he called "respectable Mohammedans" in their own interest of competing with the Hindus.[44] Though established as a literary society, this organization was occasionally consulted by the government on matters affecting the interests of the Muslims, including their political interests. For the representation of the Muslim interests in a more comprehensive form, Syed Amir Ali, a dynamic lawyer and administrator, established the Central National Mohammedan Association in 1877. All these associations, based in Calcutta, succeeded in earning the confidence of the British administrators. In founding his association, Syed Amir Ali frankly pointed out the urgent need to catch up with the advantages enjoyed by the Hindu community. By 1882, the Central National Mohammedan Association established branches in different parts of India and claimed that it was the first organized political body to represent the political and other interests of the Muslims of India.[45]

None of the associations formed in Calcutta to represent Muslim interests succeeded in gaining as wide an influence as Syed Ahmad Khan attained through his associations in North India. To be sure, he too began on a small scale. The earliest association founded by him—in 1864, called the Scientific Society—was a small literary group devoted to the dissemination of Western knowledge in India.[46] Its major purpose was to translate important Western works into Indian languages. In practice, Indian languages, as far as this organization was concerned, meant primarily Urdu.[47] This society did some useful work. Its publication efforts were directed mainly toward scientific works, with a special emphasis on the utilitarian aspects of science. In practice,

[44] See B. B. Majumdar, *Indian Political Association* (n.25 above), p. 222.
[45] By 1882 sixteen branches were operating in North India. See *ibid.*, p. 225.
[46] For details concerning this organization, see Yusuf Husain, ed., *Selected Documents from the Aligarh Archives*, especially pp. 5–31.
[47] See *ibid.*, p. 39.

the audience of this society was limited to Muslim middle classes of North India.

The restless mind of Syed Ahmad Khan could not be confined for long to such a limited educational endeavor. Through the scientific society he had earned the recognition of the British administrators and a sizeable Muslim audience. From the 1870s he took an active interest in the general problem of Muslim education and devoted his energies to the establishment of a Muslim college in the North Western Provinces. One of the first things he did was to appeal to the Muslim princes of the native states of India to contribute funds for the proposed Muslim college. He succeeded in gaining not only their support, but also a much wider one for this campaign.

In 1875 the Mohammedan Anglo-Oriental College was founded at Aligarh. This college was raised to the status of a university in 1921, when it became the Muslim University of Aligarh. The Aligarh college placed great emphasis on Muslim culture and on Urdu, although it encouraged English education at the same time. It would be a mistake to treat it merely as an educational institution; it was actually the spearhead of a rising movement for the assertion of the political and cultural demands of the Muslims. The Aligarh movement was conscious of the pride of the Muslims, which had been deeply wounded by the failure of the Sepoy Mutiny. At the same time, it was aware that only a constructive program of new education could assure their progress. It was also aware that such a program needed not only the general enthusiasm of the Muslim community but also "the cooperation of the British."[48] Working on this premise, Syed Ahmad Khan and the Aligarh movement pleaded with the Muslims to recognize the need for allaying the suspicions of the British, and tried to convince the former of the basic congruence of the Muslim and the British political interests. Initially this con-

---

[48] See I. H. Qureshi, "The Muslim Revival," in W. T. de Bary, ed., *Sources of Indian Tradition*, 2:189. The actual cooperation of the British administrators is indicated in the collection of Sir Syed Ahmad Khan's correspondence contained in the second part of the Aligarh Archives Documents cited earlier.

gruence was explained in terms of the Muslim need to explore the possibilities for self-improvement with the stability of the British empire as its prerequisite. This view was popularized by Syed Ahmad Khan also, through his Muslim Educational Conference founded in 1886. Gradually this Educational Conference helped establish Muslim educational associations in other parts of India to promote the Western education of Muslims.[49] The extension of the Aligarh movement to wider areas provided an important base for the consolidation of the newly rising westernized Muslim elite in different parts of India.

Syed Ahmad Khan was convinced that the educational consolidation of the Muslim elite was only the first step. The inevitable second step was the political mobilization of this elite. The Indian National Congress was established in 1885 as the central organization of the politically conscious nationalist forces. The earlier leaders of the Congress were admirers of Western liberalism as well as secularism, and their initial actions did not add up to more than moderate requests for greater participation of Indians in the political life of the country. Such a concept of Indian nationalism never appealed to Syed Ahmad Khan. Though in his earlier phase of public life he had occasionally preached Hindu-Muslim cooperation and had actually worked with the Hindus in many of his endeavors, he did not really believe that Hindus and Muslims constituted one nation. He thought India was essentially a cluster of several nations, and his primary concern was with what he always referred to as "the Muslim nation." He regarded the establishment of the Indian National Congress as a threat to the Muslim nation. In the first place, he viewed the advocacy of liberal nationalism as a challenge to the British rule. In the second place, he interpreted any act that tended to disturb the British rule as an act directed toward potential domination by the Hindus.

Given these perceptions and orientations, it was not surprising that in 1888 he founded the United Indian Patriotic Association

[49] See Hafeez Malik, *Moslem Nationalism in India and Pakistan*, pp. 216 ff.

with the clear objective of strengthening "the British rule in India and to wean away people from the Congress."[50] The purpose of this association was to rally anti-Congress forces together with the Indian native princes to form a unified loyal organization to protect the stability of the British rule.[51] Most of the literature of this association was written by the English principal of the Aligarh college, and one of his pamphlets frankly branded the Indian National Congress as seditious.[52] The United Indian Patriotic Association failed to evoke the response expected by its founder. The idea of a united opposition to the Indian National Congress was soon given up. In 1893 Syed Ahmad Khan founded the Mohammedan Anglo-Oriental Defence Association at Aligarh. The purpose of this organization was to represent the Muslim community and to protect its political rights. At the same time, this organization stood for intensifying loyalty to the British rule and for preventing the spread of political agitation among the Muslims. This was in continuation of the advice that Syed Ahmad Khan had given to the Muslims as early as 1886 "to keep aloof from the Congress agitation as the success of its efforts must result in the Muslims being reduced to an ineffectual minority."[53] Like its predecessor, this organization too failed to fulfill its founder's expectations.

There was, however, another trend of Muslim opinion which warned the Muslims not to associate themselves with the activities of the associations and policies of Sir Syed Ahmad Khan. This opinion was represented by a group of culturally traditionalist Muslim educators representing what is known as the Deoband school. Unlike Syed Ahmad Khan, the founders of the Deoband school had participated in the Mutiny of 1857, and

[50] For the objectives of this association, including the one cited, see Ziya-ul-Hasan Faruqi, *The Deoband School and the Demand for Pakistan*, p. 44.

[51] For details, see B. B. Majumdar, *Indian Political Associations*, pp. 227 ff.

[52] The complete title of the pamphlet is "The Seditious Character of the Indian National Congress and the Opinions Held by Eminent Natives of India Who are Opposed to the Movement," published in Allahabad in 1888.

[53] Pakistan History Board, *A Short History of Hind-Pakistan* (Karachi: Manager of Publications, 1955), pp. 428–429.

after the failure of the mutiny, they established a series of educational institutions to help Muslims reassert their pride. The Deoband school, in opposition to the Aligarh movement, remained opposed to the policy of preaching loyalty to the British rulers of India. Though culturally traditionalist, the leaders of the Deoband school were in favor of cooperation with the Hindus in "worldly matters . . . provided it did not violate any basic principle of Islam."[54] Such a policy brought the Deoband school closer to the Indian National Congress. In the conflict between the Deoband school's attitude of cooperation with the Hindus against the British rulers, and the Aligarh movement's pro-British attitude of Muslim exclusivism, the greater bulk of the Muslim elite were more and more persuaded in favor of the latter.

Why did Syed Ahmad Khan and his Aligarh movement gradually drift toward intense Muslim separatism? The answers to this question have been varied. One answer in particular demands our close attention. It has been repeatedly suggested that the Hindi language movements in North India and the conduct of the Hindi language associations had decisively contributed to the Aligarh movement's insistence on Muslim separtism. The Hindi movements, according to such a view, had convinced Syed Ahmad Khan that if the Hindus and Muslims could not agree even on the choice of a national language, and if the Hindus were so narrow-minded as to object to Urdu, which represented a linguistic compromise between Hindi and Persian, there was no possibility of a common nationhood in the subcontinent.[55]

It is true that the Hindi movement was gaining ground during the lifetime of Syed Ahmad Khan. It is also true that he perceived the anti-Urdu platform of the Hindi movement as a threat to the cultural and economic status of the Muslims. But it is equally true that this linguistic threat did not apply beyond North India, more specifically the North Western Provinces, or what was

[54] Ziya-ul-Hasan Faruqi, *Deoband School,* p. 43.
[55] Pakistan History Board, *Short History,* pp. 427–428. This work is convinced that Sir Syed's ideas on Hindu-Muslim relations were "completely changed" by anti-Urdu attitudes of the Hindus of North India.

later called the United Provinces. The Hindi movement hardly affected the majority of the Muslims inhabiting other parts of India. For example, the Bengali Muslims had no connection with Urdu, and like other Muslims outside North India, they were linguistically more concerned with their own regional language cutting across religious affiliation. And yet the Central National Mohammedan Association based in Bengal—not significantly affected by the anti-Urdu agitation—had expressed a form of Muslim separatism similar to that of the Aligarh movement of North India. This, coupled with the fact that Urdu was a regional language of only a minority of Muslims in India, seems to indicate that the emphasis on the anti-Urdu movement as an explanation of the beginning of Muslim separatism may not be so persuasive as is sometimes supposed. It should also be noted that in 1882, when Syed Ahmad Khan was a member of the viceroy's Legislative Council, he objected strongly to the Hindi leaders' opposition to the use of Urdu in the Education Commission. During this period the Urdu leaders tried to establish associations for the protection of Urdu. This effort succeeded to a limited degree only in North India. Despite the claim of the North Indian Muslim separatist leaders that the Urdu language was second only to Islam as a bond of unity of the Indian Muslims,[56] the latter did not substantiate it outside North India. The linguistic diversity of the Indian Muslims and the linguistic integration of religious groups in different regions in India have been underestimated by most historians of Muslim separatism.

Although Syed Ahmad Khan occasionally wrote as though in order to be a nation a people must profess one religion, speak one language, and have one single way of life and customs,[57] for him

[56] Some foreign writers also have supported this claim. See, for instance, M. L. Ferrar in H. A. R. Gibb, ed., *Whither Islam* (London: Gollancz, 1932), p. 182.

[57] See Syed Ahmad Khan in W. T. de Bary, ed., *Sources of Indian Tradition*, 2:194–195. One can also find isolated quotations from his earlier texts maintaining that Hindus and Muslims constituted one nation. See Rajendra Prasad, *India Divided* (Bombay: Hind Kitabs, 1947), pp. 98–99. In fact, there was rarely any conceptual consistency in his definition of nation. One can only construct a definition from his theory and practice taken together.

religion was the overriding criterion, and this was brought out clearly in his formulations and actions. He was also persuaded of the irreconciliable antagonism between the Hindus and Muslims. He believed that in the eventuality of the British leaving India, "it is necessary that one of them should conquer the other and thrust it down. To hope that both could remain equal is to desire the impossible and the inconceivable."[58] Given such a clear conviction, it would be fair to assume that though the language question might have some importance in the development of Sir Syed's policy, it could not have been a major determinant of his fundamental attitude to the Hindu-Muslim problem.

## Significance of Group Process

The above survey of the emergence and development of organized associations indicates the significance of the group process in understanding the beginning of political consciousness in India. This type of group process was something new in the Indian scene. The mediation of these organized groups in communicating modern ideas and in mobilizing people for action in a field of competition provided one of the earliest institutional frameworks for autonomous modern political action.[59] To be sure, group formation as such was not new to India. What was new was the modern structure of the associational groups and the specialized representational function performed by these groups. Each group was based on a charter of specific objectives, with a clear constitutional procedure laid down for the recruitment of members and for governing the rational hierarchy of leadership. Each group, again, tended to adopt, in varying degrees, routin-

[58] Cited in Richard Symonds, *The Making of Pakistan* (London: Tabor, 1951), p. 31. In W. T. de Bary, *Sources*, 2:195, his essay says that "at least traditionally [the Muslims] are prone to take the sword in hand when the majority oppresses them," and that given a representative government in India the Hindus will oppress the Muslims.

[59] Another dimension of this process was revealed in the emergence of important associations based on caste loyalties, which yet stretched the notion of such loyalties to suit political action and transformed categoric unities into political associations. The best discussion of this complex evolution is contained in Lloyd I. Rudolph and Susanne H. Rudolph, *The Modernity of Tradition*, esp. pp. 24–103.

ized regularity in its internal administration. The leaders of these groups used modern mass media of communication and cast their appeals in a language of rational persuasion. In all these respects they contributed significantly to gradual dissociation from the traditional norms of primordial group formation and structure, and to the growth of modern political development.

It is in this context that we propose to consider the contribution of the language-oriented groups and other groups to language rivalry in India. We should draw a distinction between the language groups as speech communities and the functionally specific language associations working in a political framework. Each speech community may be treated as a categoric group which may or may not act always as a potential support structure for the specific interest groups identifying with the language issues formulated for the speech communities.[60] It should also be noted that the structure of the interest groups and the function of interest representation through various organizational forms are equally important for our analysis. The modern structure of the associational interest group provides only one channel of interest representation. Interest may also be articulated and represented through what have been called institutional, non-associational, and anomic channels.[61] Institutional interest groups operate within established formal organizations like armies, bureaucracies, and other such institutions that do not usually articulate particular interests. And yet within such formal organizations it is not unusual to find corporate groups articulating particular interests. For our purpose the role of

[60] The terms categoric, potential, and interest groups broadly follow David Truman's definitions. However, this does not commit us to the special theory of group politics introduced by him, because for him the problems of latency and "morbific" politics are merely fringe issues. See his *Governmental Process*, pp. 23, 33, 511, and 516. See also S. Rothman, "Systematic Political Theory: Observations on the Group Approach," *American Political Science Review* 54 (March 1960); 15–33, and Truman's reply, "On the Invention of Systems," *ibid.*, June 1960, pp. 494–495, where he admits that his is a special theory with no pretension to general applicability.

[61] For elaboration, see G. A. Almond and J. S. Coleman, eds., *The Politics of the Developing Areas*, pp. 33 ff.

such interested corporate groups within the Indian bureaucracy will have significance. In contrast to the associational and institutional representation of interest, the nonassociational and the anomic processes refer to intermittent and irregular processes. Nonassociational representation of interest takes place when a sizeable segment of a categoric group articulates its interest without recourse to institutionally organized associational channels. In a country like India this is especially important because, in the transition to modernity, a large sector of potential interests at some point of time may not have organized channels of expression, and yet expediency may require a temporary organization of interests through ad hoc channels. If such ad hoc representation fails to take place at a time when certain interests seem to require an immediate spontaneous representation, popular impulse may burst forth in a sudden spurt of anomic demonstration. And as we will repeatedly witness in our study of Indian language politics, this also performs an important function in bringing dormant interests into the open arena.[62]

Given our objective of studying the representation of interest, it is necessary to clarify the crucial category of interest. Interest has often been identified with an amorphous mass of shared attitudes.[63] This identification is too broad for our purpose. We propose to use the term interest to mean a conscious desire to shape public policy in a general or specific direction. We are primarily concerned with political interest that leads to political action and its consequences. In our definition, interest is not necessarily coextensive with the self-interest of formal groups stated in economic or other narrow terms. The self-interest of a group—formal or informal—may or may not be congruent with

[62] In using Gabriel Almond's categories we are not necessarily depending on his particular functional model. As descriptive categories they are more useful for our purpose than the conceptual distinction drawn by Samuel Finer between proper interest groups and promotional groups. For a recent general statement of Almond's categories, see G. A. Almond and G. Bingham Powell, Jr., *Comparative Politics: A Developmental Approach*, chap. 4. For Samuel Finer's distinctions, see his "Interest Groups and the Political Process in Great Britain" in *Interest Groups on Four Continents*, ed. Henry W. Ehrmann, p. 117.

[63] See, for example, David Truman, *Governmental Process*, pp. 33–34.

the broader interests of other groups in a political order. We are also assuming that the interest of a particular group cannot be derived automatically from its social situation. It has to be understood in the context of the dynamic interaction and adaptation of groups in a political community. With such a flexible definition of interest, it will be possible to include expressions of emotional, intellectual, ideological, and material demands within the broad category of interest, provided these are directed to the shaping of public policy. In other words, we are not treating ideas as mere "spooks," as Bentley claimed, but rather as important factors in shaping public policy.[64] The political action necessary for shaping public policy as pursued by interest groups is not directed toward capturing governmental authority. It is this limitation that serves as the line of distinction between interest groups and political parties. It should also be evident from our study that we do not propose to describe public policies as being solely determined by interest-group action.[65] Again, for our purposes, the distinction between an interest group and a pressure group is important to the extent that pressure refers to only one of the several modes of action pursued by an interest group.[66]

Granting these assumptions and classifications, we will discuss in the subsequent chapters the politics of the interest groups engaged in language rivalry in India. For the sake of convenience we will limit our study primarily to North India. We have already surveyed the beginning of associational group politics in the first phase of the rise of modern political consciousness in India. Henceforth, the major emphasis will be on an intensive study of the political participation of the language associations of North India from the time of the consolidation of the national movements down to the contemporary period. This will involve an analysis of the structure of such associations, their performances, capabilities, interrelations, and political consequences

[64] See Joseph La Palombara's critique of Bentley in his *Interest Groups in Italian Politics*, p. 17.

[65] Cf. Harmon Zeigler, *Interest Groups in American Society*, p. iv and *passim*.

[66] Cf. V. O. Key, Jr., *Politics, Parties and Pressure Groups*, p. 18; and David Truman's criticism of Key's usage in his *Governmental Process*, p. 39.

in the context of Indian political development. The literature on these groups is extremely scanty, and no systematic study has thus far been attempted.[67] The major source materials that are available are limited to the literature published by these groups, scattered documentary evidence, some fragmentary historical accounts, and occasional newspaper reports. In addition to utilizing these materials, this study has used information concerning these groups obtained by interviews conducted in North India.[68] Wherever possible and whenever necessary, comparative materials drawn from parallel group activity in Indian language politics outside North India have been employed in order to place the findings of this study in a broader perspective. No conscious normative prescription has been attempted. It should be noted that the primary purpose of this study is exploratory and analytical and not prescriptive.

[67] The only important work on contemporary interest groups in India does not even mention them. See Myron Weiner, *The Politics of Scarcity*. B. B. Majumdar's historical work (n. 25 above) contains some useful information up to 1917.

[68] The interviews were conducted by me in 1964, primarily in Uttar Pradesh and Delhi. The persons interviewed were mainly the major leaders of interest groups connected with language policy, some active workers of these groups, eminent literary and educational scholars, leaders from various political parties, educational and cultural leaders, administrative personnel of the Union and Uttar Pradesh governments, and other persons involved in relevant processes. Many of them were interviewed again in 1967.

# IV

# *Language Associations and*
# *National Movement*

The political situation in India changed considerably after the failure of the Indian Mutiny of 1857. The events of 1857 contributed to the assertion by the crown of direct responsibility and complete control over Indian affairs. The resulting political configuration gave rise to a series of problems concerning the adjustment and adaptation of the politically conscious Indians to the new system.[1] In their attempt to come to terms with the altered political situation, the politically conscious Indians could not offer a common response. To begin with, they differed sharply among themselves in their interpretation of the situation as well as evaluation of their own roles.[2] This diversity of orientation was in a large measure due to the division of the Indian pop-

[1] See T. R. Metcalf, *The Aftermath of Revolt: India 1857–1870* (Princeton: Princeton University Press, 1964). For conflicting accounts of the mutiny, its actors, and intentions as well as its importance for Indian nationalism, see especially, S. N. Sen, *Eighteen Fifty-Seven* (Delhi: Publications Division, 1957); and R. C. Majumdar, *The Sepoy Mutiny and the Revolt of 1857*, 2d ed. (Calcutta: Firma K. L. Mukhopadhyay, 1963).

[2] For an account of the problems of this period and the responses from different quarters, see, for example, the selected documents presented by C. H. Phillips, ed., *The Evolution of India and Pakistan, 1858–1947* (London: Oxford University Press, 1962), vol. 4. Also R. C. Majumdar, *History of Freedom Movement in India*, vol. 1; and H. Malik, *Moslem Nationalism in India and Pakistan.*

ulation into a multiplicity of social, religious, cultural, and linguistic categoric groups. Also, the effect of modernization on
these groups had been uneven in terms of social, economic, and
political development.

Hindus and Muslims, in particular, tended to view the British
consolidation of power in two different perspectives. For most
Hindus, it appeared to be a transfer of political authority from
an archaic to a modern set of foreign rulers. The adjustment to
the latter was deemed to be easier and considerably more desirable for reasons of future development. Hindus were relatively
more prone to reconcile themselves to the new political system
as well as to the general processes of modernization. For Muslims
the matter was quite different.[3] They looked upon the British as
the usurpers of power. Muslims held the British responsible for
the destruction of their political power. A feeling of humiliation
and defeat persisted, especially among the Muslim aristocrats,
whose strongest center was located in North India. Even outside
the Muslim aristocracy, there was a feeling among a large number of Muslims that there might be a possibility of restoring
Muslim dominance. Though the Mutiny of 1857 was not an exclusively Muslim phenomenon, the Muslim aristocrats had a
greater stake in it than their Hindu counterparts. The ruthless
suppression of this mutiny extracted a greater psychological
price from the Muslim aristocrats than from the Hindu aristocrats. In any case, the Hindu aristocrats represented a relatively
small part of the Hindu political aspirations in India of that
time. Because of early modernization and the growth of modern
political consciousness, a sizeable westernized Hindu middle
class had already succeeded in mobilizing Hindu opinion away
from the traditional aristocracy. In fact, it was this body of new
middle classes which had been the sharpest critics of the Hindu
traditional structure of authority.[4] It is worth noting that the
modern social and political associations founded by the new

---

[3] For one view of such Muslim perception, see Aziz Ahmed, *Studies in
Islamic Culture in the Indian Environment*, pp. 263 ff.

[4] A useful survey of such criticism can be found in C. H. Heimsath, *Indian
Nationalism and Hindu Social Reform, passim.*

Hindu middle classes at the very beginning of the nineteenth century opposed the Mutiny of 1857.[5] The leaders of these associations, imbued with progressive western liberal thought, were thus able to divert Hindu political aspirations from an immediate capture of political power to patient preparation for reforming their own society in order to adapt it to the demands of modern transformation.[6]

Because westernization was consciously deferred, the Muslim society failed to produce sizeable modern middle classes such as the Hindu society had produced, and the Muslim elite was still identified primarily with the Muslim aristocracy. This aristocracy symbolized an undifferentiated elite status, and this facilitated the identification of its own goals with that of the Muslim society.[7] It is true that there were some deviant Muslim movements, but these movements were directed by fundamentalist Islamic groups which were directly opposed to modernization.[8] The landed notables, rooted in tradition, nursing a sense of humiliation and a fond hope of dislodging the new rulers, were the only articulating social group formulating Muslim interest in India before the advent of the Aligarh movement. Even the Aligarh movement depended heavily on the financial, political,

---

[5] For a sample of their opinion of the mutiny, see a collection of Bengali newspaper editorials originally published in *Sambad Prabhakar* in *Samayik Patre Banglar Samajchitra*, ed. B. Ghosh (Calcutta: Bengal Publishers, 1962), 1; 154–156 (in Bengali).

[6] The Mutiny of 1857, however, had a temporary upsetting effect on the leading political associations for more than a decade. See Ram Gopal, *British Rule in India: An Assessment* (Bombay: Asia Publishing House, 1963), p. 275.

[7] See Khalid B. Sayeed, *The Political System of Pakistan* p. 11. See also his *Pakistan: The Formative Phase* (Karachi: Pakistan Publishing House, 1960), especially chap. 2.

[8] Some of these movements were connected with the Wahabi movement. The major part of this movement was defeated in 1868. The movement was revivalistic and radically anti-English. In the Eastern part of Bengal, a fundamentalist, peasant-based movement gained some ground after 1828. The success of this movement, called the Faraiziyah movement, was extremely limited. For the Wahabi movement, see Hafeez Malik, *Muslim Nationalism*, especially chap. 6. For the impact of the Faraiziyah movement, see Anisujjaman, *Muslim Manos O Bangla Sahitya, 1757–1918* (Dacca: Lekhak Sangha, 1964), pp. 45–47 (in Bengali).

and social support of the landed notables.[9] It should be remembered that despite the violent suppression of the Mutiny of 1857, the British rulers, by and large, did not destroy the material resources of this landed aristocracy. Rather, the British policy was to recruit the loyalty of the largest possible number of the landed aristocrats of North India.[10] It remained for the Aligarh movement to direct the social energies of this landed aristocracy toward the creation of a modernized Muslim elite prepared to more effectively compete with the already ascendant modern Hindu elite. The Aligarh movement, in fact, facilitated the maintenance of the social status of the Muslim landed aristocrats of North India and also brought some of them into a position of leadership in the process of Muslim modernization. The social structure of Muslim politics thus remained fairly undisturbed, and unlike the Hindu sector of politics, social homogeneity of the Muslim elite seemed to present an obstacle to the political differentiation of Muslim interests. As a result, the initiative in Muslim politics remained concentrated in the center of Muslim aristocracy in North India, and the definition of Muslim interest in North India was eventually identified as the reference standard for Muslims all over India.

*Patterns of Conflict*

In North India one of the first open rivalries between Hindus and Muslims, during the late nineteenth century, found a political expression in the rivalry between Hindi and Urdu. The origin of this conflict and its early manifestations have been discussed in the previous chapter. Here we will describe in some detail the concrete processes of this political conflict.

[9] The organizational appeals, fund-raising campaigns, and the general correspondences of Syed Ahmad Khan bear ample testimony in this regard. See Yusuf Husain, ed., *Selected Documents from the Aligarh Archives*, especially part 2.

[10] Out of 23,543 villages in Oudh, some 22,658 were restored to the Talukdars (landed aristocrats), "in return for submission and loyalty in the form of collection and transmission of information." See S. Gopal, *British Policy in India, 1858–1905* (Cambridge: Cambridge University Press, 1965), p. 6.

By the 1830s Urdu was substituted for Persian as the language of the law courts and the administration in Bihar, North Western Provinces, and Central Provinces. The style of Urdu used in the law courts was predominantly Persianized, and was incomprehensible to most of the ordinary people in these areas. The movement against Urdu started in Bihar, then a part of the Presidency of Bengal. As we have noted before, eminent intellectual leaders initiated a series of agitations for the removal of Urdu in Bihar and for its replacement by Hindi written in Nagari script. At this stage the movement remained primarily nonassociational. Politically conscious intellectuals, drawn mainly from Bengal, urged people to impress upon the British administrators the necessity of such a change of language. Gradually, some of these intellectuals organized a series of public meetings and carried on the campaign in the newspapers. As the movement gained ground they organized public petitions, and a large number of such petitions and memoranda were submitted to the administration. As a result of this campaign some of the British administrators became personally convinced of the need for introducing Hindi, and they themselves often wrote notes to their hierarchy expressing the rationale and the urgency of the movement. One such note frankly pointed out that there was "no more reason for having in Bihar a court language other than Hindi than there is in Bengal for having one other than Bengali. The introduction of Bengali as the court language in Bengal was . . . strongly opposed at the time. Now no one ventures to suggest that it was not an improvement."[11] After about three decades of continuous campaign, the Hindi movement in Bihar finally succeeded in gaining its objectives.

In 1881 Hindi was introduced as the court language in Bihar. The Bihar administration also prohibited the use of Persian script in legal transactions. Police officers and other administrative personnel connected with court transactions were warned that if they could not read and write the Deva Nagari script, they

[11] This was a part of a forwarding letter attached to one public petition. This letter was written by the Commissioner of the Patna Division in Bihar on May 20, 1875. See Ram Gopal, *Linguistic Affairs of India*, p. 165.

would be replaced by those who could. These measures affected Muslims, who made up a high proportion of the scribes and lawyers. The only Hindu group affected was the Kayasth caste group, who were prepared to adapt to the new system. Hindus, in general, welcomed the new administrative orders. The Bihar struggle signaled only the beginning, however, of a chain of Hindi movements that gradually spread to the Central Provinces and the North Western Provinces. An expansion of the scope of this movement was also sought. From 1882 onward, the Hindi movements pressed for teaching Hindi universally in all primary and secondary schools in North India. A group of leading Bengali intellectuals, including Rajendralal Mitra, Bhudeb Mukhopadhyay, and Radhika Prosunno Mookherjea, carried on, through their influential writings, an extensive campaign in favor of the adoption of Hindi. Gradually, the leaders of the Hindi movement took the initiative in establishing local associations for the propagation of Hindi in many urban areas of North India and especially in the North Western Provinces.

The strategy of action employed by the Hindi movement in the North Western Provinces was largely similar to that adopted in Bihar earlier. But the Hindi movement in the North Western Provinces showed a tendency to use more violent language in its attack on Urdu. The constant refrain of the public petitions for Hindi in the North Western Provinces was that Urdu was an alien language. A petition signed by five hundred Hindu graduates and undergraduates declared Urdu to be an "alien and upstart language," while another petition described Urdu as "a hybrid production . . . forced upon us by our former rulers."[12] The same petition went to the extent of claiming that "no Hindu gentleman would ever condescend to educate . . . females in Urdu and Persian because the books written in these languages are generally obscene and tend to have a demoralizing effect on the character."[13] Similarly, Urdu was denounced as a survival of

[12] Cited in Rafiq Zakaria's foreword to N. S. Gorekar, *Glimpses of Urdu Literature* p. xxiv.

[13] *Ibid.*, pp. xxiv–xxv. For details see Rafiq Zakaria, "Muslims in Indian Politics, 1885–1906" (Ph.D. dissertation, London University, 1948).

Muslim tyranny and as a symbol of Muslim domination over Hindus. In general, the Hindi petitions had considerable popular support. One of the most important Hindi petitions was signed by more than 58,000 people in the North Western Provinces. At the same time, the number of local associations working for Hindi was steadily growing. In contrast to such rapid growth of the Hindi movement, there was only one petition, signed by a handful of individuals, submitted in favor of Urdu in the North Western Provinces.

The rapid progress of the Hindi movement alarmed the newly westernizing Muslim leadership belonging to the Aligarh movement. Syed Ahmad Khan denounced the Hindi movement and characterized it as a deliberate plan to injure Muslim interest. He carried on his countercampaign in his official capacity within the British administration and outside it through nonofficial efforts. He formed the Urdu Defence Association at Aligarh. Meanwhile, local associations formed by Muslim notables were making their appearance in Punjab. These associations were called the Anjuman-i-Himayat-i-Urdu. But it was the Urdu Defence Association, backed by the Aligarh movement, which came to the forefront of the Urdu movement. It issued pamphlets, collected funds, and organized meetings. The Urdu Defence Association was handicapped, however, by its self-imposed political limitation. Since the leadership was concentrated in the Aligarh movement, which did not want to disturb the British administration by any substantial political agitation, it was difficult for this movement to make much headway. In fact, Nawab Mohsin-ul-Mulk, the organizational leader of this association was also the secretary of the government-subsidized college at Aligarh. He was warned by the lieutenant governor not to participate in any openly political agitation that might disturb the administration. As a result, he retreated from his pro-Urdu agitation. Most of the aristocratic Muslim leaders of the association followed suit. By the end of 1900 the movement had virtually collapsed.

Syed Ahmad Khan sought to compensate for the lack of effectiveness and popular support for the Urdu movement through activities carried on from within official institutions. In 1882 when he was a member of the viceroy's Legislative Council, he worked actively in defense of Urdu against Hindi. One of his points of attack was that Hindi was read only by people belonging to lower ranks and by petty traders.[14] But despite all his efforts, he and his Aligarh movement could not prevent the gradual success of the Hindi movement. In 1900 a large part of the Hindi demands were conceded. Although Urdu, in this case, was not displaced, Hindi and the Nagari script gained official recognition. The Urdu Defence Association described Hindi's achievement of equal status with Urdu in official transactions as a threat to Muslim economic and cultural interests.[15] The Urdu Defence Association made a last bid to reverse this recognition. But it was of no avail. Political support for Urdu had already declined. Syed Ahmad Khan had died in 1898, and the weak Urdu movement was suffering for lack of a leader. Moreover, it was difficult to persuade the administration that it was unfair to recognize Hindi, in a province where most of the people advocated and actually needed its recognition, especially when Hindi did not displace Urdu and only gained a status of coequality.[16] The Aligarh movement was convinced, however, that it was an attack on Muslim interest and that it was an unfriendly act on the part of the British toward Muslims. It has been claimed that this conviction led to a complete disillusionment concerning the British professions of friendship for Muslims.[17] It was this disillusionment which apparently persuaded the Muslim elite to rethink their attitude of loyalty and friendship to the British rulers.

[14] See Ram Gopal, *Linguistic Affairs of India*, p. 171. See also Hafeez Malik, *Muslim Nationalism*, p. 210. Sir Syed's charge was made at a time when Bharatendu Harishchandra and some of the other great Hindi writers were actively engaged in the Hindi movement.

[15] See Malik, p. 224.

[16] It is worth noting that most pro-Urdu historians have given the impression that Hindi in fact displaced Urdu by virtue of the decision taken in 1900. This has also been the picture given by the leaders of Muslim separatism.

[17] See Ziya-ul-Hasan Faruqi, *The Deoband School and the Demand for Pakistan*, p. 47.

## Rising Communalism

The beginning of the twentieth century witnessed increasing expressions of communal tensions on an all-India scale.[18] It was at this stage that the effect of Hindu revivalism on Indian nationalism was beginning to be felt to a considerable degree. The reformist political attitudes of the earlier leaders in the Indian National Congress were under heavy pressure from Hindu revivalist leaders.[19] A strong group of Indian nationalist leaders with deep religious conviction felt that in order to expand the structure of popular support for the Indian national movement, it was imperative to discard the earlier westernized reformist dialogue and to substitute a new dialogue. This dialogue, they felt, must employ a language of politics that the greater number of the Indian masses would understand and readily accept. In other words, in order to draw support from the Hindu masses, the nation was to be identified with the religious tradition of Hinduism. Consequently, three principal ties common to both the educated and the illiterate people were increasingly emphasized. These were religion, history, and language. The myth of a glorious past, dominated by Hindu kings and philosophers, was evoked as a means to achieve solidarity and promote action. Unity was promoted through the symbol of motherland. Textbooks and literature focused the attention of the readers on the tales of Hindu heroes. Communal unity as an issue now became

[18] In Indian politics, the form "communal" is "used to describe an organization that seeks to promote the interests of a section of the population presumably to the detriment of the society as a whole, or in the name of religion or tradition opposes a social change which the speakers believe to be a progressive one." See Richard D. Lambert, "Hindu Communal Groups in Indian Politics" in *Leadership and Political Institutions in India*, ed. R. L. Park and I. Tinker (Princeton: Princeton University Press, 1959), p. 211.

[19] For representative ideas of such thinkers, see *Bal Gangadhar Tilak— His Writings and Speeches* (Madras: Ganesh, 1919); Haridas Mukherjee and Uma Mukherjee, *Sri Aurobindo's Political Thought (1893–1908)* (Calcutta: Firma K. L. Mukhopadhyay, 1958); Lajpat Rai, *India's Will to Freedom* (Madras: Ganesh, 1921); B. C. Pal, *Nationality and Empire* (Calcutta: Thacker, Spink, 1916); and C. H. Heimsath, *Indian Nationalism*, especially pp. 309 ff.

subsidiary to the more important question of recruiting support from the Hindu community against the British. Muslim separatism and the pro-British attitude of the Aligarh movement reinforced the conviction of the Hindu revivalists. With the partition of Bengal in 1906 communalism flared up, and the annulment of the partition in 1911 shocked many Muslims. In 1906, the Muslim League came into existence, and in the same year the Hindu Mahasabha was born. In 1909, the Morley-Minto reforms granted separate electorates to Muslims. All these factors taken together set the stage for a complex conflict between Hindus and Muslims expressed in various political forms.[20]

Communalism thrives on a deliberate reactivation of communal memory. The symbolic capability of revived communal memory can be increased mainly through the creation of a channel of communication between the leaders and their people. The creation of such a channel requires the identification of the people as well as the leaders of a community with a common language that can serve as a bridge for communal mobilization. Therefore, it is essential to bridge the communication gap that usually tends to exist between the elite and the masses in the underdeveloped countries. Recognizing this, many English-educated Indian leaders turned their greater attention toward their own languages. However, in India the major religious communities are not linguistically homogeneous. Neither Hindus nor Muslims could hope to politically mobilize their people through a common language. The motivation to mobilize thus inevitably focused attention on the major regional languages. For example, in Bengal, Bankim Chandra Chatterjee wrote that it is the task of the Bengalis to "disanglicize ourselves, so to speak, to a certain extent and to speak to the masses in the language which

[20] For an account of this conflict, see, for a British point of view, R. Coupland, *The Indian Problem* (New York: Oxford University Press, 1944), vol. 1; for a Muslim view, K. K. Aziz, *Britain and Muslim India* (London: Heinemann, 1963); and for accounts written by two Indian socialist nationalists, see Asoka Mehta and Achyut Patwardhan, *The Communal Triangle in India* (Allahabad: Kitabistan, 1942). See also, Ram Gopal, *Indian Muslims*; Rajendra Prasad, *India Divided*; and P. W. Kaushik, *The Congress Ideology and Programme* (Bombay, Allied Publishers, 1964), especially chap. 9.

they understand."[21] He suggested that only regional languages have the power to move people.[22] Similar attitudes gradually became popular in other parts of India as well. No wonder that the initial decades of the twentieth century proved to be a fertile period for the development of solidarity of the individual speech-communities. This was also the time when regional literatures began to flourish anew. However, just as the use of religion for mass recruitment led to the development of group solidarity in each religious group, promotion of regional languages had the effect of creating regional consciousness of solidarity. Such in-group solidarities invariably prepared the ground for potential outgroup hostility. The divisive effect of this regional language consciousness on the political cohesion of the major religious groups was appreciated much later. In any case, the rising tides of communal and regional consciousness conferred a great importance on organized language politics conducted through language associations.

## National Movement and National Language

If the demands of mass mobilization for the nationalist struggle put a premium on the use of regional languages, simultaneously there was an intense realization on the part of several nationalist leaders of the need for a common language to unify the nationalist movement. In fact, the greater part of the nationally prominent leadership was aware of the potentiality for parochialism that was inherent in the unqualified loyalty to regional languages demanded by some regional leaders. The most important advocate of a common Indian language designed to unify the national movement was Mahatma Gandhi. In this advocacy, Gandhi was ably supported by most of the important leaders of the national movement drawn from various regions.

[21] This is a part of a letter that he wrote to *Bengal: Past and Present*, vol. 8, part 2, April–June 1914, pp. 273–274. In the same letter he also mentions that interregional communication in India can be done only through the medium of English.

[22] Cited in B. B. Majumdar, *History of Political Thought from Rammohun to Dayananda (1821–1884)* (Calcutta: University of Calcutta, 1934), 1; 431.

This is not to say that Gandhi was the first leader to advocate a common language for the integration of national communication. As we have noted earlier, some of the early reform movements and associational leaders had emphasized the need for a common link language for national transactions and cohesion. Many of them were convinced that English must be replaced by Hindi for this purpose. The Brahmo Samaj, the Arya Samaj, and other such organizations had attempted to popularize Hindi for this purpose. Some of the leading intellectuals of the early nineteenth century also contributed their efforts to the cause of developing a national language transcending the barrier erected by regional languages. At the turn of the century, when revivalism was making its mark as an instrument of mass mobilization, some of the greatest national leaders with a revivalist orientation intensified the movement to accept Hindi as the national language for the integration of the national movement.

For example, it was B. G. Tilak, one of the first national leaders in the Indian National Congress, who suggested that Hindi in Deva Nagari script should be accepted as the national language of India. In fact, for Tilak the question of national language was intimately related to his national education movement. In a conference organized by the Nagari Pracharani Sabha in 1905, Tilak forcefully argued the case for the acceptance of Hindi in Deva Nagari script. He insisted that such a national langage is the most potent force for drawing a nation together.[23]

What was new in Gandhi's advocacy of Hindi was the singular persistence and organizational involvement that he brought to the cause of the national promotion of Hindi. Gandhi pointed out that there are five requirements for a language to be accepted as a national language: (1) It should be easy to learn for government officials. (2) It should be capable of serving as a medium of religious, economic, and political intercourse throughout India. (3) It should be the speech of the majority of the inhabitants of India. (4) It should be easy to learn for the whole of the country.

[23] For details, see Ram Gopal, *Lokamanya Tilak, A Biography* (Bombay: Asia Publishing House, 1956), pp. 240–242. See also L. K. Verma, ed., *Hindi Andolan* (Allahabad: Hindi Sahitya Sammelan, 1964), p. 23 (in Hindi).

(5) In choosing this language, considerations of temporary or passing interests should not count.[24] English, Gandhi declared, does not fulfill any of these requirements, and he had no hesitation in claiming that Hindi satisfied all of them. Unlike Tilak, Gandhi moreover defined Hindi in a way that was designed to bridge the stylistic differences between Hindi and Urdu and thereby to make his Hindi equally acceptable to both Hindus and Muslims.

According to Gandhi's definition, Hindi is that language which Hindus and Muslims in the North speak and which is written either in the Deva Nagari or in the Persian script. Gandhi refused to believe that Hindi and Urdu are two different languages. He pointed out that the popular speech in North India is the same, and that it is only the literary scholars who have deliberately created a barrier between Hindi and Urdu. The *Pandits* of Prayag and the *Maulvis* of Aligarh, according to him, have deliberately classicalized their usages by means of conscious borrowing from Sanskrit and Persian respectively. Such styles, he felt, are foreign to the masses, who have no use for such artificial constructions.[25] As for the script, Gandhi pointed out:

For the present Muslims will certainly use Urdu script and Hindus will mostly write in Deva Nagari. I say "mostly" because thousands of Hindus even today write in the Urdu script and some even do not know the Nagari script. Finally, when there is absolutely no suspicion left between Hindus and Muslims—when all causes for distrust between the two have been removed, the script which has greater power will be more widely used and thus become the national script. In the intervening period Hindus and Muslims who desire to write their petitions in the Urdu script should be free to do so and these should be accepted at all Government offices.[26]

---

[24] M. K. Gandhi, *Thoughts on National Language* (Ahmedabad: Navajivan, 1956), pp. 3–4. Gandhi's criticism of English dates back to 1909. See M. S. Patel, *The Educational Philosophy of Mahatma Gandhi* (Ahmedabad: Navajivan, 1956), pp. 221–222.

[25] M. K. Gandhi, *Thoughts on National Language*, p. 5.

[26] *Ibid.*, pp. 5–6. See also Gandhi's speech at Patna on December 3, 1920, in *The Collected Works of Mahatma Gandhi* (Delhi: Publications Division, 1966), 19:63.

It can readily be seen that his language program was essentially a revolt against the practices of the partisan literary elite and the political revivalists. His catholicity concerning the use of two scripts and the use of words from the common codes of communication of the ordinary people was also a political gesture for unity between Hindus and Muslims of North India and at the same time an open invitation to Indians from other speech communities to accept a broadbased Hindi as the common national language. He often referred to the Hindi of his conception as village Hindi and claimed that the sweetness which he found in it was absent in the elite usages of the educated Muslims and the Hindu *Pandits*.[27] He also believed that Sanskritized and Persianized Hindi would dry up and fade away because its support was drawn from a small circle. In other words, he thought that the separation between Hindi and Urdu was as undesirable as that between Hindus and Muslims.[28]

Gandhi often described the Hindi of his conception as Hindi-Hindustani or simply as Hindustani. In 1925 the Indian National Congress was persuaded by him to accept Hindustani as the official language for the conduct of its proceedings. The Congress amended its constitution by a resolution passed in its Kanpur session, which stated: "The proceedings of the Congress shall be conducted as far as possible in Hindustani. The English language or any provincial language may be used if the speaker is unable to speak Hindustani or whenever necessary. Proceedings of the Provincial Congress Committee shall ordinarily be conducted in the language of the Province concerned. Hindustani may also be used."[29]

Gandhi's influence persuaded many other important leaders of the national movement to accept Hindustani. Thus, Nehru declared in 1937 that Hindustani should be officially recognized as the all-India language.[30] Like Gandhi, Nehru also believed

[27] M. K. Gandhi, *Thoughts on National Language*, p. 10.
[28] *Ibid.*, p. 11.
[29] Quoted in M. P. Desai, *The Hindi Prachar Movement*, p. 14. See also, P. D. Kaushik, *Congress Ideology* (n. 20 above) p. 161.
[30] See Jawaharlal Nehru, *The Unity of India*, p. 256.

that a simple, easy-to-learn language of wide appeal could find ready acceptance in the Indian masses. The model of Basic English encouraged Nehru to think that the official language of India could be some form of basic Hindustani and that such a basic Hindustani "with a little effort from the state will spread with extreme rapidity all over the country and will help in bringing about that national unity which we all desire. It will bring Hindi and Urdu closer together and will also help in developing an all-India linguistic unity. On that solid and common foundation, even if variations grow or diversions occur, they will not lead to separatism."[31]

The same attitude to Hindi and Urdu was also expressed by Rajendra Prasad, who believed that structurally there was nothing to distinguish between these two languages. The whole Hindi-Urdu controversy seemed to him unfortunate, since these two, he felt, represent a "common heritage of both Hindus and Musalmans."[32] The acceptance of Hindi among the Congress leadership, and their efforts to propagate it, were not limited to the pro-Gandhi leaders. Within the Congress organization, non-Gandhians like Subhas Chandra Bose were equally wedded to the principle of popularizing Hindi as the national language.[33] In fact, from the 1920s till the advent of independence the most prominent political leaders in the national movement were largely united on this policy. Even when they were drawn from non-Hindi language areas, they urged the learning of Hindi as a second language to aid in establishing it as the national language.

## Hindi and Urdu Associations

The task of popularizing Hindi needed organizational efforts. The leaders of the Nagari Pracharani Sabha had identified them-

[31] *Ibid.*, p. 254.

[32] As he put it: "that structure which is the real framework of a language still common to both forms of the language known as Hindi and Urdu. The difference mainly is in respect of a portion of the vocabulary only." Both passages are in his *India Divided*, p. 54.

[33] He pointed out that Hindi, "because of its simplicity, pervasiveness and effectiveness should be the language of the nation." See L. K. Verma, ed., *Hindi Andolan* (n. 23 above), p. 32 (in Hindi).

selves too closely with the literary and political demands of the North Indian Hindi movement. Its regional image made it an inadequate organization to bear the responsibility of popularizing Hindi as the national language. In association with some of the nationally prominent leaders of North India, the leaders of the Nagari Pracharani Sabha initiated the establishment of a new organization with a wider appeal. In this way the Hindi Sahitya Sammelan was founded in Allahabad in 1910.[34] Madan Mohan Malaviya was its first president. He was a widely respected political leader, and his connection with the organization transformed it from a literary society into an effective political association working for Hindi. However, the organizational architect of this association was another prominent North Indian leader, P. D. Tandon.[35] Both Malaviya and Tandon were closely identified with Hindu revivalism.[36] They were also close to the traditional Hindi literary elite. Gandhi was aware that these factors would stand in the way of using the Sammelan to popularize Hindi on a national scale. He felt it was his duty to take a keen interest in the organizational development of the Sammelan and he became its president in 1917.

Gandhi tried to channel the work of the Sammelan in the direction in which he was interested from the perspective of national language policy. He tried to mold the Sammelan's definition of Hindi so as to make it identical with his definition of Hindi as the common language of Hindus and Muslims and as a language that would be comprehensible to the Indian people in general. At this early stage of the Sammelan's growth, the leaders of the Sammelan needed Gandhi's support, just as Gandhi himself was eager to persuade them. Therefore, Gandhi had his own way with little trouble in the earlier phase of the Sam-

[34] For details concerning the foundation, see Kantilal Joshi, "Rashtrabhasha Prachar," in *Rajat Jayanti Granth* (Wardha: Rashtrabhasha Prachar Samiti, 1962), pp. 581–582 (in Hindi).

[35] For different aspects of Tandon's life, ideas, and political career, see the felicitation volume prepared in his honor, edited by Lal Bahadur Shastri, et al., *Rajarshi Abhinandan Granth*.

[36] For Malaviya's involvements in a number of Hindu-oriented organizations in North India, see C. H. Heimsath, *Indian Nationalism*, pp. 318–319.

melan's growth. But this congruence of interests permitting the utilization of the Sammelan by Gandhi did not last long. Gradually, Gandhi came under fire both from the orthodox Hindi leaders within the Sammelan and from the Urdu leaders organized outside it.

In spite of the constant efforts of some of the greatest nationalist leaders to bring Hindi and Urdu closer to each other, neither the Hindi elite nor the Urdu elite seemed to be reconciled to this idea. Muslim leaders were determined to retain the separate identity of Urdu and to link it with Muslim cultural and political interests. After a brief period of decline of the Urdu movement in 1903, some supporters of Urdu established the Anjuman Taraqqi-i-Urdu as the focal point of a revived Urdu movement. Its first president was Thomas Walker Arnold. Maulana Shibli, its secretary, was a respected Muslim intellectual. In temperament and orientation he was far removed from the Aligarh movement, which provided the strength of the Anjuman organization. Maulana Shibli belonged to the Deoband school and ultimately became a supporter of the Indian National Congress. Initially he thought that the Anjuman would be essentially a literary and academic association for promoting Urdu. The leading members of the Anjuman were more interested, however, in making it a politically oriented language association serving the cause of the Aligarh movement. Gradually, Maulana Shibli detached himself from the Anjuman, and in 1914 he founded the Shibli Academy, which confined itself to literary and Islamic research activities.

In 1919 a dramatic change took place in the pattern of Muslim politics in India. It was at this time that the Khilafat movement brought the Deoband-oriented and the westernized Muslims closer to each other in a common cause. This brief unity of the nationalists and separatists was not brought about by any Indian internal political development. The Khilafat movement was based on the demand for the preservation of the Turkish caliphate. It was basically a pan-Islamic and anti-British movement. Neither of these aspects would have been to the taste of Syed

Ahmad Khan. But the concern for the traditional caliphate was so deep that most of the Muslim politicians plunged into mass agitation for an institution that was soon to be completely disowned by the Turkish Muslim people themselves. Be that as it may, the Khilafat movement in India not only succeeded in uniting, though briefly, different Muslim groups but also drew Muslims and Hindus together in a common anti-British movement. In 1916, by virtue of the Lucknow Pact between the Indian National Congress and the Muslim League, Hindu-Muslim relations had been relatively cordial. By 1919 there seemed to be a possibility of continued cooperation between Hindus and Muslims, which would provide a favorable ground for promoting Urdu in a context free from religious rivalry.

In 1920 the Jamiyat-ul-Ulama-i-Hind was founded by the politically conscious Deoband-oriented Ulamas to safeguard the religious and political interests of the Muslim community without bringing in Muslim separatism. The Jamiyat was favorable to and actually cooperated with the Congress. The Jamiyat's support for united nationalism provided a new background for the Urdu movement. The Jamiyat leaders were strong supporters of Urdu, but their participation in the Urdu movement was based on the detachment of Urdu demands from Muslim separatism.[37] Perhaps the best service that the Jamiyat had contributed to the Urdu movement was through the educational movement that it sponsored in the form of a unique school called the Jamia Millia Islamia. This school was founded by Maulana Mahunidul Hasan in 1920 at Aligarh. It represented "a secession movement from the official, imperialist-entangled Muslim University of the Sir Sayyid tradition; students and some teachers 'non-cooperated' by leaving the Government supported and controlled University; under a group of tents they set up a courageous but obviously improvised rival, thoroughly nationalist and free."[38] The Jamia

---

[37] See Ziya-ul-Hasan Faruqi, *The Deoband School*, pp. 67–91, for a detailed account of the Jamiyat movement and its relation to united nationalism.

[38] Wilfred Cantwell Smith, *Modern Islam in India* (Lahore: Minerva Book Shop, 1963), p. 147.

Millia Islamia quickly gained active support from Congress leaders like Gandhi and Zakir Hussain[39] and succeeded in creating a cordial atmosphere for the promotion of Urdu.

The major sections of the Muslim political leadership, however, considered the Anjuman Taraqqi-i-Urdu to be the most important vehicle of the Urdu movement. After all, the Anjuman was more in tune with the major trends of Muslim politics than any other organization working for Urdu. The Muslim League movement kept growing in the 1920s, and the astute leader of the Anjuman, Abdul Haq, maintained a close relation with the Muslim League leadership. Abdul Haq, and the Anjuman in general, did not believe that Urdu and Hindi could be brought closer to each other, as Gandhi implied.[40] He dismissed the idea that Hindi and Urdu are the same language with two different styles. Such a view, according to him, was dictated by either political expediency or ignorance. Gandhi repeatedly tried to convince Abdul Haq that the difference could be bridged and, what is more, should be bridged for the sake of national integration. Whatever might be the merit of such political persuasion, the logic of the political situation of the third decade of the nineteenth century pushed the language rivalry to a new point of crisis.

## Growth of Rivalry

From the second decade of the twentieth century, the politics of nationalism underwent several changes. A series of mass movements succeeded in extending the range of mass participation in nationalist politics. Gandhi's leadership was now an accomplished fact in the Congress sector of the national movement. In 1920, the Congress revised its constitution and provided for the

[39] Under Zakir Hussain's leadership, the teachers and the staff of the Jamia Millia Islamia formed themselves into a society called Anjuman-i-Jamia Millia and took a pledge to serve the Jamia for twenty years on a salary not exceeding 150 rupees a month. See *Jamia Millia Islamia* (New Delhi: Registrar of Jamia Millia Islamia, n.d.), p. 1; and also M. Mujeeb, "The Jamia Millia Islamia" in *Indian P.E.N.*, October 1960, pp. 291–293.

[40] See Abdul Haq's essay in Z. A. Ahmad, *National Language for India*, p. 89.

reorganization of its provincial organizations on a linguistic basis. This had the effect of fostering a sense of regional linguistic identity, and it laid the ground for the growth of regional consciousness in an increased magnitude. Meanwhile, constitutional reforms were sought to increase the scope of representation of the Indians in the government of India. After 1935, the political situation changed rapidly in India.

The Government of India Act of 1935 provided for a significant extension of the range of self-government.[41] This act envisaged a considerable measure of autonomy and responsible government in the provinces. In the general elections of 1937, the Congress had a notable success, winning clear majorities in six provinces, and pluralities in three others. Soon, Congress ministries were formed in eight provinces. The spectacular success of the Congress during this period gave it a feeling of pride, and it refused to form coalition ministries with the Muslim League in the provinces where it had obtained a majority. A major crisis developed in the United Provinces, where the victorious Congress offered terms for inviting the Muslim League, which the latter thought were too severe to allow it to live.[42] Meanwhile, the revivalist forces in Uttar Pradesh had become more aggressive, especially since Hindu orthodox leaders like Shraddhananda and Madan Mohan Malaviya initiated "Shuddhi" and "Sangathan" movements[43] to consolidate Hindu forces while Muslims reacted with their own counterparts of these movements. The Congress-League tensions and the deeper forces behind them, augmented by increasing entry of the lower classes

[41] Percival Spear notes that ministerial responsibility after 1937 "covered the whole provincial executive field and was extended to the center as well. . . . Communal representations . . . ran right through the Constitution, both in the legislatures and in the public services." See his *India* (Ann Arbor: University of Michigan Press, 1961), p. 387. For an account of the reforms and their consequences see, R. Coupland, *Indian Problem* (n. 20 above), vol. 2.

[42] See R. Coupland, *India, A Re-Statement* (London: Oxford University Press, 1945), p. 294.

[43] These two movements, led by aggressive Arya Samajist leaders, represented attempts to reclaim non-Hindus to the Hindu faith and to create strong Hindu organizations for radical action.

into politics, as well as the above-mentioned forces of revivalism —all these made the politics of the 1930s in North India highly explosive. In Uttar Pradesh (United Provinces before partition) in 1937, governmental power for the Congress was no longer a mere aspiration—to a large extent it was already at hand. A campaign was now hastily planned for "mass contact" with the uncommitted Muslims in order to win them over from the potential grip of the Muslim League. This campaign failed.[44] The Muslim League retaliated, and its organizational strength went on increasing as a result of its new determined efforts as well as because of Muslim resentment against the Congress and the Hindu revivalists.[45]

It is in this context that the intensification of the language politics in Uttar Pradesh during this and the subsequent periods can be appreciated. The leaders of the Congress ministry were now eager to introduce Hindi with the official help of their newly acquired political power.[46] As a first step, they introduced the study of Hindi in schools. The Hindi movement, as well as the Hindi elite, now came to feel an exaggerated sense of importance and power. At the same time, this new feeling contributed to an intensification of the conflict between the different factions within the Hindi movement. The leading center of this conflict was the Hindi Sahitya Sammelan. After 1935, Gandhi faced a stiff opposition from the powerful faction led by P. D. Tandon. Gandhi insisted that the Sammelan was not primarily a literary society and that its main objective was to popularize the Hindustani form of Hindi as the national language. He thought that the name of the organization was ill-chosen, because it promoted an identification of the interests of Hindi with those of the Hindi literary elite, who, according to him, were more interested in

----

[44] See R. C. Majumdar, *History of the Freedom Movement in India,* 3: 568 ff.

[45] Coupland mentions that during this period in the United Provinces the Muslim League gained spectacularly—within two or three months ninety new branches of the League were established in Uttar Pradesh alone. See his *Indian Problem,* 2:182–183.

[46] Not the Hindi of Gandhi's conception.

conserving Hindi orthodoxy than in promoting the wider objective of Hindi that he envisaged. At first, the orthodox group led by Tandon, in order to profit from Gandhi's support, assured him that the name itself was not so important and that the functions formulated by Gandhi would be performed.[47] The orthodox group was in fact concerned with the popularization of "pure Hindi" rather than Gandhi's conception of Hindi. In the Abohar session of the Sammelan in 1941, it frankly resolved that Hindi and Urdu were two different entities, and it thus refused to accommodate Urdu in the scope of its conception of Hindi. It was obvious in this conference that despite the popularity and political status of Gandhi, Nehru, and Prasad, their followers represented a minority faction in the Sammelan organization.

In 1942 Gandhi gave up the hope of utilizing the Sammelan and resigned from its leadership, though he did not give up his membership. The same year, together with Nehru and Prasad, he established the Hindustani Prachar Sabha for the dissemination of Hindustani, which would serve, he thought, as the medium of contact and intercourse between various provinces with different provincial languages, and which might come to be used throughout India for social, political, administrative, and other such purposes of the nation.[48] The new organization did not succeed appreciably in winning the bases of support that were built by the Sammelan. The orthodox group, under the leadership of Tandon, retained most of its bases. In North India, the Gandhian effort to mold the direction of the Hindi movement faced a bleak future, by and large. The split in the Hindi Sahitya Sammelan naturally affected its subsidiary organizations conducting Hindi promotional work in the non-Hindi areas. Two such organizations were prominent—the Dakshina Bharat Hindi Prachar Sabha, founded in 1918, and the Rashtrabhasha Prachar Samiti, founded in 1936. Both of these organizations were initiated by Gandhi. After the split, however, the Samiti remained closer

[47] See Gandhi's account cited in M. P. Desai, *Hindi Prachar Movement*, p. 19. See also D. G. Tendulkar, *Mahatma* (Bombay: Times of India Press, 1954), 8:295–296.
[48] See M. K. Gandhi, *Thoughts on National Language*, pp. 114–115.

to the Sammelan. The Sabha, on the other hand, consistently fol-
lowed the Gandhian leadership. It is worth noting that though
Gandhi's efforts to guide the Hindi movement failed in North
India, they were eminently successful in South India owing to
the persistent Gandhian influence on the Dakshina Bharat Hindi
Prachar Sabha.[49]

The failure of Gandhi's efforts to popularize the Hindustani
Prachar Sabha in North India—even though some of the most
prominent North Indian leaders, like Nehru, Prasad, and Azad,
were associated with the organization—can largely be explained
by the fact that the Hindi movement in this area was firmly controlled by a leadership that was closely related to the orthodox
Hindu identification of Hindi with Hindu political interests.
Gandhi was not alone in failing to promote Hindustani in this
area. From 1927 a group of literary authors and educators were
trying to promote Hindustani as a language of composite Hindu
and Muslim culture. This organization, the Hindustani Academy,[50] founded in 1927 by Rai Rajeshwar Bali, could not make
any significant mark. In 1945, a more popularly based organization, the Hindustani Culture Society, was established in Allahabad. Eminent liberal politicians and intellectuals, like Tej Bahadur Sapru, Bhagwan Das, and Tara Chand, actively tried to
promote this organization as a forum for the propagation of a
composite culture and language transcending religious barrier.[51]

[49] For details about associational work for the propagation of Hindi in
the South, see P. K. Keshavan Nayar, *Dakshin me Hindi Prachar-Andolan
ka Sankhiptatmak Itihas* (Lucknow: Hindi Sahitya Bhandar, 1963, in Hindi).
See also, *Rajat Jayanti Granth* (Wardha: Rashtrabhasha Prachar Samiti,
1962), part 5 (in Hindi). Hindi associational work in South India was started
with the support of Dr. A. Besant and Sir C. P. Ramaswany Iyer. The educational work of the Samiti was started by Devadas Gandhi, who was specially
deputed by M. K. Gandhi. Some of the information in this section was
supplied by Kaka Kalelkar in an interview in July 1964.

[50] See *Directory of Educational, Scientific, Literary and Cultural Organizations in India* (Delhi: Government of India, 1948), p. 311.

[51] See *ibid.*, p. 233. For its definition of Hindustani culture as a common
culture of Hindus and Muslims, see *Hindustani Culture Society, The In-
augural Address of Dr. B. Das* (Allahabad: Hindustani Culture Society,
1945). This pamphlet also contains Tej Bahadur Sapru's speech and the
organization's main resolutions. The leading organizer of this society was
Pandit Sundar Lal.

This organization too failed to gain any mass popularity. Pressed between the particularistic loyalties for Hindi and Urdu, the ground for the growth of any organization attempting to work for a composite language tended gradually to disappear.

*Failure of Compromise*

The widening distance between Hindi and Urdu, and the reluctance of the major associations concerned with each to reach a compromise, reflected the increasing distance between Hindus and Muslims. The attitude of the political parties of religious persuasion increasingly hardened. At the Lucknow session of the All India Muslim League held in 1937, it was declared that the League would make every effort to make Urdu the universal language of India; and similarly, in 1939, the Hindu Mahasabha declared that Sanskritized Hindi and not Hindustani rightly deserved to be the national language of India.[52] The question of national language now became a highly explosive political issue, and particularistic leaders on each side refused to compromise.[53]

[52] For these declarations see Asoka Mehta and Achyut Patwardhan, *Communal Triangle* (n. 20 above), pp. 156–157. In 1941 a Muslim fundamentalist organization, founded by Maulana Maududi, organized the Renaissance Movement which later became Jamaat-i-Islami. Maududi became the organizational "chief." The Jamaat was an extremist organization of Muslim revivalism, and its leaders championed an extreme form of Urdu particularism. The Jamaat became more influential after the birth of Pakistan than it was when it operated in undivided India. See S. A. A. Maududi, *The Islamic Law and Constitution*, trans. and ed. Khurshid Ahmad (Lahore: Islamic Publications, 1960), p. 432; and Leonard Binder, *Religion and Politics in Pakistan* (Berkeley and Los Angeles: University of California Press, 1961), pp. 80–89.

[53] In a session of the All India Muslim Educational Conference held at Poona in 1940, the report of the Kamal Yar Jung Committee revealed the attitudes of the Muslim community as defined by some of their leaders in these terms: "There is absolutely no doubt about the fact that in some places deliberate efforts are being made to replace the Urdu language from its present position and status in India. . . . There is not a doubt . . . that Urdu is being supplanted or reconditioned and unless the Muslim community now takes up the question, its ultimate effect will mean a great disaster to the best interests of Muslim education in India." See N. N. Mitra, ed., *The Indian Annual Register*, July–December 1940, p. 414. Similar suspicions and responses were expressed in the Uttar Pradesh Muslim Students' Conference held in Allahabad in 1940, where Congress governments were accused of

The only major attempt for a policy of compromise was continued by Gandhi, who claimed that as soon as a cooperation and compromise between the Hindi Sahitya Sammelan and the Anjuman could be achieved, the work of his own Hindustani Prachar Sabha would be deemed to be over.[54] In 1945, he invited P. D. Tandon (Sammelan) and Abdul Haq (Anjuman) to the Hindustani Prachar Sabha Conference at Wardha in order to devise a compromise between the two mutually hostile associations. This move did not succeed. In an important exchange of letters between Gandhi and Tandon in 1945, Tandon indicated that he regarded Urdu as a particular form of Hindi and that the Sammelan did not intend to concern itself with this form.[55] Tandon said that an intermingling of Hindi and Urdu would be possible only when writers and associations of both Hindi and Urdu manifested their belief in it. Tandon did not believe that the Urdu-speaking people would welcome it. He was not in favor of any unilateral move on the part of his organization in this regard. He also pointed out that it was a matter of the intermingling not only of two languages but also of two scripts, because experience had suggested to him that though it might be possible for ordinary purposes to have one language which could be written in either of two scripts, the same would not be possible where matters of a deeper or of a literary nature were involved. He reiterated that a permanent mixing of the two languages would be possible only when a common script developed for the country.

Gandhi was not convinced by these arguments, and he gave up his ordinary membership in the HSS, which he had retained so far, in July 1945. In his letter of resignation he wrote that he now recognized the comparatively greater difficulty in promoting Hindustani than in working for either Hindi or Urdu, but he

changing the system of education in a manner that was antagonistic to Muslim interests. One resolution protested against the use of Sanskrit religious words on the convocation degrees of the Agra University, "which hurt the feelings and susceptibilities of the Muslim students" (*ibid.*, p. 416).

[54] See M. K. Gandhi, *Thoughts on National Language*, p. 119.

[55] For the contents of the letters in this exchange see *ibid.*, pp. 133–142.

was convinced that there was no other way. However, he knew he was fighting a losing battle. His own journal, *Harijan Sevak*, which had a Urdu script edition, was facing ridicule from both Hindi and Urdu quarters. Inside the Indian National Congress organization, despite its formal acceptance of Hindustani, opposition was growing from the faction led by Tandon and other Hindi leaders. Similarly, neither the supporters of Urdu outside Congress nor the Muslim supporters of Hindustani inside Congress showed any enthusiasm to learn both the Urdu and the Nagari scripts. Even Maulana Azad seemed to be silent on this point.[56] Gandhi, however, asked the Sabha to continue its Hindustani campaigns, whether the Muslims were ready to adopt Hindustani or not. He only hoped that some day Muslims would adopt Hindustani written in the Nagari and the Urdu scripts. But a sense of despair could be clearly discerned in the feelings he expressed during the 1940s, and he knew that more difficult times lay ahead. Ultimately, his hope of reconciling the Hindu and the Muslim interests in one unified India was rudely shaken when India was divided in 1947, and his dream of making Hindustani the national language of India was largely shattered when the Congress decided in the Constituent Assembly of India that Hindi would be the official language of the federal government of independent India. In addition, no Hindi state within the Indian Union accepted Hindustani—after independence all of them chose Hindi as their official language.

## A Perspective

A number of interesting points seem to emerge from the development of language rivalry during the national movement. The juxtaposition of language interest with political interest during this phase in particular indicates how language issues are formulated through a complex tangle of interaction among social, cultural, and political factors. The conscious design of identifying the case for Hindi with the cause of Hindu solidarity, and the equally conscious endeavor to separate Hindi from its

[56] *Ibid.*, p. 172.

Hindu background and from the orthodox revivalist causes, suggest the scope of alternative definitions of the language interest, depending on the political preoccupations of mobilizing groups and leaders. The case of Urdu is even more instructive. When the Muslim League and the Aligarh movement identified Urdu as the symbol of Muslim separatism, and later of the Pakistan movement, they left several questions unanswered. In undivided India none of the Muslim majority provinces could be said to be Urdu-speaking. Even after Pakistan was born, Urdu was officially claimed to be the language of only about 7 percent of the total population. The entire Urdu movement was understandably limited to the Muslim minority in the province of Uttar Pradesh. As a second language, the scope of Urdu was extremely limited except in Punjab and in some scattered areas of Bihar and Deccan. And yet, by constant political affirmation, Urdu gained a unique symbolic status and capability in the Muslim separatist movement. The irony is that after the division of the subcontinent, the vast majority of the Urdu speakers as well as the seats of Urdu culture remained in India. Objectively speaking, it can be argued that the utilization of Urdu for political separatism was clearly against the interests of the Urdu speakers as well as the non-Urdu-speaking majority of the Muslims of undivided India.

The definition of language interest thus cannot be automatically derived from the position of a language community in the language situation of the country. It has to be understood in the context of a plurality of intervening variables of which politics is one of the most important. The question of politics also leaves a number of choices, depending on the orientation of the actors and their perceived relation to the actual situation. In the Indian national movement, Gandhi, Nehru, and a group of Deoband-oriented leaders explored one alternative. Their definition of Hindi-Urdu may have been congruent with what the technical linguists think about Hindi and Urdu, but they failed to make this definition sufficiently persuasive in the face of rising Hindu and Muslim particularism.

Whatever the outcome of the language rivalry of these enigmatic decades, the role of the developing language associations of this time must be appreciated. During this period the Hindi Sahitya Sammelan developed into a well-knit organization spreading its roots in different parts of North India. It would be a mistake to treat it as an agitational appendage of the Indian National Congress. Its leadership and the cadre were drawn from a variety of political affiliations. Within it, various factions of the Congress fought their own battles of power, status, and ideas, not always necessarily related to language. The most notable feature of the Sammelan was its lack of dependence on the Congress or for that matter on any other political organization. The Sammelan autonomously developed an extensive educational system for the dissemination of education in Hindi. The educational efforts that reached the remotest corners of North India in particular helped it to employ a large bureaucratic institution. This institution published textbooks, employed hundreds of teachers, and established a network of schools. The Sammelan's southern subsidiary proceeded in the same way.[57] Through these processes the Sammelan gradually became an established educational institution with a professional apparatus and self-sustained financing derived mainly from educational fees and the sale of publications. In this way the Sammelan was involved in a routinized year-round operation with a rich store of assets in material and personnel. These material and personnel resources could be used by the Sammelan for open political campaigns. This autonomous structure with its self-sustaining resources gave the Sammelan a unique bargaining advantage. A Gandhi or a Nehru could not hope to be in a position to control or unduly influence such a structured organization. They had to negotiate with the established apparatus of the Sammelan despite the fact that the leaders of the Sammelan continued to be Congress notables. By and large, this was also true of the Rashtrabhasha Prachar Samiti and the Dakshina Bharat Hindi Prachar Sabha. Unlike these organizations, the Anjuman Taraqqi-i-Urdu remained largely a cultural association without a large-scale edu-

[57] For details see Kantilal Joshi, (n. 34 above), pp. 583 ff.

cational and publication network, and failed to develop any imposing, self-sustained, routinized structure. In a large part this was a legacy of the organizational structure underlying the Muslim separatist movement.[58]

The organized structure of the language associations which remained close to the Indian National Congress bears testimony to the structural development and diversity that pervaded the Indian national movement. One of the notable features of this phenomenon was the network of autonomous associations, such as trade unions, peasant organizations, student organizations, teachers' associations, and a number of cultural associations, which sustained the national movement. These organizations also served important functions of financial support, continuous recruitment of new cadres, and socialization of personnel in accordance with the demands of the national movement. In this general context, the language associations performed a significant function by contributing to the organizational diversification and development of the Indian national movement. While these associations have continued to make a substantial contribution to language policy-making in independent India, in independent Pakistan the role of the organized language associations in language policy-making has been minimal. This contrast seems to arise from the variation in the structural development of the Muslim separatist and the Indian national movements in terms of associational development and diversification.

[58] For an account of the heavy reliance of the Muslim separatist movement on largely ad hoc organizational endeavors, see Khalid Bin Sayeed, *Pakistan, The Formative Phase* (n. 7 above), especially chap. 3.

# V

## Language Rivalry
## After Independence

The partition of the country into two separate states did not, in any way, facilitate the solution of the language problems in either India or Pakistan. If anything, the partition further complicated the language question and brought in its wake a complex set of new problems. At the time of the partition, Pakistan absorbed about 64 million of the Muslim population of the subcontinent, while the new state of India contained about 36 million Muslims.[1] If one accepts the principle set forth by the leaders of Muslim separatism that religion is the basic criterion of a nation, one can understand the problem of status which the creation of Pakistan undoubtedly posed for the Muslims in new India. Actually the problem was more complicated, because the leaders of the Pakistan movement were mostly drawn from the Hindu majority provinces of undivided India.[2] In practice many of these leaders solved their own problems by migrating to Pakistan. But those Muslims in post-partition India who failed to do so—and they constituted the bulk of the Muslims—were caught in a critical dilemma. On July 6, 1947, M. A. Jinnah

[1] These figures are based on the 1951 census returns. They do not include Jammu and Kashmir and the tribal areas of Assam.

[2] Most of them were from Uttar Pradesh (United Provinces till the partition). Aligarh is located in Uttar Pradesh.

advised the Muslims who were to remain in India that "the minorities should be loyal to the State to which they belong."[3] But it was not easy for the Muslim League leaders remaining in India to reconcile their earlier declarations with the role that Jinnah now expected them to perform. One such eminent leader, who stayed in India for a brief period after the partition and was at that time in charge of the Muslim League in India, now referred to the two-nation theory as one that had paid no dividends to the Muslims.[4] As he put it, especially after the partition, the two-nation theory "proved positively injurious to the Muslims of India, and on a long-view basis for Muslims everywhere."[5] These reevaluations—rarely expressed in public—were of no help in solving the predicament of millions of Muslims who had joined the Pakistan movement and yet were constrained to stay in India.

These belated reevaluations were being made when large parts of the subcontinent had already witnessed mass violence on both sides of the newly drawn border. The demand for Pakistan was based on the idea that the Hindus and Muslims cannot and should not live together. And yet after the partition Hindus and Muslims had to live together in both India and Pakistan. In post-partition India the legacy of Muslim separatism could not be undone by occasional private admissions on the part of some Muslim League leaders of the inappropriateness of communal particularism. As for Pakistan, the anomaly was not so perturbing. From the very beginning of its creation as a new state, Pakistan has been officially declared to be an Islamic state. In India, a minority of Hindu leaders thought that a similar solution could

[3] Cited in C. Khaliquzzaman, *Pathway to Pakistan* (Lahore: Longmans, Green, 1961), p. 393. M. A. Jinnah was a Gujarati Muslim who operated from Bombay in undivided India.

[4] *Ibid.*, p. 400. The author was one of the most prominent leaders of the Muslim League. He left for Pakistan in late 1947.

[5] *Ibid.*, p. 400. See also similar response to the two-nation theory from Shaheed Suhrawardy, who was one of the most prominent leaders of the Bengal Muslim League and in that capacity stayed in India for a brief period after the partition. Later on he turned against the Muslim League when he worked in Pakistan. *Ibid.*, pp. 397-399.

be reached if the state were declared a Hindu state.[6] But no such easy solution appealed to the majority of the Indian leaders, who were determined to put into practice their principle of composite nationalism.[7] However, the leaders of the Indian National Congress now faced a situation substantially more difficult than before the partition.

Hindu communal groups had always challenged the rationale of the principle of composite nationalism. They accused men like Gandhi and Nehru of being pro-Muslim, just as the Muslim League always insisted that Gandhi was a leader of the Hindus and that the Congress was a Hindu organization.[8] After the partition, the particularist Hindu groups squarely blamed the Congress for the splitting of the country. These groups also claimed that once the fact of the partition had been recognized, no gesture of conciliation should be shown to Muslims living in India. They insisted that the Congress policies of promoting a common culture should be drastically revised. These were strong views, and their emotional appeal was considerably strengthened by the violent political situation leading to and precipitated by the partition. The entire atmosphere thus posed grave difficulties for the implementation of the principles of common nationalism as cherished by the Congress and the other Indian leaders who subscribed to such principles. It is not surprising that these difficulties considerably influenced the discussion of national language questions in independent India.

[6] This idea is reflected in the demand for Hindu raj made by the Hindu Mahasabha in its election manifesto of 1951. See also D. E. Smith, *India as a Secular State* (Princeton, N. J.: Princeton University Press, 1967), pp. 461 ff. (paperback), for a representative selection of the views of the Mahasabha leaders on this question.

[7] For an analysis of this secular nationalism, see *ibid.*, pp. 139–160.

[8] One of the persistent problems of Congress-League negotiations was that the Muslim League consistently maintained that it must be accepted as the sole representative of the Muslims. This implied that the Congress should be viewed as a Hindu organization. Similarly, Jinnah also wanted Gandhi to agree that he was the spokesman of the Hindu community. See Morris Gwyer and A. Appadorai, eds., *Speeches and Documents on the Indian Constitution, 1921–47* (Bombay: Oxford University Press, 1957), vol. 1, especially pp. 429–432. See also J. Ahmed, ed., *Some Recent Speeches and Writings of Mr. Jinnah* (Lahore: S. M. Ashraf, 1943).

## Language and the Constitution

The Constituent Assembly came into existence in December 1946—a few months before the country was partitioned. During the initial sessions of the Assembly, its members were uncertain about the nature of its authority. The Muslim League boycotted the Assembly, but there was still some hope that it would eventually join. In about six months, the suspense was over, for by May 1947 the decision to partition India was in the air. The language question had engaged the attention of the Assembly from the very beginning of its existence. The nature of the debate during the initial sessions differed markedly from the pattern that followed, after it became known that the country was going to be split in two. During the initial sessions, the Rules Committee of the Assembly decided that the Assembly proceedings should be transacted primarily in Hindustani or in English. The language debates of this period reflected the persuasiveness of Hindustani.[9] This persuasiveness was virtually lost by the time the fourth Assembly session met in July 1947 under the ominous shadow of the impending partition. It was from this time that a concerted move was made by the orthodox Hindi leaders to dislodge Hindustani and to install Hindi in its place. The most prominent leaders of the Hindi movement were also important members of the Constituent Assembly. They had reluctantly accepted the term Hindustani in the initial sessions of the Assembly. But from July 1947 they gave up their support for Hindustani. Even when they had lent their support, it was simply a strategic move to avoid openly confronting the powerful advocates of Hindustani headed by Nehru. These Hindi leaders now became convinced that there was no reason for even the slightest disguise for their kind of Hindi demands. For these Hindi leaders, Hindustani was a symbol of appeasement of

[9] See, for example, the reports of the speeches and activities of the prominent Hindi leaders, especially Seth Govind Das, in Ralph H. Retzlaff, "The Constituent Assembly of India and the Problem of Indian Unity" (Ph.D. dissertation, Cornell University, 1960), pp. 363–369.

the Muslim concern for Urdu. Even if there was reason to concede to the Gandhian sentiments before early 1947, once the prospect of partition was certain, there was, according to these Hindi leaders, no ground for any such concession. Actually, they perceived that this was a signal opportunity to openly deride Hindustani as a mask for Urdu and, by depicting Urdu as a Muslim language, to identify it with the demand for Pakistan and thus to claim that there should be no legitimate occasion to concede anything to a language that had functioned as a symbol of secession.[10] The Hindi leaders accordingly made a strong move to drop all the references to Hindustani that were accepted in the early sessions. They demanded that Hindi alone, written in the Deva Nagari script, be made the official language of India. In fact, their demand in the first stage was that Hindi should be made the national language of India. Subsequently, they accepted for Hindi the status of the official language.[11]

The Constituent Assembly was overwhelmingly dominated by the Congress. Within the Assembly, the Hindi leadership enjoyed a strong position. The top leaders of the Hindi bloc in the Assembly were P. D. Tandon, Govind Das, Sampurnanand, Ravi Shankar Shukla, and K. M. Munshi. They also represented the leading Hindi associations in the country. The first four were actively involved in Hindi politics from the very inception of the Hindi Sahitya Sammelan movement and all four came from

[10] A clear example of such an attitude can be found in the writings of one of the foremost writers of the Hindi Sahitya Sammelan, who said in 1948 that "the mask of Hindustani has now been torn up and the real face of Urdu has been revealed. Hence, it is imperative that for the sake of honesty only 'Nagari Hindi' has to be declared as the language of free India." Chandrabali Pandeya, *Sasan Me Nagari* (Allahabad: Hindi Sahitya Sammelan, 1948), pp. 60–61 (in Hindi). The idea that Hindustani or Urdu was antinational was expressed by a prominent leader of the Nagari Pracharani Sabha. See Sampurnanand, in *Hindustan Times*, November 14, 1947.

[11] One commentator has suggested that this change from national language to official language indicates the use of "a tactful euphemism." In a multilingual society the distinction between national and official language is of major significance. It is not simply a distinction of tactful usage. For the cited comment, see Granville Austin, *The Indian Constitution: Cornerstone of a Nation* (London: Oxford University Press, 1966), p. 266.

Hindi areas. It was left to Tandon and Govind Das, however, to lead the Hindi bloc in the Assembly with an aggressive zeal characteristic of "true believers."

Tandon was a leader of national stature. In 1948 he was a contestant in the election for president of the Indian National Congress but lost by a narrow margin. Soon, however, he was to capture this presidency. Personally he was an orthodox Hindu and politically he usually aligned himself with Hindu revivalist causes. Through patient organizational work he had established himself in the Congress politics in Uttar Pradesh and also as the most eminent spokesman of the Hindi Sahitya Sammelan. Seth Govind Das belonged to another Hindi area—Central Provinces, now Madhya Pradesh. Although he did not have the stature of Tandon, he was always recognized as an irrepressible champion of Hindi and the most dynamic spokesman of the Hindi Sahitya Sammelan. His Hindu orthodoxy, like Tandon's, was well known.[12] By and large, similar adherence to Hindu tradition and orthodoxy characterized the personal and the political careers of Sampurnanand, Ravi Shankar Shukla, K. M. Munshi, and Dr. Raghuvira, who later reinforced the Hindi leadership in the Constituent Assembly. They all tended to identify Hindi with Hindu cultural interests as they defined them. It is doubtful to what extent they really believed in the kind of composite nationalism that the platform of the Congress organization publicly expressed.

Within the Constituent Assembly, these Hindi leaders monopolized the advocacy of Hindi. But they were aware that emotional debates would be less effective in the concrete policy-making process of the Assembly than in public campaigns. In order to be effective in the Assembly, they needed a solid bloc

---

[12] In the Constituent Assembly debates he denied that he and Tandon were communal. His argument was that neither of them had been connected with any communal organization. It is true that both of them were consistently in the Congress movement. They were not organizationally connected with the Hindu Mahasabha. But both of them identified themselves with orthodox Hindu causes. For Govind Das' defense see *Constituent Assembly Debates* (Delhi: Manager of Publications, 1949), vol. 9, no. 32, p. 1328 (hereafter cited as *C.A.D.*).

of votes. They knew that in mobilizing such votes they would encounter powerful adversary forces in support of Hindustani and under the prestigious leadership of Nehru and Azad. They were also conscious of the power of the Congress leaders drawn from the non-Hindi areas in general and from South India in particular.

For the Hindi leaders, this was a complex situation which demanded careful planning. Their strategy was first to effectively inhibit the incipient support for the retention of English for all practical purposes that was apparent in many South Indian Congressmen's participation in the language debates.[13] This move required the building of a common front of the Hindi and the Hindustani blocs, in order to assure that the case for English did not make any headway. In order to make such a common cause the Hindi leaders constantly invoked the need to maintain continuity with the Congress heritage of supporting a national language to replace English. Thus, while talking to the South Indian Assembly members, the Hindi leaders maintained the need to carry on the Gandhian mission of replacing English with Hindustani. At the same time, to the Gandhian members of the Assembly, they reiterated the need to replace Hindustani with Hindi. It was this second strategy which, more than the other, required an open struggle against the leadership of Nehru and Azad.

Throughout the history of the Congress a tradition had evolved which required the solution of controversial questions by consensual decisions.[14] For decades before the operation of the Constituent Assembly, consensual decision-making came to mean in effect the prevalence of the will of the established leader-

[13] For the most important language debates, see *C.A.D.*, vol. 1, no. 2; vol. 8, no. 3; and vol. 9, nos. 32, 33, and 34. For an analysis of these debates see R. H. Retzlaff, "Constituent Assembly," pp. 369 ff., and Granville Austin, *Indian Constitution*, chap. 12.

[14] For a perceptive discussion in general terms, see Susanne Hoeber Rudolph, "Consensus and Conflict in Indian Politics," *World Politics* 13, no. 3 (April 1961): 385–399. For a detailed discussion of the significance of the consensual norm in Indian village politics, see Ralph H. Retzlaff, *Village Government in India* (Bombay: Asia Publishing House, 1962).

ship as symbolized by Gandhi. Despite the general acceptance of democratic principles and procedures, the nationalist leaders always insisted that the adversary principle of decision-making was not consistent with the political culture of India. The insistence on consensual decision-making was due in part to the recognition that in a plural society of religious, ethnic, and linguistic diversity, solving major political problems by recourse to majority decisions might substantially affect the integration of the minority communities into the wider political community. In part, of course, this was a direct reflection of the norm of the traditional Indian system of authority concerning the solution of the basic conflicts in society and politics, which emphasized solution of conflicts by consensual procedure and conciliatory leadership.

Given the influence of such norms and their incorporation into the nationalist movement, it was difficult for the Hindi leaders of the Congress to challenge the established Gandhi-Nehru leadership into an open adversary confrontation. But they were convinced that the task of framing a constitution involved a set of long-range interests too fundamental to be settled by ephemeral conciliation and piecemeal compromise. Of these interests, the language interest was naturally perceived by them as one of unique consequence. A decision of the Assembly concerning the national or official language of India would, for example, usher in a chain of substantial changes in the educational processes, prospects of comparative mobility of social classes, and relative mobility of the regional elites in the country.

It was in this context that Govind Das clearly affirmed the adversary principle in settling national language questions facing the Constituent Assembly. Opposing the conciliatory guiding remarks on the language debate made by the president of the Assembly,[15] Govind Das declared: "We have accepted de-

[15] Rajendra Prasad, the president of the Assembly, said, "There is no other item in the whole Constitution of the country which will be required to be implemented from day to day, from hour to hour . . . from minute to minute in actual practice." This referred to the salience of the language question, and he pointed out that "Even if we succeed in getting a particular

mocracy and democracy can only function when majority opinion is honoured. If we differ on any issue, that can only be
decided by votes. Whatever decision is arrived [at] by the majority must be accepted by the minority respectfully and without
any bitterness."[16] Govind Das was not only of the opinion that
the language issue *should* be solved by votes; he was also sure
that it *could* be solved by votes. He, along with Tandon and
others, had tirelessly mobilized votes for the cause of Hindi both
inside the Assembly and, what was more important, within the
Congress caucus in the Assembly. Moreover, outside the Assembly, his Hindi Sahitya Sammelan—he was then its president—
carefully organized public pressure campaigns to influence the
Assembly's opinion on Hindi. A steady stream of letters concerning language policy was addressed to the central office of
the Congress organization on the eve of the crucial decision on
the language question. Govind Das took personal initiative in
hastily organizing a National Language Convention in New
Delhi, to which he invited a group of eminent linguists, writers,
and leaders of regional language associations in order to
strengthen the case for Hindi. The leaders of the Bangiya
Sahitya Parishad, the Kannada Sahitya Parishad, and the great
South Indian writers like Vallathol and Kunhan Raja were
among those who joined this convention.[17] It was, of course, a
highly selective group. The organizers had invited mostly those
intellectuals whose sympathy for Hindi was well known and
who were by no means representative of the language views of
their regions.[18] However, one must appreciate the organizational

proposition passed by majority, if it does not meet with the approval of any
considerable section of people in the country—either in the north or in the
south, the implementation of the Constitution will become a most difficult
problem." See *C.A.D.*, vol. 9, no. 32, p. 1312.

[16] *Ibid.*, p. 1325.

[17] *Ibid.*, p. 1327.

[18] For example, there were three participants from Bengal. K. C. Chatterjee was a professor of Sanskrit in Allahabad who had hardly any connection
with the opinions prevailing in Bengal concerning the national language
policy. Suniti Kumar Chatterjee was actively associated with the major Hindi
language associations, as was S. K. Das. None of them could be said to
represent Bengal's opinion or even the Bengali writers' opinion concerning

skill and resources of the Sammelan in quickly organizing such an apparently national convention that lent complete support to Hindi just on the eve of the most important language debate in the Assembly.[19] Tactically, it enabled the Hindi block to affirm that the cause of Hindi was not necessarily identified with Hindi particularism.

These organizational moves supplemented the basic strength that the Hindi leaders had been mobilizing inside the Congress caucus in the Assembly. The basic strength lay, of course, in the votes that the Hindi leaders succeeded in mobilizing. The most dramatic demonstration of this power of mobilization was found in a crucial voting that took place in a meeting of Congress party members of the Assembly during the crucial language debates in the Assembly in 1949. As Govind Das himself describes it, the Hindi bloc faced in this meeting a powerful Hindustani bloc, which used the influence of Nehru and that of the leading Congress ministers to defend Hindustani against Hindi. But despite such personal and official influence, in this meeting the Hindi block won by 78 against 77 votes cast for Hindustani.[20] This was an impressive demonstration of the relative strength of the Hindi bloc. At the same time it was an indication of the limit of the mobilizational capacity of the

national language policy. The four Hindi writers participating in this conference were all former officeholders and contemporary activists in the Hindi Sahitya Sammelan. For details concerning this convention, see Govind Das, *Atma-Nirikshan* (Delhi: Bharatiya Bisva Prakashan, 1958), 3:123–127, and appendix 2 (in Hindi, but the appendix cited contains an English version of the main resolution).

[19] Granville Austin suggests that this convention was intended "to be a claque for Hindi and for Govind Das." He also doubts whether the participants were really well known. In fact, the eminence of the participants cannot be doubted, nor can the convention be described merely as a claque. Actually it was a gathering of well-known writers who, for a long time, had sincerely believed that Hindi should be India's national language. For Austin's comment, see his *Indian Constitution*, p. 291.

[20] In this meeting the Hindustani bloc demanded a recount, which resulted in a tie—77 for and 77 against Hindi. The loss of one vote was due to the absence of one Hindi supporter during this recount. This account is taken from Govind Das, *Atma-Nirikshan*, 3:128–130. See also R. H. Retzlaff, "Constituent Assembly," pp. 404–405.

Hindi bloc in the Constituent Assembly. Given the almost equal strength in the Assembly of the rival blocs in the Congress party, it was obvious that these rivals both needed a measure of compromise if they cared for a viable national language policy. The mood of the house also favored a compromise. Ultimately, a compromise was reached on the basis of what became known as the Munshi-Ayyangar formula.[21] This formula did not provide for a national language. It used the term "official language of the Union" and provided that this language would be Hindi written in Deva Nagari script. The acceptance of this provision by the Constituent Assembly of India clearly suggests that in spite of many concessions on details, the Hindi bloc was successful in getting its major demand accepted by the framers of the Indian Constitution.

## Union Official Language: The Legal Position

The nature of the compromise accepted by the Constituent Assembly is revealed in the provisions in the Constitution of India relating to language. It is no wonder that these language provisions are complicated, occasionally ambiguous, and sometimes undoubtedly confusing.[22] The constitution provided that the official language of the Union should be Hindi in Deva Nagari script with international numerals.[23] For a period of fifteen years from the effective date of the constitution (1950), English should continue to be used for all the official purposes of the Union. However, Parliament could by law provide for the use after the aforesaid period of fifteen years of English or

[21] For details, see *C.A.D.*, vol. 9, no. 32, pp. 1321–1323. For an analysis of this formula, see Granville Austin, pp. 295 ff.

[22] It has been remarked: "The Constitution in its articles relating to (language) is concerned more with difficulties of achieving results than with the necessity for doing things effectively and promptly." S. Natarajan, "Pertinent Facts," *Seminar*, no. 68 (April 1965), p. 12. See also, D. D. Basu, *Introduction to the Constitution of India*, p. 206.

[23] For provisions relating to official language of the Union and a standard commentary on the provisions, see D. D. Basu, *Commentary on the Constitution of India*, 5:160–166. For the official text of the language provisions, see *The Constitution of India* (Delhi: Manager of Publications, 1965), pp. 182–187, 271.

Deva Nagari numerals for such purposes as might be specified in law. Subsequently the Official Language Act of 1963 provided for the use of English in addition to Hindi for all the official purposes of the Union and for the transaction of business in Parliament. The difference between the earlier fifteen-year period and the period after 1963 is that whereas the original clause in the constitution stated that English "shall continue to be used," the 1963 act merely says that English "may continue to be used."[24] The constitution also provides for the appointment of a commission, as well as a committee of Parliament to advise the president on certain matters relating to the official language. The duty of the commission is to make recommendations to the president regarding, among other things, the progressive use of Hindi for the official purposes of the Union and restrictions on the use of English for all or any of the official purposes of the Union. The first Official Language Commission submitted its report in 1956, which was presented to Parliament in 1957 and examined by a Joint Parliamentary Committee.

The directive for the development of Hindi, embodied in the constitution, is worth noting. It declares:

It shall be the duty of the Union to promote the spread of the Hindu language, to develop it so that it may serve as a medium of expression for all the elements of the *composite culture* of India and to secure its enrichment by *assimilating* without interfering with its genius, the forms, style and expressions used in *Hindustani* and in the other languages of India specified in the Eighth Schedule and by drawing, wherever necessary or desirable, for its vocabulary, *primarily on Sanskrit* and secondarily on other languages.[25]

This constitutional directive is a curious piece, which attempts to combine so many things in its concept of Hindi that it leaves a wide scope for conflicting interpretations. Thus, the proponents of Hindustani have interpreted this clause in a way that suggests that the Hindi of the Indian constitution is quite different from

---

[24] See Art. 343 (Clause 2) of the Constitution of India, D. D. Basu, *Commenary*, 5:160; and see Sec. 3 of the Official Languages Act, 1963.

[25] Art. 351 of the Indian constitution (emphasis added).

the orthodox concept. At the same time, the Hindi groups have apparently found in the same clause a vindication of their own ideas.

The Hindi Sahitya Sammelan, after the constitution became effective, began a systematic campaign to identify the official Hindi with Sanskritized Hindi. At the same time, the pro-Hindustani groups tried to draw a distinction between regional Hindi and national Hindi. The constitutional directive referred to the duty of the Union to promote Hindi as the expression of a composite culture and urged the assimilation of various forms and styles into Hindi. However, the Hindi Sahitya Sammelan refused to believe that there could be any special kind of national Hindi, different from the Sammelan's definition of Hindi. P. D. Tandon of the Sammelan, for instance, declared that it was impossible to separate regional Hindi from national Hindi.[26] And yet there was an ambiguity in the conception of Hindi advocated by even some of the Sammelan leaders. One of these leaders declared that he would not like to see his regional Hindi altered for the sake of making it more acceptable as a national language—he would rather see Hindi refuse the crown than have its appearance changed.[27] Another leader claimed that after independence the real appearance of Hindi had not been recognized in Delhi.[28] The ambiguity of the Hindi leaders lay in the fact that they were trying to achieve two opposite purposes at the same time: to control Hindi from its regional base, and to free it from any rigid association with a specific region in order to lend it a national color. On the other hand, the Hindustani associations were advocating the promotion of a national

[26] He said, "What a humbug it is that some few people are propagating that the U. P. regional Hindi and the all-India national Hindi are separate!" Cited in M. P. Desai, *The Hindi Prachar Movement*, p. 37.

[27] Cited in M. P. Desai, "Explanatory Note," *Report of the Official Language Commission*, 1956, p. 388.

[28] Thus, Chandrabali Pandeya compared the state of Hindi, after independence, with the condition of Shakuntala, in Kalidasa's epic, when she fondly hoped to be recognized by the king and yet had failed to achieve her end. See Gouri Shankar Gupta," "Acharya Chandrabali Pandeya," *Saptahik Hindustan*, May 13, 1962 (in Hindi).

form of Hindi that might assume different patterns in different regions, thus destroying the caretaker role of any particular regional elite over Hindi. A similar point was brought out in the report of the Bombay Hindi Teaching Committee (1951) sponsored by the government of Bombay, which stated that "Hindi as adopted in the Constitution of India does not mean Hindi the Home Language or Regional Hindi. Hindi mentioned in the Eighth Schedule and Hindi mentioned in Articles 343–351 cannot be the same. While the former is Regional Hindi, the latter is common Hindi otherwise known as Federal Language."[29] Such an interpretation of the constitutional directive is distasteful to the Hindi leadership, though for political purposes they are not averse to occasionally expressing opinions favoring the broadening of Hindi, albeit under their own guidance.

## Ambiguity and Resentment: Hindi-Urdu Struggle

The ambiguity of the Hindi leaders concerning the scope and definition of Hindi in independent India is brought out clearly in their attitude toward Urdu. In Uttar Pradesh the attitude of the Hindi leaders toward the Urdu-speaking population has always been problematic. After independence, the Urdu leaders of Uttar Pradesh resented what they perceived to be a deliberately unfair treatment of Urdu. When the Urdu leaders claimed equality of treatment for Hindi and Urdu, they were told that since Urdu and Hindi are the same language, the declaration of Hindi as the official language of the state of Uttar Pradesh automatically implied equality of status for Hindi and Urdu. This statement, coming as it did from the Hindi leaders, who overwhelmingly dominated the government of Uttar Pradesh and who were well known for their concern for the purity of Hindi, naturally failed to satisfy the Urdu leaders.

The context of the grievances of the Urdu speech community

---

[29] Cited in M. P. Desai, *Hindi Prachar Movement*, p. 34. B. G. Kher, the chief minister of Bombay—a leader of the Hindustani movement—said in 1951: "Because the name of our national language is Hindi, certain Hindi-speaking provinces are trying to foist their special brand of Hindi on the whole country as its national language" (*Harijan*, July 7, 1951).

was provided by the aggressively anti-Urdu attitude displayed by the Hindi group's leaders, inside and outside of government, during the process of enacting the Uttar Pradesh Official Languages Bill of 1950.[30] The state government had already outlined its policy in an administrative order dated October 8, 1947, which envisaged that Hindi in the Deva Nagari script would be the language of the state. The Uttar Pradesh Official Language Act, 1951, maintained the same position, reinforced by legislative authority, with the difference that it no longer deemed the use of non-Hindi languages permissible for persons not familiar with Hindi. In consonance with this view, the state government stated its keenness "to give all due facilities for speakers of the Urdu language." However, the debates on the order of 1947 as well as those preceding the official act of 1951 betrayed an attitude of Hindi leaders which provoked intense resentment among the Urdu leaders. On the one hand, the mover of the nonofficial resolution stated that "Urdu and Hindustani are no languages at all," and that, in Uttar Pradesh, after Sanskrit, Arabic, and Persian, there is only Hindi, and thus Hindi alone can be the "State Language."[31] On the other hand, the Hindi leaders assured the Urdu leaders that "the Hindi-Urdu question has been raised for nothing." Sampurnanand declared, "I don't agree that Hindi and Urdu are two languages. Nor do I admit that Urdu is a foreign language."[32] Sampurnanand's explanation

[30] For the administrative order of 1947, see *Report of the Uttar Pradesh Language Committee* (Lucknow: Superintendent, Printing and Stationery, U. P. 1963), pp. 87–88. For the Uttar Pradesh Official Language Act, 1951, see S. M. Husain, ed., *The Uttar Pradesh Local Acts, 1836–1960* (Lucknow: Eastern Book Company, 1962), 4:2550–2551.

[31] The mover was P. N. Singh. For his statements cited here, see *Proceedings of the Legislative Council of the United Provinces, Official Report* (Allahabad: Superintendent, Printing and Stationery, U. P., 1948), September 11, 1947, vol. 9, no. 6, pp. 380–383. For V. A. Ansari's response to this, see *ibid.*, pp. 385 ff.

[32] For these statements of Sampurnanand—one of the most prominent leaders of the Hindi Sahitya Sammelan—made in reply to the Urdu responses in the Uttar Pradesh Legislative Assembly, see *Uttar Pradesh Bidhan Sabha Ki Karyabali Ki Anukramanika* (Allahabad: Adhikshak, Rajkiya Mudranalaya ebam Lekhan Samagri, U. P., 1952), 66:71 (in Hindi). See also, *National Herald*, October 1, 1951.

was interpreted by the Urdu groups as an evasive strategy and the beginning of linguistic discriminations against Urdu. Begum Aizaz Rasool referred to the concrete cases of discriminations that had already begun. She said that already in the high school syllabus, "Urdu had been made an optional subject and Hindi compulsory in all groups." She added that nearly all the regional languages mentioned in the constitution were getting official support in one state or the other, but though Uttar Pradesh was the leading center of Urdu, that language was not given any protection.[33]

The sense of neglect felt by the Urdu speech community led the working committee of the Anjuman Taraqqi-i-Hind to lead a campaign on behalf of the Urdu-speaking people of Uttar Pradesh for the acceptance of Urdu as a regional language in the state. It planned to collect signatures on a mass scale and to submit a petition to the president of India for appropriate action. For this purpose, a Regional Language Committee was set up.[34] Dr. Zakir Hussain, who presided over the Regional Language Convention sponsored by the Anjuman, said that "the movement to get Urdu recognized as a regional language was a part of the democratic movement of the country."[35] Outlining the strategy of the movement, Abdul Gaffar stated that the Anjuman believed in "silent work" and that their "movement was strictly constitutional."[36] Dr. Zakir Hussain also declared in a press conference that the government of Uttar Pradesh had no

[33] See *National Herald*, October 1, 1951. In the Constituent Assembly she was assured by Nehru that Hindi-Urdu equality would be respected and that no formal action was necessary to protect this equality. She now felt that this assurance was not being respected.

[34] See *National Herald*, November 28, 1951. The committee consisted of H. U. Ansari (general secretary), K. P. Kaul (president) and prominent national Anjuman leaders like A. A. Suroor, Ehtisam Husain, M. H. Rizvi, Begum Razia Sajjad Zahir, and eight other important intellectuals and politicians.

[35] *National Herald*, December 25, 1951. At that time Dr. Zakir Hussain (who later became president of India) was the vice chancellor of the Aligarh University and the president of the Anjuman's national organization. Abdul Ghaffar was then the secretary of the Ajuman.

[36] *Ibid.*

right to decide in which language a child should start his education. The emphasis of the Anjuman was clear: it was accusing the Uttar Pradesh government of deliberately neglecting the status of and the opportunities for Urdu as declared in the Eighth Schedule of the Constitution and as set forth by various measures and assurances emanating from the leaders of the Union government of India. A directive from the Ministry of Education of the Union government issued to the state government was cited by a leader of the Anjuman in this connection. This directive of August 10, 1948, laid down the policy that in the primary or basic stages of instruction, the students should be instructed through the medium of the mother tongue.[37] However, the Urdu Regional Language Convention sponsored by the Anjuman in 1952 reported several complaints that in practice Urdu was being abolished from primary schools. The Anjuman's own enquiry about these charges substantiated these complaints.

The Anjuman launched a campaign for mass petitions from the Urdu speakers of Uttar Pradesh. Over ten thousand signatures were collected from Lucknow alone for the purpose of making a representation to the state government. A deputation of seven persons, led by Dr. Zakir Hussain, discussed the relevant issues with Sampurnanand, who was then the education minister of Uttar Pradesh. Evidently, the deputation was satisfied after the discussions. However, the convention reported in 1952 that nothing had been done to implement the assurances given in 1951. The state government's persistent silence about the question ultimately impelled the Anjuman to seek other ways. Later, it decided to send a deputation to the president of India. Article 347 of the Constitution of India offers a scope for presidential action which can direct any state to take action to redress linguistic grievances of a substantial population group in that state.[38] Before this deputation met the president, the Uttar Pra-

[37] This directive was cited by K. P. Kaul, a leader of the Anjuman. He also mentioned that the Uttar Pradesh government had endorsed this directive in a letter addressed to a member of the Legislative Assembly, which was dated August 3, 1948. See *National Herald*, January 6, 1952.

[38] Article 347 states: "On a demand being made in that behalf, the Presi-

desh unit of the Anjuman organized a number of representations, and in 1957 it organized the celebration of an Urdu Day. Meetings were organized in different parts of Uttar Pradesh on this day (August 25, 1957), and identical resolutions drafted by the Anjuman were passed in these meetings. In the same year, the Jamiat-ul-Ulama sent a representation to the commissioner for linguistic minorities which contained an approach similar to the one used by the Anjuman.[39] The commissioner—a special officer appointed by the president of India—brought such representations to the notice of the Uttar Pradesh government.[40]

A deputation of the national organization of the Anjuman met the president of India on April 29, 1958, and submitted a memorandum requesting him to issue a directive under Article 347 of the constitution to the governments of Uttar Pradesh, Bihar, Punjab, and Delhi, so that Urdu would be recognized throughout their territories for the purposes of education, and for the acceptance of Urdu documents in law courts and other government offices. The deputation consisted of eighteen members from various parts of the country.[41] In addition, the Minis-

dent may, if he is satisfied that a substantial proportion of the population of a State desires the use of any language spoken by them to be recognized by that State, direct that such language shall also be officially recognized throughout that State or any part thereof for such purpose as he may specify."

[39] See India, *Report of the Commissioner of Linguistic Minorities*, First Report (Delhi: Manager of Publications, 1959), p. 41.

[40] The Constitution (Seventh Amendment) Act, 1956, inserted the provision (Art. 350B) that it shall be the duty of the commissioner for linguistic minorities "to investigate all matters relating to the safeguards provided for linguistic minorities under this Constitution and report to the President upon those matters at such intervals as the President may direct, and the President shall cause all such reports to be laid before each house of Parliament, and sent to the Governments of the States concerned." This, as well as Art. 350A, were inserted in 1956, in order to safeguard the interests of the linguistic minorities, which created special problems as a result of the reorganization of the states. See D. D. Basu, *Commentary on the Constitution of India*, 5:165–166.

[41] The deputation consisted of H. N. Kunzru, M.P.; Hifzur Rahman, M.P.; R. B. Gaur, M.P.; Dr. Tara Chand (historian); Hukum Singh (deputy speaker of the Lok Sabha); Aruna Asaf Ali (mayor, Delhi); Sunder Lal (Hindustani Culture Society); Gopinath Aman (journalist), and other

try of Home Affairs of the government of India considered representations made by the Anjuman and "after considering the said representations and other matters" issued a press note on July 14, 1958. This note was welcomed by the Anjuman as having substantially met their demands. In a press communique issued on July 20, 1958, the government of Uttar Pradesh also fully accepted the press note.[42] The press note reiterated that Urdu and Hindi are very closely allied and may be considered to be basically the same language. But it recognized the distinctive features of Urdu, including its script, and added that Urdu "is essentially a language of our country, and its homeland is India," and that "Urdu is officially and constitutionally recognized as one of our national languages and the various provisions that apply to these languages, apply to Urdu also."[43]

It is worth noting that through the press note, the Union government recommended several facilities for Urdu and suggested that Urdu should be encouraged "in addition to other reasons, from the literary point of view." The implication is that the status of a language in India should not be decided upon merely by a quantitative criterion. The specific proposals for extending facilities to the Urdu speech community were the following:

(1) Facilities should be provided for instruction and examination in the Urdu language at the primary stage to all children whose mother tongue is declared by the parent or guardian to be Urdu.
(2) Arrangements should be made for the training of teachers and for providing textbooks in Urdu.
(3) Facilities for instruction in Urdu should also be provided in the secondary stage of education.
(4) Documents in Urdu should be accepted by all courts and offices without the necessity of translation or transliteration in any other

intellectuals and politicians like M. H. Rizvi, A. A. Suroor, B. H. Zaidi, and Dr. Syed Mahmud. See *National Herald*, April 30, 1958.

[42] See *Report of the Commissioner for Linguistic Minorities* (First Report), p. 42.

[43] See the text of the note in *Report of the Uttar Pradesh Language Committee*, pp. 79 and 80. This note also recognized that in Uttar Pradesh the use of Urdu has been widespread, though it is confined to a minority, living chiefly in towns.

language or script, and petitions and representations in Urdu should also be accepted.

(5) Important laws, rules and regulations and notifications should be issued in the Urdu language also in areas where this language is prevalent and which may be specified for this purpose.[44]

"Out of the five proposals," declared the communique of the Uttar Pradesh government, "the first four have been accepted by the U. P. Government from the very beginning."[45] As for the fifth, the state government confessed that no definite policy had been adopted in this connection. The communique admitted that the point was a valuable one and that it was the intention of the government to implement it in a befitting manner. That formal declarations are not enough was recognized by both the Union press note and the Uttar Pradesh communique. The latter stated that excess on the part of both the Hindi and the Urdu sides had sometimes retarded the progress of the government's language policy. There was an angry overtone in the communique in the passage where it refers to the role of "controversies, many of them personal, irrelevant, and of a highly objectional nature, which have been started by interested parties."[46] This reference, evidently aimed at the Urdu groups, may be contrasted with the assessment of the situation made by Nehru: "I should like to say quite clearly that I deeply regret the attempts of Hindi enthusiasts to push out Urdu . . . I think (Urdu) has a very rich inheritance which should be encouraged and nurtured."[47]

The declarations of the Union government and the Uttar Pradesh government did not solve the problem of recognizing Urdu as a regional language. Sampurnanand, the chief minister of Uttar Pradesh, stated in the Legislative Assembly in 1958 that Urdu could not be considered a regional language in Uttar Pradesh.[48] On Hindustani, Sampurnanand made the cryptic remark

---

[44] *Ibid.*, p. 80.

[45] For all references to and citations from the communique, see *ibid.*, pp. 81–82, where the communique has been reproduced.

[46] For comments on this reference, see *National Herald*, July 22, 1958.

[47] *Ibid.*, January 17, 1958.

[48] *Ibid.*, July 23, 1958.

that he knew of only fourteen languages recognized by the Constitution of India, and they did not include Hindustani.[49] Kamalapati Tripathi, then minister for education and information and for a long time a leader of Nagari Pracharani Sabha, was more explicit. He declared that there could be no legislation to safeguard the rights granted to Urdu. He warned that Urdu's rivalry with Hindi would not be allowed and reminded the proponents of Urdu that the country had suffered immensely because of the controversy over Urdu.[50]

The controversy continued, and the Urdu groups again looked to the Union government for further support. Thus, during the debate on the report of the Official Language Commission, the case for giving Urdu full scope was raised in Parliament by H. N. Kunzru, a national leader of the Anjuman. In addition to reflecting the grievances of the supporters of Urdu that have been discussed above, he also referred to the tendency to eliminate every word of Urdu origin from Hindi, which he felt to be entirely contrary to the directive contained in Article 351 of the constitution. G. B. Pant, the Union home minister, who belonged to Uttar Pradesh, appreciated the points raised by Kunzru. It was left, however, to another Congress member of Parliament from the Hindi area to utilize this occasion to spell out openly what the Hindi groups felt about Urdu. The representatives of the Hindustani groups took the opportunity to bring out the deliberate policy of the Hindi groups "to oust Urdu."[51] These attacks and counterattacks followed the usual pattern, without approaching a solution to the problem. The resulting situation, as it was perceived by the leaders of the Urdu speech community, has been summarized by a prominent leader of the Anjuman. As he put it, "Urdu is being constantly' termed as only an off-shoot or variety of Hindi, a foreign language, a language of the Muslims, an instrument of communal hatred and an enemy of Indian

[49] *Ibid.*

[50] *Ibid.*

[51] Kaka Kalelkar led this group. He thought that because of the aggressive actions of the Hindi leaders, the champions of English were getting stronger and the support for Hindi that Gandhi had secured was being destroyed. For this and other points raised in this debate, see *Hindustan Times*, September 10, 1958.

unity. All these contrary things are said in the same breath, to suppress it."[52]

The Urdu leaders, it is important to note, were not always influenced by objective considerations. Though in politics the subjective basis of an actor's perception is important as a datum, it is also necessary to look at the objective components of the situation in which the action takes place. For instance, in Uttar Pradesh, the major grievances of the Urdu groups were concerned with the language policy of the government in general, and with educational administration, recruitment to services, and encouragement to Urdu literature and language in particular. In Uttar Pradesh, according to the 1951 census, 79.8 percent of the people recorded Hindi as their mother tongue, whereas only 6.8 percent recorded Urdu. The States Reorganization Commission in its report (1955) had suggested that before a language could be considered as a second state language, the population speaking the language should be 30 percent of the total population of the state. The Union government, through a memorandum of the Ministry of Home Affairs, agreed with this proposal and advised the state government accordingly.[53] Technically, therefore, the government of Uttar Pradesh, though dominated by the leaders of the Hindi groups, did not deviate from the norm that was agreed upon by the states in the Indian Union.

In 1961, the state government appointed the Uttar Pradesh Language Committee, which submitted its report in 1962. The purpose of this committee was to investigate "the working of safeguards for Urdu and factors that would enable Urdu to occupy its due place in the cultural sphere of the State."[54] The chairman of the committee was J. B. Kripalani, who was associated with the Hindustani Prachar Sabha for a long time. The personnel of the committee included important Urdu as well as Hindi leaders and intellectuals. The findings of the committee failed to indicate any major official discrimination in respect of policies

[52] S. Ehtesam Husain, "Multilingual Aspect," *Seminar*, July 1960, p. 23.
[53] See *Report of the Uttar Pradesh Language Committee*, pp. 24–25.
[54] *Ibid.*, p. 1.

against the Urdu speech community. It appears from the report
that the difficulties experienced by the speakers of Urdu were
mainly due to lack of proper implementation of the policies and
inadequate adjustment between the psychological attitudes of
the Hindi and the Urdu speakers. The report pointed out the
importance of reconciling the feelings of the two speech communities. Without underestimating the administrative lapses, it
paid more attention to the psychological components of the
language situation.

It should be noted that in Bihar and Andhra Pradesh, the
relative size of the Urdu speech community is fairly similar to
that of Uttar Pradesh. The Urdu language associations have
rarely participated in important political movements concerning
language in these states.[55] In Bihar, the efforts of the Anjuman
were expended in representing grievances to administrative departments and seeking administrative solutions for them. In
Andhra Pradesh, Urdu is already recognized as an additional
language for the Telengana area, while Telugu continues to be
the principal language of the state. On the national level, it is
not true that Urdu has not been given recognition as a state
language in any state, for it is one of the state languages of the
state of Jammu and Kashmir.[56] The Anjuman organization itself receives substantial encouragement, financial and otherwise,
from the Union government—a fact which we will discuss later.

Why is it that in Uttar Pradesh the Hindi-Urdu conflict as-

[55] A recent exception was the movement to make Urdu the second official
language of Bihar. It was during this movement that the proponents of
Hindi clashed with the supporters of Urdu, leading to a large-scale riot in
Ranchi in August 1967, at the cost of at least seventy lives. For various demands made in the past by different Urdu organizations in Bihar and Uttar
Pradesh see *Report of the Commissioner for Linguistic Minorities,* Second
Report, pp. 43–45. It should be noted that the Bihar Anjuman urged the
recognition of Urdu as official and regional language of the state though
Urdu speakers in Bihar, according to the 1951 census, constituted only
about 7 percent of the total population. When this census figure was ques-
tioned by the Anjuman, it was pointed out to them that the 1951 figure in
Bihar was nine times the total number recorded in the 1921 census for
Bihar and Orissa combined. *Ibid.,* p. 43.

[56] For Andhra Pradesh and Jammu and Kashmir policies, see *ibid.* (First
Report), p. 138.

sumed a unique salience and succeeded in precipitating a long-drawn political conflict? The objective dimension of the language situation in that state is not likely to yield a satisfactory answer. A large part of the language conflict in Uttar Pradesh is influenced by the memories of past conflict transmitted to the Hindu and Muslim communities by the cultural and political leaders.[57] This factor of conflicting community memories is inevitably joined with and reinforced by the political preoccupations of the contemporary actors on the political scene in Uttar Pradesh. Given these complications, mere technical or administrative attempts to solve this problem in objective terms are not likely to achieve more than a partial success.

### Hindi-Punjabi Struggle

The Hindi leaders were assured of secure control over the determination of language policy in the Uttar Pradesh government. From this vantage point, it was easy for them to reject the actions of the Urdu associations as politically motivated campaigns based on parochial interest. In this manner, the Hindi leaders of the Uttar Pradesh tended to uphold official authority against linguistic agitation. In Punjab, however, the Hindi leaders faced a radically different situation. After independence, language rivalry in Punjab was expressed in the form of an intense antagonism between Hindi and Punjabi. In this conflict the Hindi leadership was largely arrayed against the Punjab state government. This was an interesting situation to the extent that the behavior of the Hindi leaders in opposition to the state government of Punjab provided a contrast with the norm of behavior that the Hindi leaders demanded from the Urdu opposition in Uttar Pradesh.

After independence, the part of Punjab that remained in India contained two major language groups. The 1961 census

[57] As Karl K. Deutsch points out, memories are essential, although they are not directly observable. Some memories can be observed by analyzing literature, mass-media transmissions, and other sources. See his "Communication Theory and Political Integration," in P. E. Jacob and J. V. Toscano, *The Integration of Political Communities* (Philadelphia: Lippincott, 1964), p. 64.

recorded 11 million Hindi and 8 million Punjabi speakers in Punjab.[58] In undivided Punjab under the British rule, the language of the courts and of district administration was Urdu in addition to English. Urdu was also the medium of instruction at the school level and a commonly used second language for Punjabis of Muslim, Hindu, and Sikh religious identification. The status of Urdu as a common language of communication began to decline with the rise of the Muslim separatist movement. Gradually, owing to particularist political persuasion, Muslims tended to learn only Urdu and English, to the deliberate exclusion of Punjabi. Similarly, Hindus and Sikhs tended to neglect Urdu and to emphasize Hindi and Punjabi respectively. Yet Urdu continued to be the most common urban second language of the literate Punjabis of all faiths, owing partially to the wide acceptance of the Urdu script by large sections of educated Punjabis irrespective of their particular linguistic affiliations.[59] The effect of the politicization of religious cleavage on linguistic cleavage assumed special importance when, after independence, Urdu script and the Urdu language were displaced from Punjab by the introduction of Hindi and Punjabi, written in Deva Nagari and Gurumukhi scripts respectively, as the only media of instruction at the school level.

The language issues assumed great political importance from 1948, when an extremist group of Sikh leaders voiced their demand for a linguistically homogeneous Punjabi state.[60] This group defined Punjabi in a very special way. Punjabi was not

[58] The corresponding figures for 1951 were not published because of widespread political interference led by interested groups. For the 1961 figures, see *Census of India, 1961*, vol. 1, part II-c (ii), pp. 15–16.

[59] For a detailed discussion of the language problem in Punjab, see Satya M. Rai, *Partition of the Punjab*, chap. 9. For the specific question of Urdu, see p. 219. The author points out that the position of Urdu as a common language was limited to the male population of Punjab. However, even during the worst period of the Hindi-Punjabi conflict, the leaders of both sides frequently used Urdu in attacking each other.

[60] The story of the Punjabi Suba movement and Sikh-Hindu political conflict has been treated in Baldev Raj Nayar, *Minority Politics in the Punjab*. For another angle on the Sikh-Hindu political conflict, see Khushwant Singh's *A History of the Sikhs*, pp. 289–305. I have not brought in the details of the Punjabi language for reasons explained earlier.

dissociated from its common background transcending religious affiliation and was exclusively identified with what the Sikh particularist leaders called Gurumukhi culture and Gurumukhi script.[61] In this way Punjabi was identified with the religious particularism of the orthodox Sikhs. This exclusive identification of Punjabi with Sikh particularism impelled large sections of the Hindu community to repudiate Punjabi and to declare Hindi written in Deva Nagari script as their mother tongue.[62] These moves led to strong Hindu-Sikh rivalry, which led to organized political agitations to influence census language returns. As a result of these political agitations the census authorities were constrained to abandon the separate tabulation of Hindi and Punjabi speakers in 1951.[63] One interesting consequence of this battle over census returns was that in the All-India Census tables, Hindi, Urdu, Punjabi, and Hindustani were grouped together. At the national level the Hindi leaders claimed the combined total of these language speakers as the legitimate total for Hindi speakers, whereas at the state level the Hindi leaders were engaged in bitter struggles against Urdu, Punjabi, and Hindustani. Evidently, the propensity to conveniently expand and contract the definition of Hindi was dictated by the need to use Hindi as a political resource in specific conflicts.

Hindi and Punjabi are closely related languages.[64] As they are spoken in Punjab, these two languages are mutually comprehensible and on many occasions overlapping. The difference between them tends to widen in their written forms. In the late

[61] See Satya M. Rai, *Partition of the Punjab*, pp. 224–225.

[62] See *Report of the States Reorganization Commission* (Delhi, 1955), p. 141.

[63] For details, see India, Punjab Boundary Commission, *Report* (Delhi: Manager of Publications, 1966), pp. 11–12.

[64] For details concerning the linguistic relation between Hindi and Punjabi see G. A. Grierson, *Linguistic Survey of India* (Calcutta: Government of India, Central Publication Branch, 1927), vol. 1; part 1, pp. 135, 138, and 168–170. See also *Census of India, 1961*, vol. 1, part II-c (ii), pp. ccxv to ccxvi. For an analysis of the pattern of bilingualism of a specific group of Punjabi speakers, see John J. Gumperz, "Hindi-Punjabi Code-switching in Delhi," in *Proceedings of the Ninth International Congress of Linguists* (The Hague: Mouton, 1964), pp. 1115–1124.

nineteenth century, the Hindu revivalist organization, the Arya Samaj, attempted to introduce Deva Nagari script among the Hindu literates of Punjab. This move was joined with the propagation of literary Hindi divested as far as possible from the common Punjabi speech and linked maximally with Sanskrit. From this time onward, the Deva Nagari script and the literary Hindi language were publicized as marks of Hindu identity in Punjab.[65]

By the beginning of the twentieth century, the common basis of popular Punjabi speech was undermined by the religious and political particularism of the emerging modernized elites, who utilized religious comunities as their political resources. In this process, it is difficult to determine who initiated the first thrust leading to the chain of Hindu, Sikh, and Muslim particularistic political moves. More important is the fact that linguistic particularism is not an isolated product manufactured by any one specific religious group. It is the cumulative product of a complex of moves and countermoves by various sections of the Punjab elite in their quest for social and political ascendance from the very beginning of modernization in Punjab. The development of linguistic rivalry following the demand for an autonomous Sikh state has to be seen in the broader context of the Hindu-Sikh rivalry dating back to the days before independence. To a certain extent, the Hindu-Sikh rivalry was submerged by their common cause against Muslim dominance in Punjab before independence. After independence the Hindu-Sikh rivalry developed a greater intensity and militancy.

Until the fourth general elections of 1967 the Congress organization managed to control the state government of Punjab. The Congress leadership proposed a formula for solving some of the basic issues arising out of Hindi-Punjabi language rivalry. The Sachar formula, as it was popularly known, was aimed essentially at delineating two separate linguistic regions for Punjabi and

[65] It has been said that owing to the Arya Samaj movement, "the Hindi language and the Deva Nagari script acquired religious significance" for a section of the Hindus of Punjab. See Punjab Boundary Commission, *Report*, p. 3.

Hindi in the state. This delineation was based on the perceived educational needs of the Hindi and Punjabi speakers, and it provided that the medium of instruction in each region would be its own language through pre-university education, and the students were required to learn the other language at the secondary stage.[66] Though this formula was concerned mainly with the medium of instruction, its long-term impact emphasized the linguistic division of the state in terms of Hindu and Sikh areas.[67] However, the formula itself did not provide for the acceptance of Hindi and Punjabi as the official languages of Punjab. It merely decided that these two languages were to progressively replace English and Urdu as the official languages. It was in 1960 that the Official Languages Act of Punjab established Hindi in Deva Nagari script in the Hindi area and Punjabi in the Gurumukhi script in the Punjabi area as the official languages in the districts belonging to these respective areas.[68]

The Hindi leaders of Punjab interpreted the gradual crystallization of the regional division of Punjab as the progressive victory of the Sikh demands. Thus, while the Sikh extremists acclaimed the Sachar formula, the Hindi leadership was determined to fight it. They specifically opposed the policy of compelling the Hindi speakers of the Hindi area to learn Punjabi and the Gurumukhi script in addition to their own language and script. In this opposition, the leadership of the Hindi movement in Punjab was drawn predominantly from Hindu particularist organizations like the Arya Samaj and the Jana Sangh. This leadership was not backed by any established language association rooted in Punjab. Moreover, unlike the Hindi Sahitya Sammelan leadership in Uttar Pradesh, the Hindi leaders in Punjab did not have the advantage of fully utilizing the Congress organization and government of the state. These associational and institutional lags in the Punjab Hindi movement turned the Hindi

[66] For details see Satya M. Rai, *Partition of the Punjab*, pp. 220 ff.

[67] For the wider impact of the formula, see Baldev Raj Nayar, *Minority Politics*, pp. 218 ff.

[68] For the text of the act, see *Report of the Commissioner for Linguistic Minorities* (Fourth Report), pp. 206–207.

leaders' attention to the creation of an ad hoc organization for the defense of Hindi.

In creating such an organization, the Hindi leaders of Punjab had to depend primarily on the support of the Hindu communal organizations opposing the Congress government in Punjab. In 1957 the Hindi leaders sponsored the Hindi Raksha Samiti for the protection of the interests of Hindi in Punjab. Explaining the background of the new organization, Swami Atmanand Saraswati stated: "When Punjabi is used to gain political power in the form of Punjabi Suba or Punjabi region, and Hindi, which is our national language as well as regional language, is relegated to a secondary position to appease the Akalis, the whole complexion of the problem changes."[69] The new organization published a charter of demands. The major demands were as follows: (*a*) the medium of instruction in the educational institutions should be left entirely to the choice of the parents; (*b*) there should be no compulsion to teach either of the two languages—Hindi and Punjabi—as a second language at any particular stage; (*c*) Hindi should replace English at all levels of administration; (*d*) office records up to the district level should be in both scripts—Deva Nagari and Gurumukhi; and (*e*) there should be one language "formula" in the whole state of Punjab.[70] These demands were substantially related to the Hindu communalists' movement to counter the demand for a Sikh state. This Hindu movement, initiated by the Jana Sangh, was directed toward the creation of a greater Punjab in order to contain the influence of the Sikhs in the politics of Punjab.[71] The Hindi leaders were not merely confident that because of a Hindu majority in Punjab, Hindu dominance could be assured; they were also convinced that through the linkage of Hindi with Hindu demands, they would be able to draw considerable support from the Hindu-oriented Hindi movements of the other North Indian states.

It is in this context that the Hindi Raksha Simiti staged its

---

[69] See *National Herald*, June 29, 1957.

[70] See *Ibid.*, December 28, 1957.

[71] For details of their demands, see Baldev Raj Nayar, *Minority Politics*, pp. 42 ff., and Satya M. Rai, *Partition of the Punjab*, pp. 236–238.

"Save Hindi" agitation in Punjab in 1957. It quickly succeeded in spreading to almost the entire Hindi area of Punjab. One striking feature of this agitation was that the neighboring Hindi states took an active interest and large numbers of volunteers were dispatched from these states to Punjab to augment the resources of the Hindi Raksha Samiti. By November 1957, six thousand volunteers were arrested for violating law and order. The agitation continued uninterrupted for seven months, and in all, about thirty thousand volunteers participated in this massive move to challenge the Punjab government.[72] This movement did not meet with any immediate success. But its violent attitudes, its aggressive techniques, and its open identification with militant Hindu revivalist forces evoked strong criticism from many parts of the nation.[73] However, even after the withdrawal of the movement, the Hindi leaders of Punjab, as well as revivalist Hindu leaders outside Punjab, were committed to mobilize their resources for future struggles.[74] Meanwhile, language leaders from the non-Hindi regions of India, and of course, the Punjabi language leaders, watched with interest the militant stance of the Hindi movement and the involvement of Hindi volunteers from outside Punjab in this Hindu movement. One prominent South Indian anti-Hindi leader declared that the entire mass of non-Hindi-speaking Indians "should take a lesson from what is happening in [the] Punjab."[75]

[72] See Observer, "Changing Shape of the Punjab Agitation," *National Herald*, November 24, 1957. According to another account, the number of the arrested was 4,000. See *National Herald*, December 28, 1957. The Arya Samaj's role in the Hindi movement was not confined to this agitation. Even after the "Save Hindi" agitation "came to a formal end," it continued the movement in other forms. Mahasay Krishan made it clear: "We shall have to solve the Hindi problem in Punjab. . . . We will not tolerate Hindi becoming a slave to Gurumukhi" (*Hindustan Times*, December 26, 1959).

[73] The editorial of a liberal daily newspaper maintained that the more this particular Hindi agitation was "defended and explained, the more it seems to be a political agitation inspired by reactionary Hindu forces. . . ." *National Herald*, June 25, 1957.

[74] In Delhi, Swami Abhedanand, president of the Sarvadeshik Arya Pratinidhi Sabha, "urged lovers of Hindi to keep themselves in readiness, to march into Punjab if and when it was considered necessary to resume 'Save Hindi' struggle" (*Ibid.*, March 10, 1958).

[75] *Ibid.*, March 9, 1958.

The Hindi movement in Punjab served as a convenient lever for a wide range of political interests. Though it was a movement against the Congress government, Hindu Congress leaders from the Hindi area of Punjab used it for their purposes. Thus, thirty Congress legislators, all from the Haryana area of Punjab, tried to utilize this movement to reinforce their demand for a 50 percent share for the Hindi areas of Punjab in the appointment of ministers, deputy ministers, and presiding officers of the Legislative Assembly and the Council as well as administrative officers and high court judges. The use of the language movement as an extension of a faction fight within the dominant Congress party was made clear by the chief minister of the state, who saw the language movement as a political instrument of the Hindi leaders employed against the Punjabi leadership of the Congress government. The Haryana faction of the Congress, he pointed out, could make their demands inside the Congress party, but instead, they preferred to use the language movement "to harass the Government" in order to avenge the defeat they had suffered previously within the Congress party.[76] Be that as it may, the totality of language conflict mixed with religious intransigence eventually led to the division of Punjab into two states at the close of 1966.[77]

Neither the treatment of Urdu interests in Uttar Pradesh and elsewhere nor the militant involvement in the anti-Punjabi movement has contributed to the creation of a better image for Hindi among the non-Hindi people in India. On the national level, the Hindi leaders often demand a broad role for Hindi and its general acceptance among Indians. But nearer to their own

[76] Pratap Singh Kairon asked, "For the last eight years there has been no opposition to the teaching of the second language (Punjabi) from the last stage of the primary standard. Then why this agitation now?" His answer: "It is because I have beaten thoroughly some persons politically that they have come together to harass the Government." On the Haryana legislators, he said that they could "put forward their demands within the Congress Party and every demand would be considered on its merits." See *ibid.*, June 26, 1957.

[77] For background information, see Punjab Boundary Commission, *Report*, and Jagjit Singh Anand et al., *Punjabi Suba, A Symposium* (New Delhi: National Book Club, 1966).

homes, they are found to be involved in bitter struggles against languages that are closely related to Hindi. In these struggles, the Hindi leaders sometimes claim that Urdu and Punjabi are mere variations of Hindi and at the same time try to create the impression that Hindi is, in fact, a pure language having an authentic style which admits of little variation. These contrary attitudes do not seem to convince the leaders of the non-Hindi areas that the Hindi language politics is not an extension of the quest for exclusive power and status on the part of the Hindi regional elite. In fact, the non-Hindi leaders are increasingly persuaded that the Hindi language demands and the activities of the Hindi associations as well as of their leaders undoubtedly represent a threat to the political and social interests of the non-Hindi language communities. In order to evaluate this perception concerning the use of language politics for achieving broader social and political interests, we turn our attention to the struggle between the proponents and opponents of Hindi as the only official language of India.

# VI

## *Official Language: Policy and Implementation*

The formal provisions in the Constitution of India regarding the official-language question set a formidable task for the Indian political authorities at both the federal and state levels. The democratic structure of politics, the federal form of the polity, and the plural basis of the Indian society added to the complication of the above task. It may appear that one mitigating factor lay in the dominance of the Congress party at both the federal and the state levels of political operation in India. It cannot be denied that the dominance of the Congress party, for about two decades after independence, did provide a unifying structure of leadership. But it should also be noted that the dominant party, over these decades, was a relatively loose coalition of diverse groups, leaders, and orientations. Given this nature, the Congress party tended more to reflect the difficulties of implementing the language provisions than to offer a single-minded direction for solving them.

The constitution envisaged the replacement of English by Hindi for the official purposes of the Union and as the language of communication between the states and the Union and between one state and another. The legislatures of the component states of the Indian Union were given the authority to adopt any one or more of the languages in use in the state, or Hindi, as the official language or languages of the state concerned. At the Union level, Hindi was to be introduced as the official language in accordance with a phased program. In the first stage, Hindi was to be used in addition to English for purposes specified by the president by order. In the second stage, restrictions could be imposed on the use of English, and the progressive use of Hindi could be introduced during the first fifteen years following the effective date of the constitution after an investigation of the problem by an Official Language Commission and a Joint Committee of Parliament. In making its recommendations, the Official Language Commission was required to pay due regard to the industrial, cultural, and scientific advancement of India, and to "the just claims" and the interests of persons belonging to the non-Hindi areas in regards to the public services. The deadline for the replacement of English by Hindi—initially fifteen years— could be extended further by Parliament by law. In addition, the constitution charged the Union with the duty to promote the spread of Hindi and to develop it so that it might serve as a medium of expression for all the elements of "the composite culture of India."[1]

### Language Commission

The first report of the Official Language Commission was submitted in 1956. The chairman of the commission, B. G. Kher, was for a long time a leader of the Hindustani Prachar Sabha and was renowned for his advocacy of replacing English with Hindustani. The basic assumption of this report was that language is important only "at the level of instrumentality" and hence language "is of no intrinsic consequence."[2] Given this basic assumption, it was not difficult for the commission to suggest an active role for the federal government in implementing a comprehensive policy for the introduction of Hindi. The measures suggested by the commission and accepted by the Committee of Parliament on Official Language in 1958 envisaged that English would be replaced by Hindi after 1965 and that English would

---

[1] Some problems relating to this directive have been discussed earlier.

[2] *Report of the Official Language Commission*, 1956 (*R.O.L.C.*), p. 269.

continue as the subsidiary official language only. In addition, it attached considerable importance to the development of Hindi by the central government. In pursuance of the recommendations of this parliamentary committee, the president issued an order on April 27, 1960, which contained directions for implementing the above recommendations.[3]

Of these directions, the major one was concerned with the evolution of Hindi terminology for scientific, administrative, and legal purposes and with the translation of materials on administration and procedure into Hindi. The president's order also included the following provisions. (*a*) English shall continue to be the medium of examination for the recruitments through the Union Public Service Commission, but later, Hindi may be admitted as an alternative medium. (*b*) An authorized translation of parliamentary legislation in English should be provided in Hindi. (*c*) When the time comes for the changeover, the language of the Supreme Court shall be Hindi. (*d*) As for the language of the high courts, when the time for the changeover comes, Hindi shall ordinarily be the language of judgments, decrees, or orders, in all regions. However, by undertaking the necessary legislation with the previous consent of the president, the use of a regional language as the official language instead of Hindi may be made optional. Thus the president's order made the intentions of the government clear: from that time on the introduction of Hindi shall be an active concern of the government. The range for the introduction of Hindi, as envisaged in the reports of the commission and the committee and in the president's order, was comprehensive enough, however, to provoke opposition from the non-Hindi areas and groups.

The minutes of dissent and the notes attached to the reports of the commission and the committee reveal that some members from the non-Hindi groups widely disagreed with the recom-

[3] See D. D. Basu, *Commentary on the Constitution of India*, 5:162. See also the *Report of the Committee of Parliament on Official Language, 1958* (New Delhi: Government of India Press, 1959), for the basis of the president's order. This report was submitted to Parliament and the president in 1959. The chairman of this committee was G. B. Pant.

mendations. Thus, one note of dissent to the report of the Official Language Commission, prepared by an eminent linguist and a former advocate of Hindi, stated that the entire outlook of the commission was one of the "Hindi speakers who are to profit immediately and for a long time to come, if not forever."[4] He thought the attitude of the commission was far from democratic, because it tried to impose Hindi on the non-Hindi speakers of India. He added that the recommendations would bring about two classes of citizens in India—Hindi speakers as first-class citizens and the rest as second-class citizens. He detected an incipient "Hindi Imperialism" in the direction of events initiated by the Hindi politicians.[5] In a similar vein, Dr. P. Subbarayan, expressing the suspicions of the southern states, characterized Hindi enthusiasm as a "militant chauvinism" which was creating "a considerable amount of misgivings and opposition among speakers of languages other than Hindi."[6]

Perhaps the strongest voice of dissent came from the representative of the English-language group. Thus, Frank Anthony, in his minute attached to the report of the Committee of Parliament on Official Language, stated that owing to the "increasing intolerance and aggression of the Hindi protagonists," the new Hindi had become a negation of secular democracy and that "it spells the inevitable disintegration of the country and the ultimate destruction of minority languages."[7] In another note, on the other hand, two leaders of the Hindi areas—P. D. Tandon and Govind Das—thought that the committee's recommendations were halting and unsatisfactory in respect to spreading the use of Hindi. These two members were in favor of a drastic re-

[4] *R.O.L.C.*, p. 276. This Minority Report was prepared by Dr. Suniti Kumar Chatterjee. He was the chairman of the West Bengal Legislative Council. For over a decade, he presided over the West Bengal unit of the Rashtrabhasha Prachar Samiti sponsored by the Hindi Sahitya Sammelan. He was made an honorary member of the Nagari Pracharani Sabha, and the Hindi Sahitya Sammelan conferred on him an honorific title for his services to Hindi. See *ibid.*, pp. 277–278.

[5] *Ibid.*, p. 278.

[6] *Ibid.*, p. 320.

[7] See *Report of the Committee of Parliament on Official Language, 1958*, p. 92. Frank Anthony is an eminent Anglo-Indian leader.

striction of the use of English for official purposes. Expressing dissatisfaction at the slow rate of introduction of Hindi, they characterized the recommendations of the committee as pro-English.[8]

## Politics of Implementation

The pattern of implementation of the official-language policy at the level of the Union government was criticized by the Hindi groups from the very beginning. The fundamental point of attack was that the non-Hindi faction was deliberately delaying the replacement of English. The Hindi leaders expressed the fear that the purpose of this delay was to extend the deadline beyond fifteen years. The major target of open attack was, of course, the Ministry of Education. Maulana Azad, who was minister of education during the crucial decade, was a famous writer in Urdu and one of the founders of the Hindustani Prachar Sabha. The attacks against Maulana Azad were directed, however, in fact, against Nehru, who as the prime minister was in charge of leading the policy processes of the government. If Azad was attacked on the ground of frustrating the advancement of Hindi for the sake of his interest in Urdu, Nehru was attacked more for his attachment to English.

The guiding soul of the Hindi faction, during the first decade in Parliament, was P. D. Tandon. Although in personal relations Tandon and Nehru were friends, in political relations they represented two polar opposites both in terms of political principles and in terms of factional struggles within the Congress party.[9] In 1950 Tandon fought for and won the presidency of the Indian National Congress. Tandon's victory was widely perceived as

---

[8] *Ibid.*, pp. 76–81.

[9] The conflict of political principles in this case refers mainly to the questions of secular westernizing and religiously oriented traditionalizing propensities—the former associated with Nehru and the latter associated with Tandon. The question of ideology was relatively less important in this particular conflict. See Paul R. Brass, *Factional Politics in an Indian State: The Congress Party in Uttar Pradesh* (Berkeley and Los Angeles: University of California Press, 1965), pp. 35–37. See also Myron Weiner, *Party Politics in India* (Princeton, N.J.: Princeton University Press, 1957), chap. 4.

Nehru's defeat although Nehru was not a direct contestant—he had supported a candidate against Tandon. At this time the Congress was beginning its preparations for the first general elections in India. Nehru was confident that the victory of the Congress in the general elections depended heavily on his active leadership of the Congress organization. Even the supporters of Tandon agreed with this assessment.[10] Given this situation, it was not difficult for Nehru to dislodge Tandon from the presidency of Congress. Through various kinds of pressure, Nehru and his faction succeeded in this task very soon. Tandon, in giving up the presidency, felt that it was not merely his own personal defeat, it also indicated the aggressively hostile stance of the Nehru faction against the causes advocated by Tandon. Of these causes, the promotion of Hindi was obviously one of the dearest to Tandon. He was aware, however, that in his encounter with Nehru, he had the solid support of the majority of the Uttar Pradesh Congressmen.

The identification of the Hindi faction in Parliament with Tandon's leadership naturally made it more difficult for the Hindi faction to use Nehru's leadership in Parliament for the active promotion of Hindi. On the other hand, Nehru's role as one of the founders of the Hindustani Prachar Sabha, his sympathy for the role of English as a language of higher education, his hostility to the revivalist forces in the Congress, and above all, his basic premise that an official language cannot be imposed on the people—all these factors made it difficult for him to come close to the Hindi groups. "A number of Hindi enthusiasts," Nehru declared in 1958, "in the past had thrown their weight about and had been trying generally to impose their will on others which was highly improper and harmful."[11] Aside from his own attitudes, for Nehru there was also the question of draw-

[10] See the reflections of Govind Das on the resignation of Tandon from the presidency of the Congress in his *Atma-Nirikshan*, 3:191–197 (in Hindi).

[11] See *National Herald*, April 5, 1958. On the same occasion he explained his attitude toward English: "It is beyond my conception . . . that English should be called the national language of India. That is a falsehood which I will never accept, though I am all for spreading the English language" (*ibid*).

ing the maximum support both inside and outside Parliament from all sections of the Congress leadership and the Indian people to strengthen his image as a symbol of the nation. It is no wonder, then, that the forces of opposition to Hindi, both in the Hindi and the non-Hindi areas, had always looked to Nehru as the moderating influence in Parliament and the Congress party. However, the strength of the Hindi groups in Parliament could not be ignored. Most of the members of Parliament from the Hindi states were behind the Hindi faction led by Tandon and Das. Their efforts, backed up by the extra-parliamentary campaigns and influences of the leading Hindi associations, led eventually to elaborate preparations on the part of the Indian government for the eventual replacement of English by Hindi.

*Implementation and Administration*

The actual task of implementing the Union government's policy of developing and promoting Hindi is under the auspices of the Ministry of Education. This ministry has been responsible for the organizational translation of a number of ideas concerning innovation, control, and coordination in the implementation of the Hindi policy. In 1950 it sponsored a Board of Scientific Terminology, which was assigned the job of preparing 350,000 new terms in Hindi, of which 290,000 were produced by 1963.[12] The board was later replaced by a standing Commission for Scientific and Technical Terminology. By 1967–1968, 200,000 terms related to the sciences, humanities, and social sciences had been produced and 125,000 had been published in twelve glossaries released by the commission.[13] Apart from terms pertaining to academic fields, considerable effort has been invested in the production of specific terms relating to various departments and ministries.

The responsibility for translation and publication of standard

[12] See India, Ministry of Education, *Educational Activities of the Government of India* (Delhi: Manager of Publications, 1963), p. 134.

[13] See India, Ministry of Education, *Report, 1967–1968* (New Delhi, 1968), p. 119. For sample of the official efforts see, for example, India, Ministry of Education, *A Consolidated Glossary of Technical Terms, (English-Hindi)* (Delhi: Central Hindi Directorate, 1962).

works in Hindi is entrusted to whole-time, authorized cells for specified subjects. During 1967–1968 five such cells were located in universities. For example, one cell in Delhi University is working in the fields of mathematics, zoology, and political science, and another cell (in Ranchi University) has been assigned botany. University departments and other academic bodies also provide agencies for the translation of various subjects. In addition, work is carried on through individual assignment and through the commission's own staff.[14]

The terms evolved and authorized by the commission are gradually being incorporated in officially sponsored dictionaries, manuals, and "books of knowledge."[15] The policy of subsidizing nonofficial bodies for the dissemination of the products of Hindi planning was apparent in the act of officially assigning to the Nagari Pracharani Sabha the task of preparing a ten-volume encyclopedia in Hindi. This work has been running behind schedule, and the nine volumes published thus far have not set any enviable standard. In fact, the policy of giving liberal grants to nonofficial organizations to promote and develop Hindi initially raised many problems of coordination and control of quality. The routinized system of a standard ministry in India was inadequate to handle such problems.

One measure of innovation in the system was reflected in the creation in 1960 of the Central Hindi Directorate as a "subordinate office" of the Ministry of Education. Operationally, the directorate is a supplement to the commission. Formally, the job

[14] See Ministry of Education, *Report, 1967–1968*, pp. 119–120. On translation problems, plans, and programs, see *The Art of Translation* (New Delhi: Ministry of Scientific Research and Cultural Affairs, 1962). On the problem of translating legal works, see M. C. Sharma, *Rendering of Laws in Hindi—Its Problems* (New Delhi: Ministry of Law, Government of India), 1964.

[15] At least twelve dictionaries are at different stages of production. These include Hindi-English, English-Hindi, and Hindi and various Indian-language dictionaries. Manuals include administrative as well as academic standard handbooks. Books of knowledge refer primarily to encyclopedias. Work concerning these items is distributed among departmental, university, and voluntary organizations.

of the directorate is to undertake programs for the development and dissemination of Hindi as well as to get the administrative materials of the government of India translated. The first task endows the directorate with wide coordinating authority. The magnitude of the second task may be appreciated by the fact that on an average, one hundred manuals and two thousand forms are being translated by this office annually.

Production and distribution of printed words, whether created or translated, represents, however, only one dimension of the implementation of Hindi planning. Language education is equally important. This education has been planned on two levels. In the first place, a central organization has been set up to promote technical expertise and guidance for teaching Hindi. The training of Hindi teachers is systematically undertaken in this project.[16] In the second place, the Ministry of Education provides facilities and financing for the teaching of Hindi in non-Hindi-speaking states. In 1968 an extensive system of correspondence courses to teach Hindi was planned. In addition, the total cost of setting up Hindi teacher-training colleges in non-Hindi-speaking states is borne by the Ministry of Education.

The Hindi publication program of the Ministry of Education deserves special attention. The works of the commission and the directorate represent only a part of the total program. The ministry handles an extensive program for publishing Hindi primers and readers. It also offers facilities for publishing works of non-Hindi literature, either translated into Hindi or transcribed in Deva Nagari; it offers various prizes to Hindi authors and subsidies to Hindi publishers; and it maintains an elaborate system for the distribution of Hindi books free of cost to the non-Hindi-speaking states for schools, colleges, and public libraries.

The leadership of the Ministry of Education in respect of certain technical innovations for the promotion and development of Hindi should be noted. The reform of Deva Nagari script,

[16] The central body set up in 1960 is known as Kendriya Hindi Shikshana Mandal. This body has sponsored a teacher-training organization for Hindi in Agra.

standardization of Hindi shorthand, and rationalization of keyboard designs for typewriter, teleprinter, and linotype machines are some of the most important moves in this direction.

Hindi planning, however, is not conducted under the auspices of the Ministry of Education alone. Three other ministries participate in this planning process. The Ministry of Home Affairs started a project of teaching Hindi to central government employees in 1955. Since 1960, training in Hindi has been made obligatory for all central government employees, with certain exceptions.[17] During 1968, 38,039 employees were enrolled in courses for training in Hindi. Approximately 70 percent of the candidates completed these courses. The Ministry of Home Affairs is also responsible for matters relating to the progressive use of Hindi for official transactions. An advisory board called the Hindi Salahkar Samiti has been formed to assist the ministry in this direction.[18] The Ministry of Law has been busy in getting the major texts of law translated into Hindi and in promoting the progressive use of these Hindi versions in the courts of India. The role of the Ministry of Information and Broadcasting in the implementation of Hindi planning will be discussed later.

All of these implementation efforts require the investment of a sizeable sum of money. These funds are ultimately used to employ thousands of Hindi authors, experts, teachers, and scribes. The actual output of these personnel has been oriented more toward contribution in quantity than quality. Success has been measured by the number of terms, volumes, schools, incentives, and even programs. The actual use of the products of Hindi planning has rarely been subjected to systematic investigation. This is not surprising, since administrative leadership in India has generally been interested in measuring any plan more by its monetary investment than by substantial results. In the case of

[17] The exceptions are employees aged over forty-five in 1961 and those below Class III status. Central government employees in industrial establishments are also excepted. "No penalties are attached to failure to pass the prescribed examinations." However, there are elaborate incentives for passing the examinations. See India, Ministry of Home Affairs, *Report, 1967–1968* (New Delhi, 1968), p. 91.

[18] *Ibid*, p. 92.

Hindi the emphasis on volume and speed has been more marked because very few of the senior administrators have so far revealed a genuine commitment to Hindi as opposed to English.[19] In any case, the extensive patronage for the promotion of Hindi unfolded a world of employment opportunity for the educated people of the Hindi areas. The pattern of public expenditure for Hindi promotion as channeled through the Ministry of Education alone is presented in table 16.

*Aid to the Associations*

In its report the Committee of Parliament on Official Language accepted the recommendation of the Official Language Commission that the central government should give "liberal financial assistance" to voluntary associations "for enlarging and improving their activities" for the systematic organization and expansion of the work of propagation of Hindi.[20] Long before the declaration of this policy, substantial funds were being channeled to the Hindi associations. This generated a strong rivalry among the different Hindi and Hindustani associations in securing funds from the central government. The Hindi associations opposed the idea of giving aid to the Hindustani groups, though the largest part of the aid was going to the Hindi associations themselves. This rivalry found its expression in Parliament and outside through the concerted attack waged by the Hindi leaders on the Ministry of Education. Thus P. D. Tandon and Govind Das deprecated what they alleged to be the policy of the Ministry of Education—of helping Hindustani and Urdu and deliberately neglecting the cause of Hindi.[21] In the Sixth Annual

[19] Even the matter of speed is doubtful. One prominent Hindi literary author, who has himself served on various expert committees for coining new terms, confessed to me in an interview that the output of such projects is rather poor in quantity and quality. He mentioned a specific case when ten experts were assembled for four days and were given the assistance of a staff of two hundred together with excellent financial support. The output on this occasion was forty words of doubtful quality.

[20] See *Report of the Committee of Parliament on Official Language, 1958,* pp. 53–54.

[21] See M. P. Desai, "Hindi, Hindustani and Urdu," *Harijan,* April 17, 1954.

TABLE 16

FINANCIAL PROVISIONS FOR LANGUAGE PLANNING, UNION MINISTRY OF
EDUCATION, 1967–1969. PROMOTION AND DEVELOPMENT OF HINDI

| | 1967–1968<br>Revised estimates | 1968–1969<br>Budget estimates |
| --- | --- | --- |
| | (in hundred thousand rupees) | |
| *Projects of the ministry* | | |
| Hindi teachers: | | |
| appointment and training | 114.00 | 121.20 |
| Voluntary Hindi organizations | 11.00 | 11.00 |
| Hindi encyclopedia | 0.74 | 1.50 |
| Hindi book gifts | | |
| to non-Hindi states | 1.00 | 1.00 |
| Prizes on Hindi books | 0.20 | 0.25 |
| Subtotals | 126.94 | 134.95 |
| *Projects of the Central Hindi Directorate* | | |
| Terminological index preparation | 0.10 | 0.10 |
| Dictionary preparation | 0.92 | 1.00 |
| Popular books | 1.00 | 1.20 |
| Primers and readers | 0.09 | 0.15 |
| Omnibus volumes | 0.14 | 0.15 |
| Seminars and exhibitions | 0.50 | 0.70 |
| Script reform | 0.03 | 0.10 |
| Correspondence courses | 1.00 | 2.00 |
| Basic Hindi grammar | 0.02 | .. |
| Hindi shorthand | 0.25 | 0.20 |
| Hindu library | 0.45 | 0.20 |
| Journals | 0.22 | 0.37 |
| Offices and travel | 9.57 | 9.09 |
| Subtotals | 14.29 | 15.26 |
| *Projects of the Commission for Scientific and Technical Terminology* | | |
| Translation of standard works: | | |
| university level | 11.90 | 14.00 |
| Manuals based on evolved terms | 0.10 | 0.05 |
| Journal of Commission's terms | 0.05 | 0.05 |
| Staff pay and allowances | 12.22 | 16.53 |
| Cell work and | | |
| non-official travel | 2.55 | 2.55 |
| Subtotals | 26.82 | 33.18 |
| Totals | 168.05 | 183.39 |

SOURCE: India, Ministry of Education, *Report, 1967–1968,* pp. 121–123.

Conference of the Uttar Pradesh Hindi Sahitya Sammelan, a resolution was passed which even demanded a separate ministry for Hindi at the center. In this conference Rahul Sankritayan accused Maulana Azad, then the education minister, of trying to "drive a wedge between Hindi and its sister languages," and of "trying to stab the cause of Hindi in the back."[22] In the same conference, P. D. Tandon disclosed, as evidence of the indifference of the Ministry of Education to Hindi, that none of the three principal secretaries of the Ministry of Education knew Hindi.[23] B. L. Varma, the president of the conference, opposed the grants to the Hindustani Culture Society because the latter "drew no inspiration from Sanskrit."[24] In order to press these points, an organized campaign was conducted by the Sammelan leaders in the Indian press. One statement appearing in the press alleged that the Ministry of Education, while always neglecting the Hindi Sahitya Sammelan, had favored Urdu organizations by financial and other aids—the organizations being the Anjuman, Jamia Millia Islamia, and the Shibli Academy—and that the policy of giving grants to the Hindustani Cultural Society was crippling Hindi. For all these developments, the statement frankly blamed Maulana Azad as the central obstacle to the development of Hindi.[25]

Despite the charges of discrimination against Hindi, there seems to be no doubt about the fact that ever since central government funds began to flow for the development of Hindi, the Hindi associations have secured the bulk of such funds. Through

[22] *National Herald*, June 8, 1954.

[23] *Ibid.*

[24] *Ibid.* Brindaban Lal Varma is a noted Hindi novelist and playwright. It is worth noting that in this conference, while Communist intellectual leader Rahul Sankritayan was attacking Hindustani, one leading target of attack was a fellow-traveler, Sunder Lal—the leader of the Hindustani Culture Society. The conference site and its approaches were decorated with colorful gates bearing the names of famous Hindu communalist leaders of the R.S.S. and the Jana Sangh, like Golwalkar and Dr. S. P. Mukharjee. The slogans shouted in the conference included "Drive out Maulana Azad" and "Stop the nonsense of Urdu" (*ibid*).

[25] See *National Herald*, April 9, 1954.

contracts for the preparation of dictionaries, encyclopedias, coinage of terms, translation, and for teaching and propagating Hindi, these Hindi organizations have received substantial sums of money from the central government. The first five-year plan to develop Hindi, drawn up by the government of India in 1952, showed an estimated expenditure of 1,708,000 rupees. During the period 1949 to 1951, the Ministry of Education had already spent 385,000 rupees in grants to organizations, of which the Hindi Sahitya Sammelan and the Akhil Bharatiya Hindi Parishad and other Hindi organizations received the major portions for the preparation of "post-literacy literature in India."[26] In 1954–1955, the Nagari Pracharani Sabha received a total grant of 100,000 rupees to publish a revised edition of *Hindi Shabda Sagar*. In 1956, the same organization was entrusted with the job of preparing a Hindi encyclopedia for which it received a grant of 700,000 rupees. Similarly, the Hindi Sahitya Sammelan was given a generous financial grant for bringing out an English-Hindi dictionary. Table 17 will provide some idea of the general direction of the funds received by the Hindi organizations. It also indicates the sums paid to the Hindustani organizations for the promotion of Hindi.

Table 17 shows that the strongest Hindi associations working specifically in the Hindi areas have received by far the largest proportion of the central government funds for the promotion of Hindi. It should be noted that this table does not indicate all the channels of financial assistance to the organizations working for Hindi. Except for one or two organizations mentioned in the table, the funds that usually go for buildings and equipment, for example, have not been included. Since the governmental funds for Hindi are distributed through various departments and agencies, one can assume that the figures released by the Ministry of Education represent only part of what the organizations devoted to Hindi actually received.

Apart from the governmental assistance, the Hindi organizations also collect large sums of money through the process of

[26] See *ibid.*, January 26, 1952.

TABLE 17

GRANTS FROM THE UNION GOVERNMENT PAID TO THE ORGANIZATIONS
WORKING FOR THE PROMOTION OF HINDI, 1951–1960

| Organization | Rupees |
|---|---|
| Hindi Sahitya Sammelan, Allahabad | 360,125 |
| Nagari Pracharani Sabha, Varanasi | 360,000 |
| Akhil Bharatiya Hindi Parishad, Agra | 163,203 |
| Hindustani Prachar Sabha, Wardha* | 156,000 |
| Hindustani Cultural Society, Allahabad | 90,000 |
| Dakshin Bharat Hindi Prachar Sabha, Madras | 52,500 |
| Hindi Association of Parliament | 46,000 |
| Hindustani Prachar Sabha, Hyderabad | 31,750 |
| Hindi Prachar Sabha, Hyderabad | 31,500 |
| Mysore Riyasat Hindi Prachar Samiti, Bangalore | 25,000 |
| Sahityakar Sansad, Allahabad | 25,000 |
| Bharatiya Hindi Parishad, Allahabad | 15,000 |
| Hindustani Prachar Sabha, Bombay | 10,000 |
| Rashtra Bhasha Prachar Samiti, Wardha | 9,000 |
| Hindustani Hindi Sabha, Hyderabad | 3,000 |
| Total | 1,378,078† |

SOURCE: Computed from the data in India, Ministry of Education, *Programme for the Development and Propagation of Hindi* (New Delhi: Central Hindi Directorate, 1960), pp. 74–87.

* Later moved to New Delhi.

† Not including the grant of 26,950 rupees given to the Hindi Bhawan of New Delhi.

conducting examinations in Hindi—a practice which is facilitated by the Union government's recognition of these examinations.[27] Important individuals conected with the Hindi organizations are awarded cash prizes from the governmental sources through Hindi book "contests." Thus, in 1952, seventeen writers shared an award of 24,000 rupees; in 1953–54, seven writers shared 14,000 rupees; and in 1955, fourteen writers shared 28,000

[27] The government-recognized organizations for Hindi examination are: Hindi Sahitya Sammelan, Allahabad; Rashtrabhasha Prachar Samiti, Wardha; Prayag Mahila Vidyapith, Allahabad; Hindi Vidyapith, Deoghar; Travancore Hindi Prachar Sabha, Trivandrum; Assam Rashtrabhasha Prachar Samiti, Gauhati; Hindi Prachar Sabha, Poona; Akhil Bharatiya Hindi Parishad, Agra; Manipur Hindi Parishad, Imphal; Mysore Hindi Prachar Parishad, Bangalore; Gujarat Vidyapith, Ahmedabad; Dakshina Bharat Hindi Prachar Sabha, Madras; and Hindustani Prachar Sabha, Bombay.

rupees.[28] In addition, Hindi writers are awarded cash prizes for writing for "neo-literates." From 1954 to 1959 the sum of 23,000 rupees was spent for this purpose. Sometimes the works of some Hindi writers are purchased outright for publication and distribution by the government. Large-scale employment of Hindi writers, teachers, and publicists as well as other personnel, has been facilitated by the Union government's policy of making generous grants to the non-Hindi states to promote Hindi. For such work the Union Ministry of Education alone provided the grants shown in table 18. These grants represent roughly 60 per-

TABLE 18

UNION MINISTRY OF EDUCATION'S HINDI GRANTS TO STATE GOVERNMENTS

| Year | Budget provision (rupees) | Amount sanctioned (rupees) | Amount utilized (rupees) |
|---|---|---|---|
| 1954–55 | 445,000 | 279,001 | 100,567 |
| 1955–56 | 500,000 | 540,915 | 325,040 |
| 1956–57 | 800,000 | 283,905 | 164,963 |
| 1957–58 | 500,000* | 643,783 | 366,550 |
| 1958–59 | 564,000 | † | † |

SOURCE: *Programme for the Development and Propagation of Hindi*, pp. 31 and 46–69.
NOTE: The figures presented include those for the non-Hindi Union territories.
    * Why this provision is lower than the amount sanctioned is not explained in the source.
    † From this year forward, lump grants are paid in accordance with a different procedure. Hence the corresponding figures have not been cited in the source.

cent of the expenditures for the Hindi projects conducted by the non-Hindi states. The actual employment potentiality of the projects is greater, therefore, than the monetary amounts in table 18 would suggest. Besides, the Ministry of Home Affairs employs a large number of Hindi teachers for its Hindi-teaching scheme. The annual expenditure on this program was about 1,600,000 rupees in 1961–1962.[29]

We have referred only to the enterprises for promoting Hindi

[28] See India, Ministry of Education, *Programme for the Development and Propagation of Hindi* (New Delhi: Central Hindi Directorate, 1960), pp. 41–42.
[29] See *Educational Activities of the Government of India*, p. 283.

conducted under the auspices of the government at the Union level. A more comprehensive picture would have to include the projects that are in operation in the Hindi states under their own monetary and bureaucratic supervision.[30]

In any event, the charge that during the crucial years after the constitution took effect the pressures of the Hindustani groups and the non-Hindi groups led to a concerted effort on the part of a faction within the Congress party cannot possibly be sustained. Nevertheless, it appears to be true that the pressures of the Hindi associations to completely neglect the interests of the Hindustani or the non-Hindi groups were, to some extent, counteracted by the representatives of the latter working mainly through a process of coalition of the relevant factions within the Congress party.

## Hindi and Broadcasting

The effect of rival pressures on the Union government's role in promoting Hindi can perhaps be seen in the case of the Hindi policy followed by the All-India Radio. As the monopoly broadcasting organization operated by the government of India, the All-India Radio has an especially important role in promoting Hindi as the official language of India. In December 1949, it started a program of Hindi lessons, which were broadcast from every radio station in the non-Hindi areas. The unimaginative way in which this program was conducted defeated its purpose to a great extent and it was discontinued because of the emergency situation in 1962.[31] An expert committee appointed by the government of India noted that "the fact that this discontinuation has not raised a murmur of protest anywhere seems to indicate that these lessons have not enthused people."[32]

---

[30] For various projects undertaken by the leading Hindi state see *Uttar Pradesh me Hindi* (Lucknow: Bhasha Bibhag, Government of U.P., 1959); and *Bhasha Neeti Par Svet-Patra* (Lucknow: Bhasha Bibhag, Government of U.P., 1961) (both in Hindi).

[31] See G. C. Awasthy, *Broadcasting in India*, p. 131.

[32] India, Ministry of Information and Broadcasting, *Radio and Television: Report of the Committee on Broadcasting and Information Media*, 1966, p. 68.

The most important controversy concerning the Hindi policy of the All-India Radio has been centered around the question of the Hindi used in the news bulletins. In November 1949, the term "news in Hindustani" was suddenly changed to "news in Hindi." Together with this change, the language of the Hindi news bulletins also became highly Sanskritized. When B. V. Keskar became the minister of information and broadcasting, the policy of Sanskritization was extended further. It was during this period that Nehru once complained that he could not understand the language in which his own Hindi speeches were being broadcast.[33] When it was pointed out that the style of Hindi used in the news bulletins was incomprehensible to the masses for whom such bulletins were broadcast, the officials supporting Keskar replied that the masses would learn it by constant listening. Under Keskar a number of Hindi writers and intellectuals were appointed as advisers and producers. They resisted all efforts to simplify the language style of the Hindi news broadcasts. One important secretary in the Ministry of Information and Broadcasting tried to press the point that the ordinary listeners would not benefit from unnecessary Sanskritization of Hindi, but his efforts failed.[34] In 1962 Keskar was defeated in the general election, and Gopala Reddi replaced him as the minister of information and broadcasting. Reddi was interested in bringing Hindi and Urdu closer to each other and, in July 1962, he sponsored an experimental policy of using the same language for both the Hindi and Urdu news broadcasts. The Hindi groups in Parliament refused to accept any such dilution of Hindi, and in Parliament their spokesmen vehemently opposed the alleged policy of Urduizing Hindi.

Almost simultaneously the important Hindi writers employed by the All-India Radio in various capacities started mobilizing support from the established Hindi associations in order to frustrate Reddi's moves. Using the slogan that the purity of Hindi was in danger, several Hindi writers appealed to others in their

[33] See G. C. Awasthy, *Broadcasting*, p. 132; and *National Herald*, April 5, 1958.

[34] The official concerned was P. M. Lad, who tried this in 1954.

profession to refuse to cooperate with the All-India Radio. The Delhi unit of the Hindi Sahitya Sammelan set out to collect one hundred thousand signatures on a petition of protest addressed to the prime minister. Ultimately, however, a compromise was reached through Nehru's initiative, though the agitation was really stopped only after Reddi was replaced—for another reason —by S. N. Sinha, who enjoyed the confidence of the Hindi groups in respect of language policy. Meanwhile, as a writer on Indian broadcasting puts it, 'the basic issue continues to be shirked: is the language used in A.I.R.'s Hindi news bulletins understood by the vast majority of the people for whom they are intended?'[35] Those who have advocated and introduced the "pure" form of Hindi for such broadcasts do not wait for any systematic listener-survey for an answer to the above question. For them, the demands of linguistic standardization in terms of orthodoxy would seem to be more important—especially since these demands coincide with the political interests of the leaders of the Hindi associations.

### The Hindi Literati and Language Planning

The principle of the purity of a language depends to a large extent on the definition offered by those who are reputed to be in command over the language. In the case of Hindi, the commanding heights of the language are still monopolized by the literary authors. The scientific and the technical personnel drawn from the Hindi-speaking areas rarely speak Hindi in the communications relating to their profession. This is also true about the academic transactions in the social sciences. It is not surprising that the leadership of the Hindi movement, both in the past as well as the present has been composed almost entirely of personnel drawn from literary and rhetorical sectors of social life. This is not to say that all those who write in Hindi or use Hindi ora-

---

[35] G. C. Awasthy, *Broadcasting*, p. 135. The author, a former member of the program staff of the All-India Radio, writes with an intimate knowledge of the working of radio broadcasting in India. For some examples of reactions to Reddi's move, see, among others, the letters published in the *Statesman*, July 6, 8, and 9, 1962.

torial persuasion are involved in the Hindi movement or in the Hindi associations. What is important is that the literary purists have tended to dominate the Hindi movement and the higher echelons of the leadership of the Hindi associations.[36] In part, this is understandable because the scientific and technical personnel are more interested in investigating relations between materials than in relations between words or in the function of words to move men.

Whatever the reason, the lack of functional diversification among the leaders of the Hindi movement, and the monopolization of the movement by an organized literary elite, inevitably tend to put a premium on the purity of the language and continuity with the tradition of the Hindi literati than on the use of language for functional efficiency and the expansion of communication.

This tendency is invariably reflected in the course of language planning followed by the program of development of the Hindi language as undertaken under the official and the nonofficial auspices. All the efforts of the Union government to develop Hindi have been marked by a sense of urgency. In their hurry to meet the fifteen-year deadline, the administrators gathered around them whatever experts were available in the Hindi intellectual circles. Most of those who were available happened to be the literary leaders who were associated with the Hindi movement through the Hindi organizations. For a long time, these were the only people who had given serious thoughts to the development of Hindi. Some of them, like Dr. Raghuvira and Dr. Dhirendra Varma—eminent linguists in their own right—had undertaken the cause of developing Hindi long before official patronage came onto the scene. By virtue of their conviction for the

---

[36] This will be apparent from the professional backgrounds of the listing of the leading office-holders of, for example, the Hindi Sahitya Sammelan. These listings, dating back to the foundation of the Sammelan and extending to the contemporary period, are usually appended to the annual reports of the Sammelan. Usually these leaders are either literary authors or active political leaders with literary reputations. For a sample, see *Hindi Sahitya Sammelan Ka Unchaswa Barshik Bibaran, 1962–1963* (Prayag: Hindi Sahitya Sammelan, 1963), pp. 97–101 (in Hindi).

cause and their competence to handle the task, it was natural that the literary authors as well as the linguists oriented to literary norms with experience in the field of language development would supply the major part of the necessary expertise.

Once pressed into service, these Hindi experts were quick to bring their basic conviction to bear on their task of language planning. One of the most respected Hindi experts has articulated some of these convictions in clear terms.[37] He began with the premise that the development of Hindi is dependent on the creation of a vocabulary that is consistent with the genius of the Indian languages.[38] The question of genius is emphasized because, according to him, this is a way of rescuing India from the denationalizing effect of English. As he puts the question and answers it himself:

Shall we be anglicized, shall we be turned into Greeks and Latins and shall we then alone pick up the few crumbs thrown to us as refuse . . . by the West? We have a grain of sense. We have our respect to attend to. . . . Our languages will again go into the lap of mother Sanskrit, the language of India, when she was free. We shall have again our own words. . . . When this is done Indians will be free of the thraldom of the European languages.[39]

Specifying a program, Dr. Raghuvira claimed that within a short span of ten years it should be the duty of the experts to create a vocabulary of two million words.[40] In creating these words the soul of the nation must be attended to.[41] For this purpose, "Sanskrit will be a mighty weapon for forging all our linguistic needs."[42] According to him, this will save Indians from the clutches of English, which, as he puts it, is "one of the most

---

[37] The reference is to Dr. Raghuvira. A representative selection of his writings on language development can be found in his *India's National Language* (New Delhi: International Academy of Indian Culture, 1965). Some of the articles are in Hindi.

[38] See *ibid.*, p. 221.

[39] *Ibid.*, pp. 206–207.

[40] See *ibid.*, p. 204.

[41] See *ibid.*, p. 188.

[42] *Ibid.*, p. 222.

erratic languages of the world."[43] It should be noted that Dr. Raghuvira thought that if the newly developing Hindi were Sanskritized, it would be brought closer to the other Indian languages. But the idea of bringing Hindi closer to the other Indian languages by simplifying its grammar or style was out of the question for these experts. As another expert suggested, he preferred that Hindi should remain regionally isolated in order to maintain its "purity intact."[44]

There are, of course, variations of opinion among the Hindi experts as to how far the above objectives can be pursued in practice. But most of them seem to agree on the basic thrust of the logic behind these objectives. Fundamentally, they agree that language development depends on scholarly language planning, and if the products of the planners are not intelligible to even the educated Hindi speakers, the blame should lie on the latter. As they perceive the problem, the primary responsibility of the experts is to create the new product. The responsibility of the people is to invest the time and in the training required for the use of such products.[45]

### Problems of Language Planning

What emerges from the discussion of the above objectives set forth for the development of Hindi is the element of arbitrariness in setting the norms of development which seems to be unavoidable. Any act of planning requires a formulation of the basic objectives of planning, an assessment of the available resources, a working out of the proper strategy, and an actual implementation of the strategy in the most economical way. Though invariably tied to the resources, the planning objectives are likely to reflect the arbitrary choice of norms of the planners. In this sense, the element of arbitrariness in the normative setup

[43] *Ibid.*, p. 188.

[44] See Dhirendra Varma's essay in Z. A. Ahmad, ed., *National Language for India*, p. 270.

[45] The idea that the people at "the receiving end" must apply efforts to catch up with the scholarly linguistic developments is the same as the one that we found in the attitude of the Hindi planners involved in the All-India Radio.

constructed by the Hindi experts cannot be measured by completely objective criteria.

Comprehensive language-planning carried out under the auspices of the state in cooperation with various public organizations is relatively new.[46] Positive planning of this type, involving extensive language development and propagation directed by the authority of the state, unfolds a new dimension of modernization. Though some elements of these processes were implied in the language reform processes related to Italian and French during the sixteenth and the seventeenth centuries, these were at best precursors to the kind of positive language-planning that was witnessed in nineteenth-century Europe. It is this kind that one finds in many contemporary Asian countries. The novelty of this politically directed enterprise has been aptly described as follows: "The typical source of language planning in our day is neither the stately academies of the Enlightenment nor the eager entrepreneurs of the Romantic era, but the expert commission of the Technological Age. . . . They are normally appointed by a branch of the government . . . and they are asked to furnish materials and analyses while serving in a purely advisory capacity."[47]

This description apparently assumes a basic congruence of objectives between the political authority and the appointed experts concerning language planning. This assumption of congruence holds good under two conditions. Either this planning is undertaken by an autocratic state where the experts do not assume the role of politicians, or it is undertaken in a democratic state where the experts work under fairly institutionalized norms separating policy from administration. The first of these alternatives worked well in Turkey under the Kemalist regime.[48] But it is inconsistent with the political structure of India. The second

---

[46] One view of academic rationale for such planning is contained in V. Tauli, *Introduction to a Theory of Language Planning*, pp. 15–28.

[47] Einar Haugen, *Language Conflict and Language Planning*, pp. 14–15.

[48] For the function of the Turkish Linguistic Society, see Uriel Heyd, *Language Reform in Modern Turkey* (Jerusalem: The Israel Oriental Society, 1954), pp. 25 ff. For a recent account, see Yucel Ozmen, "A Socio-Linguistic Analysis of Language Reform in Turkey, 1932–1967," (Ph.D. dissertation, Stanford University, 1967).

alternative might work in India were it not for the explicitly political role performed by the experts through organized interest-
group action in the various stages of linguistic decision-making
in India. It is this factor which has made it possible for the
experts to attempt to impose their own objectives on Indian
language-planning.

Assuming that there are no objective criteria for evaluating
the goals of language planning, and given the nature of the Indian situation, is it fair to assert that language planning in India
should be guided by standards based on the outcome of a political rule-making process? Are there any possibilities of at least
setting some limits drawn from a store of linguistic expertise
which may be above political interests? Some linguists have suggested a set of norms to guide language planning under any situation.[49] One suggestion invites attention to three components
that should go into language planning—efficiency, rationality,
and commonalty.[50] Efficiency refers to the economy of the learning efforts, while rationality implies the intellectual capacity of
a language to correspond to available knowledge. The third component refers to "maximal adoption as token of a unified life of
language use."[51] These components may serve as criteria for the
guidance of the language planners. The Hindi language-planners
are aware of these criteria. But the question of efficiency is
subsidiary to the question of nationalist pride as defined by them.
Similarly, rationality is perceived by them as a criterion which
can be met by classicalizing the language according to their intellectual propensities. This, too, is rooted in their nationalist
orientation. In general, their attitude tends to be more prescriptive than functional—oriented more toward the creation of a
formal structure of an ideal Hindi than to the actual function
that this structure is capable of performing as the official language of the Union. It is because of this orientation that they
tend to interpret commonalty with some ambiguity. Sometimes

[49] See, for example, Punya Sloka Ray, *Language Standardization,* and V.
Tauli, *Introduction to a Theory of Language Planning.*
[50] See Punya Sloka Ray, *Language Standardization,* p. 12.
[51] *Ibid.*

they clearly say that the scope of commonalty should be restricted to a group that has the capacity to adhere to the strict standards set up by the experts. At other times, they assure us that commonalty should be imposed by politically forcing greater numbers to use the experts' products.

Most of the time the Hindi language-planners have given more emphasis to the codification of the form of standard Hindi than to the ability of this Hindi to gain the acceptance of the widest possible audience. This preoccupation with codification has led, in practice, to a disproportionate emphasis on the vocabulary problems rather than on the communicational capacity of the artificially increased lexical stock. This is not surprising, because lexical production and prescription are easier to control than any other part of the complex task of language planning. It would be a mistake, however, to assume that the entire energy of the Hindi planners has been directed to the lexical dimension. Following their literary orientation, they have introduced a number of new grammatical features into modern Hindi.[52] In doing this, they have attempted to move the new Hindi as far away as possible from the commonly accepted Hindi speech in nonliterary communication. For example, a set of new derivative suffixes are being introduced in the new Hindi. These suffixes follow a set of derivational rules and require certain vowel alternations which are more characteristic of Sanskrit than of Hindi as used till recently. The new syntax, similarly, is oriented more toward Sanskrit than toward colloquial Hindi. With the growing Sanskritization of Hindi, the sounds of the language are also being considerably affected. The gradual introduction of Sanskritic consonant clusters and final short vowels, for example, is causing the new Hindi to diverge significantly from Hindi colloquial speech. All of these planned changes are indications of the growing classicalization of the language and a consequent

[52] For illustrative examples, see J. Das Gupta and J. J. Gumperz, "Language, Communication and Control in North India," in *Language Problems of Developing Nations,* ed. J. A. Fishman, et al., pp. 151–166. See also, Alfred Pietrzyk, "Problems in Language Planning: The Case of Hindi," in *Contemporary India,* ed. B. N. Varma (Bombay: Asia Publishing House, 1964), pp. 247–270.

erection of a set of new barriers between the newly standardizing Hindi and the commonly comprehended Hindi as spoken and written in the Hindi areas till recently.

Hindi planning, however, is not the work of a completely homogeneous group. Though most of the planning efforts have been controlled by the literary experts who belonged to the group described above, there has been another group which tends to differ from the former. The dominant group, or the Hindi leaders, as we have called them, carried their normative orthodoxy to such an extreme that soon they provoked widespread criticism against their activities. When the Indian constitution was being drafted, Dr. Raghuvira and his committee were in charge of preparing a Hindi translation of the draft constitution. When the translation was completed, Nehru complained that though a Hindi speaker himself, he did not understand a word of the Hindi version.[53] But Dr. Raghuvira thought that the translation was an eminent success. He defended the highly Sanskritized style adopted in the translation and suggested that the attitude of the educated Hindi speakers to the new style should be "that of a learner, a receiver."[54]

Men like Nehru and Azad were not easily persuaded that their role was that of a mere receiver. Gradually, they tried to gather support from a group of technically oriented experts who were recruited to represent their specialty subjects on the officially appointed boards of the government of India, entrusted with the task of coining technical terms. The terms evolved by this group tended to differ significantly from those of the Hindi experts who dominated the Hindi language movement. The deviant experts emphasized intelligibility more than regularity and rigidity in codification.[55] They pursued a policy of flexible borrowing from English and of maintaining a closer relation with commonly intelligible Hindi speech. In spite of their influence on

[53] See Granville Austin, *The Indian Constitution: Cornerstone of a Nation* (London: Oxford University Press, 1966), p. 282.

[54] See his *India's National Language* (n.37 above), p. 223.

[55] For results of their influence on the coinage of scientific terms, see *A Consolidated Glossary of Technical Terms* (n.13 above), *passim*.

the official evolution of scientific terms, and the support that they enjoyed from the Hindustani-oriented group in the Indian government, their efforts were too specialized and their scope was too narrow to stem the tide of the general influence exercised by the Hindi leaders on language planning. In this connection, it is important to note that a large part of Hindi development is promoted by the established Hindi associations working both through official and unofficial channels. These associations have also wider political support in the Hindi areas. It is therefore natural that with their experience, resources, and institutional support, the Hindi leaders were in a position to more than offset the influence of the deviant experts in the general structure of the development of Hindi.[56]

## Effects of Divergence

In confronting the critics of Sanskritization, the Hindi leaders often resorted to the argument that Sanskritization would enable Hindi to come closer to most of the other Indian languages with the exception of Urdu. It is true that the history of modernization of several Indian languages, such as Bengali, Marathi, and Gujarati, has been one of borrowing extensively from Sanskrit. Apparently, this common feature is likely to persuade many that Sanskritization may act as a bridge from one Indian language to another. This belief is based in part on an oversimplification. In respect of inheritance and borrowing, some of these languages do have a common source in Sanskrit. But the ways in which they have borrowed and the results of borrowing have varied considerably among these languages. The common source has not necessarily led to a convergence of the borrowing languages. As it has been pointed out, "Even when mutually intelligible, and this is not always true, the Sanskrit loanwords in the different languages may be felt as mutually grotesque and barbarous."[57] The divergent borrowing in these related languages cancels to a large extent the Hindi leaders' expectation of building

---

[56] These deviant experts were mostly academic people without any significant institutional support from outside the official administration.

[57] Punya Sloka Ray, *Language Standardization*, pp. 72–73.

a linguistic bridge through Sanskritization. In any case, the Hindi experts' own efforts have tended to augment this divergence.

In fact, the Hindi planners have not paid adequate attention to the institutional language-development efforts in various regions of India. Many of the problems faced by the contemporary Hindi planners were given considerable attention by the intelligentsia in several regional language communities as early as the nineteenth century. These efforts were aimed at translating educational books from English into the regional languages. The Bombay Native School Book and School Society, the Deccan Vernacular Translation Society, and the School Book Society of Calcutta devoted systematic efforts to bringing western literature in arts and science to the people through their own language media. These efforts were substantially augmented by the general attempts of their respective language societies to modernize regional languages. These enterprises were especially successful in the cases of the Marathi, Gujarati, Tamil, and Bengali languages.[58] Apart from these regional efforts there were also attempts to develop technical terms which would have a national acceptance in India. In this connection one can mention the report of the Scientific Terminology Committee of the Central Advisory Board of Education of India published in 1941.[59] The recommendations in this report, as well as similar recommendations emerging from nonofficial sources, suggested a large measure of acceptance of foreign names and terms.[60] None of them recommended a complete Indianization of the terminology. Rather, each of them cautioned against the complete isolationism

[58] The reference here is to the organizational efforts of the Maharashtra Sahitya Parishad, the Maharashtra Shabda Kosh Mandal, the Gujarat Vidya Pith, Gujarat Vernacular Society, Bangiya Shaitya Parishad, and the Tamil Cultural Society.

[59] This report was based on a note prepared by B. N. Seal in 1939. For a discussion of this report, see Suniti Kumar Chatterjee in *Report Regarding the Indian Languages Development Conference* (Poona: University of Poona, 1953), pp. 39–41.

[60] One of the earliest systematic efforts in this direction was by Rajendra Lal Mitra in Bengal during the middle of the nineteenth century. For a discussion of his ideas, see *ibid.*, pp. 37–39.

that could result from a blind policy of Indianization, especially in the field of scientific knowledge. These efforts were also marked by an awareness that modern science is a western development and that nothing would be gained by an obsessional purification of the language of science by the Indianization of scientific symbols based on Roman and Greek letters and other accepted signs.

Most of the Hindi planners, especially the Hindi leaders involved in developing Hindi, have not shown any eagerness to learn from the above-mentioned processes of language development in the relatively advanced regional languages of India.[61] Moreover, they have an ideological inclination for complete Indianization which is not shared by the modernizers of these regional languages. These Hindi leaders and experts are not merely in favor of replacing international numerals with Deva Nagari numerals for use all over India; they also want to introduce Deva Nagari symbols to replace the widely used scientific symbols based on Roman and Greek letters and other symbols in mathematics and science.[62] The insistence on the use of Deva Nagari symbols for these purposes is likely to provoke other regional languages to adopt their own symbols in the place of the widely accepted international symbols currently used by them. These developments would naturally compartmentalize Indian scientific literature in regional quarters and thus retard scientific communication and development in India.

The manner in which the Hindi experts have sought to develop Hindi has given rise to several problems. The guiding norm of going back to "mother Sanskrit," and the unremitting

[61] An interesting compilation of a sixteen-language dictionary (including English) has been edited by V. D. Narawane. See his *Bharatiya Vyavahara Kosa* (Bombay: The Author, 1961).

[62] For examples of the use of Nagari symbols in the standard Hindi encyclopedia financed by the government of India and prepared by the Nagari Pracharani Sabha, see *Hindi Bishwakosha* (Benaras: Nagari Pracharani Sabha, 1966), 6:154–157. For a contrast see the standard Bengali encyclopedia which uses all the widely accepted mathematical and scientific symbols. See, for example, *Bharatkosha* (Calcutta: Bangiya Sahitya Parishad, 1964), 1:277–279.

zeal in purifying Hindi from all "alien" influences, have created a language which may satisfy the regional pride of the Hindi leaders, but it is not likely to facilitate either the cause or the function of Hindi as the official language of India. Even within the Hindi area the artificial product has tended to erect barriers between literary communication and mass communication on the one hand, and between the proposed literary language and the actually used scientific language on the other. Outside the Hindi area, the new Hindi has not excited the imagination of the people. The manner in which the formal development of Hindi has proceeded has thus failed to keep pace with its own functional need. In the political sphere the use of official resources to force the adoption of Hindi has been more conspicuous than any persuasion for its adoption. The actions of the Hindi planners themselves have rarely been of a persuasive nature. The cumulative effect of these factors has been to reinforce the opposition against Hindi from the non-Hindi language communities and associations.

### Non-Hindi Response

The attempts to implement the language provisions have generated more intense language rivalry than unity. When the Constitution of India took effect, initially there was a hope on the part of the non-Hindi leaders that the development of Hindi as the official language would involve more persuasion than imposition. But within a few years they felt that the Hindi leaders were interpreting the constitutional provisions as justifications for an immediate imposition of Hindi. In this context, every single move to replace English by Hindi tended to evoke an increasing degree of suspicion concerning the motives of the Hindi leaders. The fifteen-year deadline failed to mitigate this suspicion—it only postponed its extreme political expressions.

In a country like India, where the pace of life is slow and where the structure of life rarely moves one to anticipate radical changes, it was difficult at first for most educated Indians to believe that within the span of a decade an established language like English was really going to be replaced. But the report of the

Official Language Commission, and the subsequent intensification of governmental action to actually implement Hindi, gradually created the impression that the official language provisions were, in fact, meant to be real and were going to be implemented by the power of the political authority. This, in the perception of the non-Hindi leaders, posed a grave threat to their sense of regional community, interregional balance of power, and personal status security. As a legacy of the colonial rule, politically conscious Indians had developed an exaggerated image of the potency of governmental action. In independent India the extensive scope of state action tended to confirm the image of government as a mighty, authoritative instrument. If such an authority seriously attempted to replace English, there was no reason to assume, it was believed, that it could not be done. This belief was strengthened by the fact that the dominance of the Congress party was assured all over India, and that within the Congress party the leaders of the Hindi states enjoyed a relative dominance during the first decade after Indian independence.

Given this background, it was not surprising that as soon as the non-Hindi leaders found that concrete steps were being taken to implement the official language policy, they felt an immediate need for organized political action to put pressures on the Union government and the dominant party in order to counteract the influence of the Hindi leaders. One of the problems of organizing the non-Hindi opposition was the difficulty of unifying the leaders drawn from various non-Hindi language communities around a comon symbol of protest. In the past most of these leaders had made an emotional commitment in favor of replacing English by an Indian official language. Because of this commitment, it was difficult to demand a complete reversal of the constitutional provisions in favor of English. Their best initial symbol of protest could only be built around a common case for implementing the official language provisions through gradual persuasion instead of political imposition. This meant formulating demands for the continuation of English as an additional official language even after Hindi was implemented as an official language. In practice, this implied a demand for the extension of the fifteen-year deadline and also a flexible treatment of the very notion of deadline. Some non-Hindi leaders even urged that English alone should be made the official language of India.[63] Though popular in parts of South India, this extreme form of support for English was generally felt to be unnecessary, and probably unwise, for mobilizing a united opposition from the non-Hindi areas againt Hindi extremism. It was in this context that organized opposition to Hindi was initially built around demands for gradualism and persuasiveness in the implementation of the constitutional provisions rather than for a complete reversal of the substantive constitutional provisions regarding the official language of the Union. Later, the procedural protest gradually changed into a strong demand to revise the substantive provisions.

The opposition to Hindi found its strongest political expression in the southern states, especially in Madras. In these states there had been a long tradition of suspicion against the North. Even during the national movement, political leaders from the North were sometimes treated as cultural outsiders in the South.[64] For many leaders of the Dravidian movement, the North symbolized a potential source of Aryan domination. In part this was tied in with the anti-Brahmin resentment expressed by the non-Brahmin leaders of the Dravidian movement in South India.[65] But the scope of the resentment was not limited to the internal politics of South India. Gradually this scope was extended to include a systematic campaign against the northern part of India as a whole. It is not difficult to imagine why the identification of the southern Brahmins with Sanskritic culture, and of the latter with the Aryan symbolism evoked by the northern leaders, could attain a unique symbolic capability for political mobilization of the masses in the South. The northern

[63] See, for example, C. Rajagopalachari, "English for Unity," *Seminar,* no. 68 (April 1965), pp. 18–26.

[64] See S. S. Harrison, *India: The Most Dangerous Decades,* p. 278.

[65] For an account of the evolution of the politics of the Dravidian movement, see Robert L. Hardgrave, Jr., *The Dravidian Movement.*

leaders themselves were largely responsible for generating this resentment, if not consciously, at least by virtue of their actions.

As we have seen before, political mass mobilization in the North was substantially facilitated by the actions of many Hindu traditionalist leaders who constantly invoked a chain of Aryan symbols. Phrases like Arya Samaj, Arya Sanskriti, Arya Bhasha, Arya Lipi—referring to the greatness of Hindu organization, culture, language, and script respectively—were extensively used, not only by the Hindu communal leaders but also by many of the leading lights of the Congress organization in North India, especially in Uttar Pradesh and Punjab. Some of the national leaders like Tilak and Lajpat Rai defended the cause of Hindi and Deva Nagari by claiming that these were sacred Aryan inheritances. It was precisely the use of these Aryan symbols which substantially contributed to the alienation of Muslims. These Hindu leaders weighed this loss against the great mobilizational capacity of these symbols among the Hindu masses. What they failed to see was the power of the Aryan symbols to alienate southern Hindus. They failed to develop a sensitivity to the idea that what is functional for mobilization in the North may be dysfunctional for communal unity in the North as well as for national unity in general.

Dravidian regionalism made spectacular inroads into southern politics from the beginning of the Self-Respect movement in 1925. The Self-Respect movement differed from its predecessor, the Justice party, founded in 1916, to the extent that it gave a more militant, dynamic, and antireligious quality to Dravidian regionalism. The successors of the Self-Respect movement—the Dravida Kazagham, and later the Dravida Munnetra Kazagham —intensified the militancy of Dravidian regionalism. The alliance between Kamaraj Nadar and the Dravidian movement to displace the Brahmin dominance in Tamilnad, while strengthening the support base of Congress party, also strengthened the Dravidian movement at the same time. In 1955, in response to the Union government's moves to introduce Hindi, E. V. Ramaswamy Naicker appealed to the members of the Dravida Kazagham to burn the national flag as a symbolic act of resentment against the imposition of Hindi on an unwilling people.[66] The efforts of Kamaraj to pacify the Tamil patriots effected some measures of compromise, to be sure. But these measures did not solve the problem.

In 1956 the Academy of Tamil Culture convened in Madras the Union Language Convention, which stated in a resolution that it would be "greatly unjust to make any other language take the place of English, when to a population of about a hundred million . . . it would be a language with which, for all practical purposes, they are totally unacquainted."[67] Significantly, this convention included sponsors from diverse political organizations.[68] Simultaneously, the southern leaders attempted to seek bases of support for their stand from other non-Hindi regions. They knew that a coalition of the political groups of the major non-Hindi states was not difficult to achieve because of the similarity of responses that had already been provoked among the leaders of the political groups in other non-Hindi states. Thus, a conference was convened by some representatives of the Tamil, Malayalam, Telugu, Assamese, Oriya, Marathi, Kannada, and Bengali languages under the initiative of C. Rajagopalachari.

In this All-India Language Conference (March 8, 1958), C. Rajagopalachari declared that "Hindi is as much foreign to the non-Hindi speaking people as English to the protagonists of Hindi." In explaining the objective of the rallied persons, he said that "they were engaged in a 'fight' with those who wanted

[66] See *ibid.*, pp. 45 ff. "The people of Tamilnad have not received justice under the flag of the Indian Union," declared Naicker, as a reason for choosing the national flag as a symbol of oppression. See also the *Hindu*, July 22, 1955.

[67] See the report of this convention in *The Language Problem of India* (Calcutta: Association for the Advancement of the National Languages of India, 1957), pp. 15–17.

[68] The sponsors of this convention were C. Rajagopalachari, E. V. Ramaswamy Naicker (D.K.), P. T. Rajan (Justice party), C. N. Annadurai (D.M.K.), A. Ratnam (Tamilnad Scheduled Caste Federation), S. R. Venkataraman (Servants of India Society), and many other prominent leaders drawn from various organizations.

to impose Hindi."[69] In this conference Frank Anthony stated that not even one percent of the "so-called Hindi-speaking people" know the Hindi that is disseminated by the All-India Radio. But, he added,

Worse than the stylized unreal character of the new Hindi is the fact that it has become, increasingly, the symbol of all that is reactionary and retrograde in the country. The new Hindi today is the symbol of communalism; it is a symbol of religion; it is the symbol of language chauvinism, and worst of all, it is the symbol of oppression of the minority languages. . . . There is an unanswerable case for a complete revision of the language provision [in the Constitution] in the light of the experience of the past several years.[70]

In the same conference, Tara Singh referred to the aggressive nature of the Hindi agitation in Punjab and the way in which organized Hindi groups identified Hindi with Hinduism and Hindustan, and he concluded that the Hindi imperialism was a new menace posing a grave danger to Indian unity.[71] The resolutions passed in this conference demanded "the continuance of English as the Union language without any time limit," and that "no attempt should be made to give any particular regional language the position of the Union official language for the transaction of the business of the Union or inter-state affairs." This conference, it should be noted, brought together political leaders of diverse orientations, ranging from Marxism to Dravidianism. The same diversity could be noticed in the composition of the language association that sponsored the conference—the Association for the Advancement of the National Languages of India. The activities of the language associations in the non-Hindi areas intensified spectacularly on the eve of the expiry of the fifteen-year deadline in 1965 when violent opposition to Hindi broke

[69] *National Herald*, March 9, 1958.

[70] See Frank Anthony's address to the All-India Language Conference, reproduced in *Modern India Rejects Hindi, Report of the All-India Language Conference* (Calcutta: Association for the Advancement of National Languages of India, 1958), pp. 56–57.

[71] See *ibid.*, pp. 47–54.

out in different parts of India, especially in the South. The pattern of this violence and its consequences will be discussed later.

Meanwhile, it should be noted that the response of the non-Hindi language leaders to the question of Hindi represents a complex of diverse motivations. The westernized urban middle classes seem to oppose Hindi in order to defend English because their control over the latter gives them a relatively easy access to social status and administrative jobs and offers a prospect of interstate mobility. In addition, English provides a window to the intellectual and technical achievements of the modern world. For the westernized middle classes, therefore, the introduction of Hindi signifies a situation of comparative economic and intellectual disadvantage.[72] With the increasing politicization of the rural areas, however, a new generation of leaders is increasingly utilizing the representative political processes to assert its own voice, which differs in many ways from that of the urban westernized elite.[73] The rural support structure behind these leaders often constrains them to confine their vision to the narrow range set by the limited perceptions of their audience. The relatively less mobile rural masses of India, handicapped by lack of literacy and adequate means for living, have little concern for the nature of the Union official language—both Hindi and English being equally inconsequential for their daily activities. If any language really matters to them, it is invariably the local dialect or a popular form of their regional language.

The new generation of leaders is aware of the political potentialities of the regional media of communication. In order to retain and expand their bases of political power, they have to converse with the illiterate masses in their dialects and with the neo-literates in either dialects or popular forms of the regional languages. In addition, such leaders have to find means to relate

---

[72] For examples of such arguments, see for instance, Suniti Kumar Chatterjee's "Minority Report" in *R.O.L.C.*, especially pp. 300–302.

[73] For an account of the increasing importance of the rural leadership see, for example, Myron Weiner, *Political Change in South Asia* (Calcutta: Firma K. L. Mukhopadhyay, 1963), pp. 176–227. See also F. G. Bailey, *Politics and Social Change, Orissa in 1959* (Berkeley and Los Angeles: University of California Press, 1963).

the relatively upward-mobile[74] sections of the rural areas to centers of power—power at the local, district, or state level. For all of these processes the only relevant language of communication can be the regional language together with its variants.

It is not surprising, therefore, that at the state level, the importance of the regional language has been steadily increasing. After the effective date of the constitution, all the states gradually adopted a regional language as their official language.[75] Despite the limited effect of the formal declarations regarding the adoption of regional language as official language in the states, the fact remains that the use of regional language for official transactions is growing. At the same time, regional language as the medium of instruction is also increasingly displacing English. In most of the states, college education up to the level of graduation is now making use of regional languages.[76] To be sure, at present, the regional-language media of instruction have been more popular in the "arts" instructions than in the "science" instructions. Gradually, many universities are adopting, or proposing to adopt soon, regional languages as media of instruction for postgraduate education. The products of such education are likely to be engaged in a rivalry with the corresponding products of English education.

The emerging trends are worth noting. In both the rural and the urban areas, the demands for extending opportunities for those who speak or who are trained in only the regional language are likely to gain more attention than the corresponding demands of those who have control over both English and the regional language. As a result, the tension between the new generation of leaders with greater regional involvement and the

[74] The use of this term here does not bind it to the typological scheme in which Robert Presthus uses this term in a different context in his *The Organizational Society* (New York: Knopf, 1962), p. 9.

[75] Punjab was an exception. The division of Punjab into two unilingual states has brought the new Punjab and Haryana in line with the other states in India.

[76] For information about the adoption of the Indian languages in the universities, see India, Ministry of Education, *Report of the Committee on Emotional Integration* (Delhi, 1962), pp. 226–34.

westernized leadership is likely to increase. In the non-Hindi areas, because of common hostility to Hindi, both these classes of leaders may enter into a temporary coalition to defend the status of English against Hindi as the official language of the Union. But the motivations of these groups for defending English are different in each case. Thus the intensity of the defense of English as the official language of the Union would vary in accordance with the particular motivation of the defender concerned. In fact, within the non-Hindi areas, there are significant levels of language rivalry that are perhaps as important as the rivalry between the Hindi and the non-Hindi areas of India. The intraregional and the interregional language rivalries in the non-Hindi areas, therefore, provide important contextual factors for the understanding of the complexity of the politics of language rivalry in India.

# VII

## *Language Associations: Organizational Pattern*

In order to understand the role of the associations active in the language politics of India, it is necessary to study the organizational form adopted by them. Organization has been defined as a social unit deliberately patterned and constructed to seek specific goals.[1] One basic feature of organizations is their conscious attempt to control their structure, nature, and performances.[2] It is this feature that distinguishes organizations from other social groups. Organizations reflect the broad social situation and the normative frame of society in which they operate. Hence, one can understand the purpose of an organization and the means of realization adopted by it more clearly in the broad context of the social processes which make up the background of organizational operation.

[1] See Talcott Parsons, *Structure and Process in Modern Societies*, p. 17. See also his, *The Social System* (New York: Free Press, 1964), p. 279 (paperback).

[2] The nature of an organization as envisaged by an organization theory varies with the orientation of different theorists. For a mechanistic orientation, see Herbert Simon, *Administrative Behavior* (New York: Macmillan, 1957), p. 122; for a different orientation employing a natural system model, see Philip Selznick, "Foundations of the Theory of Organization," *American Sociological Review* 13 (February 1948): 25–35. See also, Alvin Gouldner in R. K. Merton et al., eds., *Sociology Today* (New York: Basic Books, 1959), for a discussion of different orientations in organization theory.

Organizational patterns tend to vary with the social patterns in which they operate. Despite the situational variations, organizations in modern societies reveal certain similarities. Usually, organizations are marked by divisions of labor, power, and communication responsibilities.[3] In every organization there is a system of control that patterns the efforts of the organizations and directs them toward their goals. One primary requirement of every organization is an institutionalized concern for mobilization of resources directed toward the attainment of its purpose. The conscious direction necessary for the implementation of the organizational programs, in its turn, requires institutionalized leadership, plans for coordination between the leaders and followers, and the devising of the best means for the utilization of the resources. Control and consent, therefore, seem to be indivisible for the achievement of a cooperative system that characterizes an organization.[4] For this reason, a proper understanding of an organization would involve a study of both the formal and the informal relationships which build, sustain, and develop organizations.

The organizational structure of the voluntary associations in the developing areas reveal a considerable discrepancy between their declared formal pattern and their actual operative pattern. Hence, it will be necessary, for our purpose, to go beyond the formal pattern and to investigate the informal relations which add up to a more realistic picture of the organizations—especially the political organizations in India. In general, the organizational pattern of the voluntary associations in India reveals a mixed picture. Thus, one may find highly modernized organizational structures of some business associations,[5] and at the same time, at the other end of the continuum, a number of organizations like some caste associations which reveal only rudimentary

[3] See Amitai Etzioni, *Modern Organizations*, p. 3.
[4] See Philip Selznick, "Foundations"; for an analysis of organizations as cooperative systems, see Chester I. Bernard, *The Functions of the Executive* (Cambridge, Mass.: Harvard University Press, 1938), pp. 65 ff.
[5] Cf. Bernard E. Brown, "Organized Business in India," *Indian Journal of Political Science*, April–June 1962, pp. 126–143.

modernization.[6] But a simple dichotomous distinction in terms
of modernity and traditionally, as applied to the organizations
in a country such as India, may be misleading.[7] In a transitional
society the structure of the political organizations tends, in fact,
to combine the elements of tradition and modernity in various
proportions. In this respect the political organizations in India
are not exceptions. A study of the organizational forms of the
major voluntary associations engaged in the language politics
of India would seem to substantiate this point.

## Hindi Organizations

The oldest organization advocating the cause of Hindi was
founded in 1893. The Nagari Pracharani Sabha of Benaras grew
into a leading Hindi organization from a very small beginning.[8]
Today it is one of the largest language associations of India. Initially, the declared purpose of the Sabha was to establish itself
as an important center for the advancement of the Hindi language and the Nagari script. However, as we have seen before,
it soon transformed itself into the leading organization for the
protection of the interests of the Hindi speakers, as opposed to
the Urdu speakers.[9] Gradually, it assumed the role of an organized protector of the purity of Hindi—thereby identifying
Hindi with its predominantly Sanskritized version, as advocated
by many prominent traditionalist Hindu leaders. During the
national movement, it advocated the case for Hindi as the national language of India. It was during this time that its leadership became increasingly associated with the prominent leaders
of the national movement.

The structure of the Sabha management, as described in its

[6] Cf. Lloyd Rudolph and Susan Rudolph, "The Political Role of
India's Caste Associations," *Pacific Affairs*, March 1960, pp. 37–38.

[7] See Myron Weiner, *The Politics of Scarcity*, pp. 37–38.

[8] For an account of the development of the Nagari Pracharani Sabha, see
*Bigata Shat Barson ka Sinhabalokan* (Benaras: Nagari Pracharani Sabha,
Sambat 2010), p. 3, and *Hirak Jayanti Granth*, pp. 3 ff. (both in Hindi). See
also *Hindi Bishwawakosha* (Benaras: Nagari Pracharani Sabha, 1966), 6: pp.
284–286 (in Hindi).

[9] See chapter 3.

constitution, vests the highest power in an executive committee consisting of thirty-four ordinary members led by a chairman, two vice-chairmen, one general secretary, and one or more departmental secretaries. Of this committee, as many as fifteen must be from Benaras and six others from other parts of Uttar Pradesh. Only nine members may come from the other states of India. The essential core of this organization is thus concentrated in Uttar Pradesh. Membership is limited to those adults who "love the Hindi language and the Nagari script." The members of the executive committee are elected for three years—one third of the members each year. Formally then, a democratic management is envisaged in general, with some reserved status for the members of proved special eminence.[10]

An analysis in 1963 of the ages of the members of the executive committee and the elected officials shows that out of a total of sixty-three persons in these categories, twenty-one were aged from fifty to sixty, eight from forty to fifty, five from thirty to forty, and ten were aged sixty and above. At the top level of the leadership there is a predominance of those who are above fifty. A historical analysis of the ages of the Sabha's leadership shows that it is only since the independence of India that the leaders belonging to the group aged forty or below have assumed some importance. One may assume that the expansion of the organization since Hindi was made the official language of the Union and of the Hindi-speaking states has allowed young aspirants for leadership to become relatively more active. In fact, one of the reasons for the increasing entry of the younger members seems to be the range of opportunities offered by the expanding governmental support given to the Nagari Pracharani Sabha.

In terms of occupations, about sixty percent of the members of the executive committee and the officeholders of the Nagari Pracharani Sabha in 1963 belonged to the teaching profession. About 20 percent of these leaders were classified as lawyers, 10 percent as social workers, 5 percent as businessmen—industrial

[10] For the provisions of the constitution of the Nagari Pracharani Sabha, see *Sambidhan* (Benaras: Nagari Pracharani Sabha, Sambat 2011) (in Hindi).

and commercial—and the rest belonged to other professions. The relative proportion of the leaders in terms of occupation has remained fairly constant during the recent decades except in one respect: since independence, the role of the princes and the zamindars has been replaced by that of the businessmen.[11] In any case, the most important component of the leadership is drawn from the intellectually oriented members of the middle classes.

The Hindi Sahitya Sammelan, another major organization promoting the Hindi language, represented a form of structural organization somewhat different from that of the Sabha until 1962. Like the Sabha, it provided for different categories of membership, with a favored status being assigned to the higher category of members.[12] However, unlike the Sabha, the responsibility for directing the organization formally belonged to a Standing Committee.[13]

The committee was an unwieldy body made up of representatives of state committees, constituent associations, former officeholders, writers honored by the organization, and other associates. Thus, it was rarely in a position to perform a managing role. As a result, the real directing responsibility belonged to the officeholders, including the departmental secretaries. This meant that organizational power was concentrated mainly in a small body consisting of the chairman, the vice-chairmen, the general secretary, and the secretaries of seven important departments, and twenty elected members. The important departments were concerned with the executive office, conducting Hindi examinations, coordinating literary activity, publication, publicity, mobilizing

---

[11] For most of the data about the social composition of the current leadership I had to rely on the materials furnished to me in interviews with some important officeholders in 1964. These data were checked against the Sabha's published reports and other accounts.

[12] The higher category refers to permanent members, members honored with titles, the recipients of awards from the Sammelan, and the representatives of the state and the constituent functional units of the national organization. See *Niyamabali* (Allahabad: Hindi Sahitya Sammelan, Sambat 2018), p. 3 (in Hindi).

[13] For details, see *ibid.*, pp. 6 ff.

financial resources, and enlisting support for Hindi as the national language.

The organizational differences between the Sabha and the Sammelan lie mainly in the types of work that they are supposed to perform. From the very beginning, compared to the Sabha, the Sammelan was supposed to aim at a much larger audience and a wider range of work. In fact, the Sabha was one of the main sponsors of the Sammelan. Formal relations between these two organizations were maintained. The founders of the Sammelan had originally expected it to be a forum for writers and a center for training in Hindi, just as the Nagari Pracharani Sabha was initially supposed to be primarily a center for research and the promotion of Hindi. In the course of time, the organizational objectives of the Sammelan became less directly concerned with Hindi literature, and it devoted its resources mainly to teaching Hindi and campaigning for Hindi as the national language of India. These objectives were closely related to the language policies advocated by a strong section of the leadership of the national movement. We have already seen how a bitter conflict arose among these leaders concerning various definitions of Hindi. During this debate the leadership of the Sammelan gradually alienated the Gandhian group and veered toward a section of the Congress leadership in Uttar Pradesh led by P. D. Tandon.

The organizational strength of the Sammelan was derived primarily from two sources. The more spectacular source was, of course, the association of the important national leaders with the Sammelan. The first chairman of the Sammelan was Madan Mohan Malaviya, and its first general secretary was P. D. Tandon. Later, political leaders such as Gandhi and Rajendra Prasad became its chairmen. Such personal associations unmistakably enhanced the strength of the Sammelan. But a less spectacular, yet organizationally more important, source of strength for the Sammelan was to be found in its work devoted to the teaching of Hindi. Through its own centers and the centers conducted by its branches and associate organizations like the Rashtrabhasha Prachar Samiti, the Sammelan developed an extensive network of activity in various states of India. After Hindi was declared to be the official language of India, the educational role of the Sammelan increased further. Through the training courses and examinations in Hindi, the Sammelan has reached a large audience that serves as a potential recruiting ground of support for the views of the Sammelan.[14] Financially, these educational activities provide substantial earnings. In terms of personnel, the large number of persons who conduct the training programs and the examinations serve as the "field-workers" of the Sammelan.

If the educational activities of the Sammelan have contributed to its financial and personnel strength, they have also served as a source of intraorganizational tension and discord.[15] The educational activities of the Sammelan necessitated the creation of a large bureaucratic setup. Those who control this bureaucratic apparatus automatically secure a major vantage point for controlling the organization. This apparatus commands a large capacity to dispense favors—the most important of them being prospects of employment, offers of contracts to intellectuals, and approval of textbooks written by those who are close to the apparatus. Indeed, the problem of the "textbook racket" has haunted the organizational integrity of the Sammelan for a long time. It has been a source of constant conflict among the factions within the Sammelan. However, as a greasing mechanism, it has bound together many disparate personalities and cliques in its relatively cohesive collective blocs. For the attainment of public status, these blocs seek coalition with the political leaders of the Sammelan, just as the political leaders who want to mobilize support groups in their favor find such coalitions to be equally welcome. This usually involves a process of reciprocal support

[14] For an indication of the number of students who take the Sammelan examinations every year, it may be noted that in 1957 more than 27,000 students received various diplomas from the Sammelan. In 1961 the corresponding figure was 34,166. See Kantilal Joshi, "Rashtrabhasha Prachar" in *Rajat Jayanti Granth* (Wardha: Rashtrabhasha Prachar Samiti, 1962), p. 593.

[15] Some of the materials used here rely on the information supplied by Prabhakar Machwe in the course of interviews in 1964, and, during the same year, from interviews with other important persons connected with the Sammelan.

in which the political leaders confer a tacit approval on such greasing mechanisms in the interest of keeping the organizational apparatus operating at a stable level. Because such a stable operation provides an important support for the political leaders, the organizational leaders who manage the apparatus enjoy a tacit assurance that they in fact have a large measure of autonomy independent of the political leaders' control. These organizations thus cannot be understood simply with reference to what happens at the level of public visibility. The incentive system that keeps the bureaucratic apparatus going represents a sphere of pragmatic transactions which is organizationally functional though publicly invisible.

The bureaucratic apparatus is often so powerful that, at times, it succeeds in overwhelming the political leadership in respect of the policy-making processes of the organization. However eminent, the political leaders operating at the top of the organization cannot neglect the power of the organizational control groups operating through the apparatus. Thus, even a leader of the stature of P. D. Tandon, who was able to dislodge the Gandhian leaders from the Hindi Sahitya Sammelan, did not always succeed in challenging the power of such groups within the Sammelan. After independence, Tandon repeatedly attempted to alter the constitution of the Sammelan in a radical way. But the bureaucratic control groups organized themselves in a coalition to frustrate Tandon's moves. This brought out the fact that neither Tandon's national eminence nor his long leadership of the Sammelan was adequate to give him a decisive dominance over the internal affairs of the Sammelan. The only way of assuring such a dominance was to build a coalition with the dominant factions within the bureaucratic apparatus. But on questions which affect the basic structure of the organization, the factions within the bureaucratic system tend to preserve the status quo. Tandon's moves, in this case, were perceived as a threat to the status quo, hence it was difficult for him to recruit support from these dominant factions.

In such a case, when the political leaders and the organizational control groups revealed divergent interests, and the link

of reciprocity broke down, the organization itself faced a stalemate. As a result, the Sammelan central organization was
immobilized for some time. By 1950 the organizational headquarters of the Sammelan was virtually paralyzed. A continued
stalemate, however, would be detrimental to the very interest
of the organizational control groups. The political leaders were
less affected by this stalemate because, after all, the Sammelan
represented only a part of their total organizational involvements in different aspects of public life. The organizational
leaders of the Sammelan thus turned their attention to an immediate solution through the intervention of a third party. As it
happens in many factional struggles in India, the third party in
this case was the law court of the area. From 1951 onward, a
series of litigations followed among the contenders for the control of the Sammelan's headquarters. Rather than facilitating a
solution, these litigations and the resulting court actions further
crippled the central organization of the Sammelan.

All this happened in Uttar Pradesh, which is considered to
be the center of the *Hindi Sansar*, or the Hindi community.
These developments, though affecting the Sammelan activities
in Uttar Pradesh, did not significantly affect the operation of
the Sammelan's work outside Uttar Pradesh. In Uttar Pradesh
the situation continued without any change for about five years.
Eventually, the political leaders of the Sammelan sought legislative action in order to revive the activities of the central body
of the Sammelan. This was not difficult to achieve, in view of the
predominance of these leaders in the Congress party which then
dominated the Uttar Pradesh Assembly. Thus followed the
Uttar Pradesh Hindi Sahitya Sammelan Act of 1956, which attempted to reorganize the central body of the Sammelan. Political intervention to save the Sammelan was reinforced by the
actions of the Union Parliament, which in 1962 passed the Hindi
Sahitya Sammelan Act. By this act the Sammelan was declared
an institution of national importance.[16] The government of

---

[16] See *Hindustan Times*, March 31, 1962, for a report of the debate in
Parliament on the Hindi Sahitya Sammelan Bill. As an indicator of critical
opinion in the non-Hindi press the following may be cited: "The mischie-

India nominated a Governing Council which, in addition to acting as the receiver, was given the responsibility for framing a new set of rules for reorganization and for conducting new elections. In 1963 the receivership was terminated but the crisis was by no means over.[17] The continued stalemate at the headquarters had by then considerably weakened the coalition of the factions of 1951. Some of them were still seeking judicial intervention,[18] but with the support of the Union and the state government of Uttar Pradesh, the political leaders of the Sammelan gradually succeeded in reconstituting the central headquarters. With the official intervention, the Sammelan's position appeared, for a while, to be that of an academic institution. However, despite the official recognition of the Sammelan, it continues to be one of the most important voluntary associations working for Hindi. That, institutionally, it has not been reduced to a mere academic body will be apparent in our analysis later of its continued political role. Meanwhile, it is worth noting that despite the power conflict at the level of the controlling center of the Hindi Sahitya Sammelan, the day-to-day work of this organization, including its Hindi promotional activities, maintained a remarkable continuity. This was due mainly to the vitality of the major branch organizations and the uninterrupted effectiveness of the educational institutions operated by the Sammelan.

The Hindi associations of Uttar Pradesh have been so closely tied to the faction-ridden politics of the state that their activi-

vous provisions are that the Hindi Sahitya Sammelan of Allahabad can distribute degrees and diplomas in Hindi and these will enjoy equal status in securing Government jobs with the degrees and diplomas awarded by the universities. This Act creates channels for the flow of large amounts of money to this organisation from the University Grants Commission." From a letter published in *Hindusthan Standard*, April 15, 1962. The same criticism was offered in the editorial in *Desh* (in Bengali), April 21, 1962.

[17] From information supplied by C. B. Rao, formerly of the Indian Civil Service and currently one of the most important leaders of the Hindi Sahitya Sammelan.

[18] Information from G. C. Sinha, who was appointed by the government of India to guide the reorganization of the Sammelan. He was replaced in 1965.

ties are always identified with the interests of the major political factions of Uttar Pradesh. This local and sectional identification is absent in the case of the most important Hindi association which operates in the non-Hindi areas. The Dakshina Bharat Hindi Prachar Sabha of Madras concentrates its activities mainly in the South.[19] It was founded by Gandhi in 1918 in Madras, and from its very beginning, he tried to dissociate the image of Hindi which it promoted from the regional interests of the Hindi areas. As we have seen before, this organization consistently attempted to promote Hindi as the necessary second language in the non-Hindi areas. It took special care to popularize a style of Hindi that followed Gandhi's definition. Initially, it was operated as a specialized part of Gandhian constructive work. Since then its leadership has consistently remained in the hands of Gandhi's political followers and their associates.

It is obvious that this organization chose to operate in an area that was by no means naturally inclined to support its work. But by persistent efforts, the Sabha has grown from a small beginning to one of the largest language associations in India. From 1922 to 1930, it could organize only 73 centers for the propagation of Hindi in South India. By 1963, however, it had extended its operation to 1,352 centers. So far it has trained 7,000 field-workers for Hindi promotion. Its organizational network is built on the foundation of 800 local associations spread all over South India. The responsibility of the management of this organization belongs to an executive council composed of six officeholders and seven members. Special care is taken to recruit most of the executive members from South India.[20] The hard core of the organizational leadership consists of tried Gandhian leaders. But the central organization as well as the state units

[19] Information on the Sabha has been collected from, among other sources, B. C. Apte, general secretary of the Sabha's branch in Delhi, and from the survey of the Sabha's work published by the Sabha in a mimeographed report released in 1964.

[20] In 1964, out of six officeholders of the council, five were from South India. Only the president—Lal Bahadur Shastri—was from North India. Similarly, all the seven members were from South India.

of the Sabha also include non-Gandhian leaders. Most of the
prominent leaders of the Sabha were Congress leaders and this
trend continues.[21]

All the operations of the Sabha are planned, supervised, controlled, and managed by an Executive Council. This council is
elected by a Governing Body. This body consists of representatives of the state units, and individual members of the Sabha.
Unlike the Hindi associations of the Hindi areas, the leadership
of this Sabha is not tied to any particular state. Again, unlike
those Hindi associations, this Sabha insists on an equal status
for Hindi and the regional languages, thereby dissociating Hindi
from any regional pride, status, or power. Like the Hindi Sahitya
Sammelan, however, it has developed a professional institutionalized structure that relies mainly on Hindi propagation,
publication, and promotion. It has been recognized by the
government of India as an institution of national importance.
This signifies, among other things, that it will have a greater
access to the Hindi funds provided by the government than
before. In fact, large-scale aids from the government of India
and the income from its own educational activities have already
contributed substantially to its financial and organizational stability and have assured it of a larger scale of operation. Because
the Sabha has been closely allied with the Hindustani Prachar
Sabha, and because of its ability to attract a large number of
nationally prominent leaders from outside the Hindi areas to
work for it, it has succeeded in recruiting an impressive support
for Hindi from the non-Hindi areas.

The Sabha is not the only Hindi association, however, that is
working in the non-Hindi areas. In 1936 the Rashtrabhasha
Prachar Samiti was organized in Wardha.[22] Its original program
was to supplement the work of the Sabha in the non-Hindi
areas outside South India. The organizational foundation of
the Samiti was strengthened by the persistent efforts of the
Gandhian constructive workers. It gradually established itself

[21] For example, S. Nijalingappa (Mysore), C. Subramaniam (Madras), and
B. Gopala Reddi (Andhra).
[22] For details, see Kantilal Joshi (n.14 above), pp. 602 ff.

as a leading Hindi association in the non-Hindi areas not covered by the Sabha. Structurally, it resembles the organizational system of the Sabha. But its central leadership is closely allied with the Hindi Sahitya Sammelan. It is not surprising that the factional quarrels of the Sammelan have repeatedly spilled over to the controlling centers of this organization. It is this linkage which has apparently hindered its organizational appeal in the non-Hindi areas, especially after the intensification of language rivalry in contemporary India.

## Urdu Organizations

The Anjuman Taraqqi-i-Urdu (Hind) is the most important organization serving the cause of Urdu in India. Its parent organization was established in 1903, and after the partition of India, it was split into two separate organizations, one working in Pakistan and another in India. The reorganized Anjuman in India seeks to adopt all possible measures for promoting Urdu and "to popularize its simpler form, the Hindustani."[23] Anyone interested in the progress of Urdu is entitled to be a member of the Anjuman. Technically, the governing body of this organization is referred to as "the Anjuman," and the number of the governing members varies from thirty to forty. Not all the members of this body are elected—five are nominated by the president of the organization and two by the government of India. The executive committee of the Anjuman consists of thirteen members. The chief executive officer of the Anjuman is the general secretary. The president of the reorganized Anjuman exercises powerful authority, although the normal organizational responsibilities are discharged by the general secretary. Among the architects of the reorganized Anjuman, two were especially important: Kazi Abdul Gaffar, the general secretary of the Anjuman in 1948; and Zakir Hussain, who served as its president from 1948 to 1956.[24] The Anjuman has branches in ten

[23] For this and other provisions referred to later, see *Rules and Regulations* (Aligarh: Anjuman Taraqqi-i-Urdu (Hind), 1950).

[24] From information supplied by Ehtesam Husain in an interview in 1964. Dr. Husain is the chairman of the Department of Urdu in the University of

states of India.[25] Its major concentration of strength, however, is in Uttar Pradesh and its headquarters is in Aligarh. The reorganized Anjuman is different in many respects from its prepartition predecessor. The changed political situation of the Indian Muslims has made it much less militant than before.

The upper echelon of the Anjuman leadership is divided into two main generational groups—leaders like Zakir Hussain and H. N. Kunzru who belong to the old generation and are firmly committed to nonagitational political work, and the leaders who belong to the middle-aged group and are more radical. Among the middle-aged leaders there is a strong group with a broadly Marxist orientation. The organizational apparatus of the Anjuman is weak, and in terms of continuous educational activity for the promotion of its aims, it cannot claim much to its credit. It comes to life only when political grievances concerning Urdu are prominent. Because of its lack of substantial continuous activity, its leadership is less institutionalized and more personal than that of either the Hindi Sahitya Sammelan or the Nagari Pracharani Sabha. The central organization of the Anjuman, as far as its daily activities are concerned, looks more like a small personal secretariat of its chief executive officer, the general secretary.

In the initial years after independence, when Kazi Abdul Gaffar held the position of general secretary, his role as a full-time official brought a measure of professionalism to the organization. Since his death in 1957 that factor has been largely absent. Professor A. A. Suroor, whom Zakir Hussain appointed as the general secretary, devotes only a small part of his busy time to his role as the pivot of the central Anjuman organization. However, because of his pro-Marxian orientation and his important position in the leadership of the Aligarh University, he has been able to coordinate the activities of both the radical and the con-

Allahabad and an eminent leader of the Anjuman. His intellectual convictions are Marxian.

[25] One important official of the Anjuman central office claimed the existence of 355 local branches. Most of these, however, seem to be active only intermittently.

servative factions within the Anjuman.[26] In view of the fact that the Urdu speech community is represented by only one important language association, the Anjuman, the latter can ill afford debilitating factionalism within its organization. So far it has been able to maintain a cohesive leadership.

One reason for the continuity of this cohesion lies in the fact that, though the Muslim politicians of North India are politically divided into several factions, all of them have recognized the utility of a united language association in protecting and promoting Urdu. Muslim politics in North India has found Urdu to be a potent issue to mobilize their political resources in the Muslim community in independent India. Because of the fragmented nature of the Muslim leadership, it is in the interest of all the factions to utilize the Anjuman as a common rallying center. The other Muslim organizations are too specialized in their primary fields to protect the language interest of the Muslim minority in North India as a whole. For example, the Jamia Millia Islamia of Delhi, though a highly institutionalized educational association, is too involved in its academic work and too localized in its effect to perform any large-scale mobilizational function. Moreover, the fact that it is recognized as a "central university" by the University Grants Commission makes it difficult for this organization to participate in open politics. It can, however, supplement the public political support of Urdu by influencing the language policy of the Union government through institutional channels. The prestige, respectability, and confidence enjoyed by the leaders of the Jamia among the non-Muslims tend to facilitate this kind of supplemental effort.[27]

The Muslim organizations which operate in the open political field perform the function of articulating Urdu interests in their own specialized way. The Jamiat-ul-Ulama and the Jamaat-i-

---

[26] He is currently the chairman of the Department of Urdu in the Aligarh University. In 1964, he was the dean of the Faculty of Arts in this university.

[27] For structural details on the Jamia, see *Jamia Millia Islamia, Review of Aims, History and Scope of Work* (Delhi: Jamia Millia Islami, 1956). The most famous leaders of the Jamia organization are M. Mujeeb, S. Abid Husain, Z. H. Faruqi, and the former president of India (1967–1969), Zakir Hussain.

Islami have performed this function for a long time. Because of their traditionalist and fundamentalist associations, their mobilizational capability is limited, however. The Jamiat, owing to its long association with the nationalist movement, did appeal to a more differentiated audience. But its effectiveness has of late been retarded because of its division into two rival factions diverging increasingly from each other.[28] The Jamaat-i-Islami has all along been noted for its political extremism based on communalism, and it has been identified with Urdu extremism as well. In contrast to its effectiveness in Pakistan, its Indian counterpart has had an extremely limited success.[29] Its communal identification serves more as a liability to the Urdu movement than as an asset. The Anjuman leaders constantly strive to keep the organization away from such extremist groups. In 1964 some Muslim leaders belonging to various political groups—operating mainly in North India—attempted to build a broad alliance of Muslim political organizations. This organization is called the Muslim Majlis-i-Mushawarat.[30] This broad front, unlike a political party, does not contest the elections, serving more as a rallying platform. Its support or opposition to Muslim candidates is deemed to be important in many parts of North India. If it continues to provide a broad unity of various Muslim political

[28] For the details of this split, see Theodore P. Wright, Jr., "Muslim Education in India at the Crossroads," *Pacific Affairs* 39, nos. 1 and 2 (Spring-Summer 1966): 60–61. For the background of the Jamiat, see Ziya-ul-Hasan Faruqi, *The Deoband School*, pp. 67–91 and *passim*.

[29] It was founded in 1941 by Maulana Maududi in Lahore. For its importance in Pakistan, see Leonard Binder, *Religion and Politics in Pakistan* (Berkeley and Los Angeles: University of California Press, 1961). For its general ideals influencing the Jamaat, both in India and Pakistan, see S. A. A. Maududi, *The Islamic Law and Constitution*, trans. and ed. by Khurshid Ahmad (Lahore: Islamic Publications, 1960). See also Charles J. Adams, "The Ideology of Maulana Maududi," in *South Asian Politics and Religion*, ed. D. E. Smith (Princeton, N.J.: Princeton University Press, 1966), pp. 371–397; and F. Abbott, *Islam and Pakistan* (Ithaca, N.Y.: Cornell University Press, 1968), esp. chap. 6.

[30] It means Muslim Consultative Committee. For details, see Theodore P. Wright, Jr., "Muslim Education in India at the Crossroads," p. 55. See also Imtiaz Ahmed, "Indian Muslims and Electoral Politics," *Economic and Political Weekly* 2, no. 10 (March 11, 1967): 521–523.

groups in a common front which is not directly involved in the battle for political power, it can perform a significant function of supplementing the specific language associations like the Anjuman in promoting the Urdu interests.

The language associations which are active in the movement to oppose Hindi are, organizationally speaking, nothing more than temporary coalitions of various regional language associations brought together intermittently by some political leaders who take persistent interest in the official language policies. Such coalitions have not been successfully institutionalized in a continuous organization. One attempt to build such a continuous organization was reflected in the establishment of the Association for the Advancement of the National Languages of India. This association succeeds more in bringing together various organized representations in different regions in a common front during periods of intense popular resentment against Hindi. There is hardly any year-round activity of this organization. It maintains a skeleton bureaucratic apparatus, which functions, however, more as an adjunct to other associational enterprises than as an autonomous organization. The intermittence of the organizational activities in the anti-Hindi movement is not surprising when we consider the essentially negative nature of the anti-Hindi movement itself. The sporadic nature of this movement stands in sharp contrast to the institutionally consolidated regional language associations built around the positive interests of the regional language communities, such as the Tamil Cultural Society, Bangiya Sahitya Parishad, the Kannada Sahitya Parishad, and other similar language associations.

### Organizational Finance

The financial statements released by the leading language associations provide some important glimpses into the scale of their operation and their relative strength. These statements, usually contained in their annual budgets, do not, of course, present a comprehensive picture. But in the absence of intensive studies of the organizational finance of the language associations, even the partial light offered by these financial statements can be of some value. Since the size of the membership of the language associations is very limited—the leading associations rarely having more than two thousand members each—it is apparent that membership subscriptions furnish but a small part of the financial resources of these organizations. Most of them depend heavily on other sources of income. Before the abolition of the native states in India, the Hindi and Urdu language associations received substantial donations from some of these states. The ruler of Baroda was the most important single contributor to the funds of the Hindi Sahitya Sammelan. Similarly, the most important contributor to the major Urdu associations was the Nizam of Hyderabad. The literature of the Hindi and Urdu associations often mentioned the generous contributions of many other smaller states. After independence, these sources dried up. The largest contributors to the funds of the Hindi, Hindustani, Urdu, and other regional language organizations are now the government of India and various states within the Indian Union. Several states have also established their own institutional language organizations, especially in the Hindi areas. Examples are the Hindi Samiti of Uttar Pradesh, the Rashtrabhasha Parishad of Bihar, and the Shasan Sahitya Parishad of Madhya Pradesh.[31] In addition, by giving legislative recognition to voluntary associations such as the Hindi Sahitya Sammelan and the Dakshina Bharat Hindi Prachar Sabha, and by accepting them as organizations of national importance, the Union government has taken an indirect financial responsibility for them.

Some organizations have other sources of income in addition to those stated above. For instance, large-scale printing and publishing enterprises, various endowment funds, trust funds, and private donations from wealthy individuals have been important sources of income for the Nagari Pracharani Sabha. The total annual income of the Nagari Pracharani Sabha for 1965 was estimated to be more than one million rupees. The major sources

---

[31] See *Report of the Official Language Commission*, 1956, pp. 213 ff.

of income, as cited in its budgetary estimate for 1965, were printing, publication, and subsidy from the government of India for its encyclopedia project.[32] The budget of the Hindi Sahitya Sammelan for 1962–1963 showed a fairly similar pattern, with the difference that Hindi educational work forms one of its major sources of income and that, instead of a major publication project like that of an encyclopedia, it earns a considerable sum from smaller publications.[33] In comparison, the total budget of the Anjuman for 1963–1964 revealed an income of 49,500 rupees, out of which 44,000 rupees were cited as grants from the government of India. This grant was expected to be increased by 10,000 rupees in 1964–1965, in addition to a new grant of 5,000 rupees from the government of Kashmir.[34]

It appears that those language associations which tend to diversify their operations tend also to depend relatively less on governmental subsidy. It is also apparent that the Hindi organizations, for obvious reasons, are in a stronger position in terms of finance. Even apart from governmental promotion of Hindi, these organizations are institutionally better organized to secure larger financial resources. Again, the Hindi writers—an important source of strength for the Hindi associations—are in a comparatively better financial position than their non-Hindi counterparts. The Hindi market for intellectual products is larger than any other Indian language market. The inducements

[32] From the official budget statement of the Nagari Pracharani Sabha, submitted to the Sahitya Akademi in New Delhi in 1964. Income under the item of publication is cited as 282,050 rupees, whereas the corresponding sum for the encyclopedia was 266,225 rupees. Printing yielded 130,856 rupees. The income from membership subscriptions was only about 2,000 rupees.

[33] The total expenditure envisaged in the budget was more than 1,300,000 rupees. Its income from examinations alone was 393,800 rupees, and from printing, 143,240 rupees. See the budget statement of the Hindi Sahitya Sammelan, appended to *Hindi Sahitya Sammelan ka Unchaswa Barshik Bibaran* (Allahabad: Hindi Sahitya Sammelan, 1963, in Hindi).

[34] From the budget statement of the Anjuman, submitted to the Sahitya Akademi, New Delhi, in 1964. The estimated budget of the Anjuman for 1964–1965 was 100,950 rupees. This unusual increase was due to the expected increase of financial support from the government of India, and other large donations.

offered to the Hindi writers from the governmental sources are also considerably larger. In 1958, for example, the deputy minister for education told Parliament that the financial assistance provided to Hindi, Sanskrit, and Urdu poets and writers during the preceding three years amounted to 51,610 rupees, of which 45,270 were given to Hindi poets and writers, 5,840 to Urdu, and 500 to Sanskrit literateurs.[35] The relative prosperity of the writers in Hindi indirectly strengthens the Hindi organizations because these writers realize that their identification with the Hindi organizations will strengthen the cause of Hindi, the advancement of which, in its turn, will benefit both the writers and the organization.

The Hindi organizations also benefit from the fact of the preeminence of the Marwari businessmen in the Indian economic scene. The magnitude of the financial support provided by such businessmen is difficult to assess, though some indications can be had from one instance. On the occasion of the Nagari Pracharani Sabha's sixtieth anniversary a substantial drive for funds was undertaken by some of the leading Marwari businessmen.[36] The leading industrialist of India, G. D. Birla, contributed 25,000 rupees. He was followed by others.[37] In fact, from the very beginning of the consolidation of the Hindi movement during the national movement, the Marwari businessmen were repeatedly referred to as great sources of financial support for Hindi. Gandhi himself referred to them as "Hindi-loving Marwaris" and appealed to them to support the Hindi organizations.[38] The re-

[35] See *National Herald*, February 15, 1958.

[36] They were M. Kedia, G. P. Kejriwal, and B. Kanoria—all of them leaders of the Indian Chamber of Commerce.

[37] A sample of the donations from the Marwari business circles can be cited: Ramkumar Bhowalka paid 15,000 rupees; Ramkumar Kejriwal, 1101 rupees; and one Dalmia enterprise paid 5,000 rupees. On this occasion the Nagari Pracharani Sabha also received substantial amounts from the state governments in the Hindi areas. Thus, the Uttar Pradesh government promised to pay 125,000 rupees; the Bihar government, 6,000; the Madhya Pradesh government, 5,000; and the Vindhya Pradesh government, 1,000 rupees. See *Bigata Shat Barson ka Sinhabalokan* (n.8 above), pp. 83–84 (in Hindi).

[38] See M. K. Gandhi, *Thoughts on National Language*, p. 38. In his work

sponse to this appeal was mostly favorable. To cite only one example, when the Rashtrabhasha Prachar Samiti was founded, Gandhi succeeded in making its financial foundation secure by persuading one leading Marwari industrialist, Padampat Singhania, to donate 75,000 rupees and to promise an annual donation of 15,000 rupees for five years after the founding of the Samiti.[39] In sum, in terms of financial resources, no language association in India comes anywhere near the actual as well as the potential resources that the Hindi associations can mobilize.

*Factionalism*

In the non-Hindi areas, it is usually believed that the Hindi associations are endowed with a homogeneous leadership, guided from a single center and motivated by a unity of purpose that is automatically generated by a clearly defined interest of the Hindi elite.[40] Such a belief credits the Hindi leaders with a degree of unity and homogeneity which, in fact, they do not have. From the very beginning of the Hindi associations there has been a continuous sense of crisis in their leadership. The source of this crisis lay in a series of conflicts which arose as a result of bitter struggles among the different factions within the upper levels of the leadership.

A variety of motives and interests have guided these factions. We have already seen how, in the Hindi Sahitya Sammelan, the traditionalist group led by P. D. Tandon fought the Gandhian group and eventually displaced them from the leadership as well as from the organization. The outcome of this struggle was determined less by ideological factors than by the grip that the respective groups had on the organization. Tandon's victory in this struggle was due, to a great extent, to the keen interest that

for Hindi, Gandhi was continuously supported by eminent industrialists like Ramnath Goenka and Jamnalal Bajaj. The latter was an active organizer in the Gandhian Hindi movement.

[39] See Kantilal Joshi (n.14 above), p. 604. Padampat Singhania was the founder of the third largest industrial combine of India known as the J. K. Industries. The center of this combine is in Kanpur, Uttar Pradesh.

[40] In this section we will consider only the Hindi associations. Leadership in the Urdu associations has been discussed before.

he took in the day-to-day organizational processes of the Sammelan, and to the successful coalition that he had built up during
that period between the political leaders of a revivalist persuasion
and a section of Hindi intellectuals. Thus, he was able to bring
together personalities of mutually incompatible ideological per-
suasions like Rahul Sankritayan and Govind Das. The former
was a reputed Marxist intellectual and had intimate relations
with the Communist movement. Rahul Sankritayan believed
that "all the two dozen odd 'dialects' spoken in the length and
breadth of North India should be given the status of 'national'
languages."[41] Govind Das, on the other hand, believed in an
identification commonly summed up as "Hindi, Hindu and Hindustan." In addition, Govind Das seriously believed in an intimate relation between the interest of Hindi and the interest of
cow-protection.[42] As he explicated his point in one of his recent
formulations, "cow-protection and serving Hindi—these are related in the way the body is related to mind—are inseparable . . .
as we need Hindi for the development of our mental faculties,
so we need in the same way, the protection of cow for the sake
of our body."[43]

That Tandon could unite the advocates of such diverse orientations demonstrated his capacity to generate a sense of organizational purpose transcending the individual eccentricities of his
associates. However, after independence, when the Sammelan
devoted the greater attention to political campaigns, lobbying,
and publicity at the level of the Union government to promote
the case for Hindi, Tandon's efforts were concentrated more on
convincing the national leaders than in maintaining his grip
over the Sammelan's organization. Meanwhile, the Sammelan
had already become an established organization with its appropriate bureaucratic setup, and another faction, based on a dif-

[41] See S. S. Narula, *Scientific History of the Hindi Language*, p. 107.

[42] He is still one of the most important leaders in the Cow Protection Association and took an active part in organizing a series of cow protection
agitations which assumed considerable prominence in the North Indian
politics of 1966.

[43] See his address as reported in *Bihar Rashtrabhasha Parishad ka Barshik
Karyabibaran* (Patna: Bihar Rashtrabhasha Parishad, 1960), p. 43 (in Hindi).

ferent coalition and well entrenched in the organizational apparatus, had consolidated its grip over the central headquarters of the Sammelan. The details of the faction struggle and the resulting judicial action and legislative intervention have been discussed before.[44] After 1962, the dominant factions realigned themselves in accordance with the exigencies of the new situation created by the Union government's recognition of the Sammelan as an organization of national importance.

The leadership of the Nagari Pracharani Sabha is equally torn among conflicting factions. These factions are usually based on coalitions of various literary and political cliques with occasional caste overtones. Factionalism invaded the Sabha as soon as it attained a unique importance in the politics of Hindi. During the national movement and also after independence, one important influence on the formation of its factions as well as their success or failure has been connected with the politics of the Benaras Hindu University.[45] In this sense the immediate environment of the central organization of the Sabha located in Benaras has had an important influence on it. This is comparable to some extent with the effect that the Aligarh Muslim University has always had on the central organization of the Anjuman located in Aligarh.

The other important influence on the Sabha's factionalism is exercised by the leaders of the Uttar Pradesh Congress party.[46] Since the 1940s, one faction led by Kamalapati Tripathi has

[44] Legalism and judicial remedy have sometimes cast an unusual spell on some Sammelan leaders. Once, a group of leaders threatened to prosecute Gandhi. Malaviya's intervention saved the situation. This incident is cited in a speech of B. Chaturvedi in the Rajya Sabha on March 19, 1962. See *Modern Review*, April 1962, p. 267. From 1951 to the present day, the Sammelan has been involved in several judicial disputes raised by its factions.

[45] For this and other information used in this whole section, I have relied on my interviews in 1964 with important officeholders, members, observers, and critics of the Hindi Sahitya Sammelan, Nagari Pracharani Sabha, and other organizations.

[46] For details concerning the internal politics of the Congress party in Uttar Pradesh, see Paul R. Brass, *Factional Politics in an Indian State: The Congress Party in Uttar Pradesh* (Berkeley and Los Angeles: University of California Press, 1965).

dominated the leadership of the Sabha.[47] But the power of Tripathi's faction has not remained unchallenged. For example, Acharya Narendra Deva tried to challenge Tripathi's control over the Sabha during the early 1950s. At this time Narendra Deva was the vice-chancellor of the Benaras Hindu University. He utilized his control over the university by organizing a group around the famous Hindi writer, Hazari Prasad Dwivedi. Dwivedi himself was specially brought to the Indology faculty of the university in order that he might have a local base in Benaras. The Hindi and the Indology faculties of the university have long been important factors in influencing the Sabha's leadership. These are prize faculties for many of the intellectuals involved in the Hindi movement. Dwivedi, therefore, was set up in a strategic point to influence the faction system in the Sabha. With the vice-chancellor behind him, he was doubly assured of a secure base of operation. But it was not easy to gain access to the established leadership of the Sabha. Dwivedi's wide literary and scholarly reputation was not enough for this purpose. What really helped him was the fact that Tripathi was a former student of Narendra Deva, and the traditional system of social reverence for the teacher helped Narendra Deva to persuade Tripathi to secure for Dwivedi the necessary access. Even after this, the personal relationship between Narendra Deva and Tripathi made it easier for Dwivedi to consolidate the position of his faction in the Sabha's leadership.

Narendra Deva was Marxist in his political orientation and one of the most respected socialist leaders of India.[48] With his help Dwivedi brought a group of radical intellectuals—some of them with a Marxist persuasion—into the leadership of the Sabha. This was a move to challenge the traditionalist intellectuals who

[47] Tripathi leads one of the two most important factions in the Uttar Pradesh Congress party.

[48] See Paul R. Brass, pp. 37–40, for some aspects of Narendra Deva's political career in the background of Uttar Pradesh politics. For his political views, see his *Socialism and the National Revolution* (Bombay: Padma, 1946), and L. P. Sinha, *The Left-Wing in India* (Muzaffarpur: New Publishers, 1965), chap. 6.

enjoyed dominance by virtue of their association with Tripathi and his group. But the struggle was more than ideological. Till 1934 the Sabha's leadership was largely dominated by Brahmins, and from 1934 to 1953 the Agarwals maintained a controlling voice in the Sabha. Dwivedi attempted to destroy this dominance by bringing in a number of Rajputs who were his ideological friends. With Nambar Singh, Chandrabali Singh, and B. S. Upadhyay, Dwivedi succeeded in forming a mixed coalition which challenged the social and ideological basis of the traditionalist leadership of Tripathi. The solidarity of this coalition was not based on any one single factor. It was partly a case of ideological solidarity, partly based on a caste coalition, and partly due to the fact that most of the members of the Dwivedi faction came from the Balia and the Deoria districts of Uttar Pradesh. The success of this faction was short-lived, however, because it identified itself mainly with the smaller opposition parties, and it could not withstand for long the challenge of the Tripathi group, which drew sustenance from the resources of the Congress party and a strong group of traditionalist intellectuals aligned with the Congress. After 1957, the Tripathi group recaptured the leadership of the Sabha and has maintained it since then.

In the art of managing power in a language association dominated by the intellectuals the use of intellectual persuasion or complex factional coalitions is not always sufficient. On some occasions, faction struggles tend to reach such a high intensity that violence is used to supplement conventional political instruments. For example, despite the democratic constitution of the Nagari Pracharani Sabha, the factional leaders, especially those of the dominant faction, have at times used acts of physical violence to maintain their power. In such informal techniques of power management, the patronage-oriented younger supporters of the dominant faction have in recent times provided an important arm of support. From November 1963 to February 1964, to cite one period of recent history, on two important occasions of power struggle in the Nagari Pracharani Sabha headquarters, physical violence was employed in order to silence inconvenient challenges against the established leadership.[49] Such incidents are not rare in the history of the power management in the Sabha, though it must be admitted that the use of force is a marginal phenomenon in the management of power of the Sabha as well as other such associations.

## Problem of Categories

It should now be evident that the major language associations in North India are highly organized. In most cases they have developed a structure of resources which can be compared favorably with some of the most developed interest groups built around the problems of labor or business policies in India. The leadership of the language associations is recruited from a wide variety of personnel, including political leaders, literary authors, professional teachers, and bureaucratic managers. This leadership cuts across diverse ideologies within almost every major language association. Financially, some associations are more dependent on government patronage than others, but none of them can be said to rely exclusively on any single, specific financial source. In fact, most of them have developed a diversified structure of financial support. All of these organizations have institutionalized bureaucratic structure characterized by varying degrees of professionalism. Most of these associations have a democratic structure of recruitment and management. Some of these democratic principles are contradicted by the informal mechanisms that are brought to bear on these organizations through faction rivalries. In general, however, the violations of the democratic norm do not seem to be so severe as to cancel the norm itself. In any case, such occasional violations are not inconsistent with the normal practices of the democratic institutions operating in the other sectors of Indian political life and possibly in other democratic systems of the world.

In spite of these features, there has been a persistent tendency

[49] It is possible that the role of violence has been overestimated by the losing factions, the members of which were most vocal about these incidents during my interviews with them.

to view these language associations as mere conspiratorial clusters of primordial ties. This view is shared by many Indian and non-Indian observers. It appears that one reason for adopting such a view lies in the inability to differentiate the structural development from the formal goals of the language associations. The facts that the formal goal of these associations is based on language, and that language is usually dismissed as a primordial question, have persuaded many to neglect the contribution of the language associations to the development of institutionalized politics in India. The question whether language goals are primordial goals will be discussed later. Even assuming the validity of such an equation, the question remains whether an association having a language goal, or for that matter any other similar goals, can contribute to the institutional development of political life. To this question many westernized Indians as well as Western observers have given a negative answer. In this connection, one ingenuous attempt at theorizing deserves mention. Fred Riggs proposes an interesting typology according to which political associations having primordial goals should be called clects.[50] The term *clect* is a juxtaposition of the terms *clique* and *sect*. According to him, what characterizes a clect is that it draws its membership from a particular community. It applies its norms in a selective manner to members of that community, involving a particularist attachment to the community and a discrimination against the outsiders. In this way, a clect may have an apparently modern organization with a modern norm for its members, but because of selectivism and particularism, it ultimately fails to be modern. What is more, clects end up by retarding political modernization because, more often than not, they frustrate the necessary functions of the political order.[51]

Is it profitable to describe the major language associations in India as clects?[52] No major language association restricts its mem-

---

[50] For details, see Fred W. Riggs, *Administration in Developing Countries* (Boston: Houghton Mifflin, 1964), pp. 169–173.

[51] *Ibid.*, p. 455.

[52] Riggs does not explicitly discuss language associations, though he treats

bership to its own community.[53] We have seen how, during the national movement, non-Hindi speakers took an active part in the Hindi movement and associations. Even since independence the Hindi associations have drawn support from non-Hindi communities. The Hindi community itself defies a homogeneous definition. The interest of Hindi is not inherently incompatible with the interests of Hindustani, Urdu, and even with languages from outside what is roughly called the Hindi area. This is not to deny that major sections of the Hindi intellectuals and politicians have often been involved in particularism and selectivistic application of norms. But the recruitment to the Hindi associations has never been exclusively restricted to those who conform to such leaders' definitions. More or less the same can be said about the other associations that we have described before. The best that one can say is that these associations occasionally reveal "clectic" propensities. But that is not enough to dismiss these organizations as sheer clects. Such typological labels would tend to overlook the complexity of the composition of a community and its interests involved in language politics. What is more, these easy labels do not clarify the positive contributions of the language associations to the organizational development of Indian politics.[54] In our later discussion, we will analyze some of the positive contributions of the language associations to the processes of modernization and political development in India.

language loyalty on the same level as religious, tribal, and caste loyalties. *Ibid.*, p. 452.

[53] The reference here is to the associations included in this study.

[54] In part, Riggs himself misses this opportunity because he relies exclusively on one partial study of the Indian interest groups.

# VIII

## *Conflict, Integration, and Development*

The public pronouncements of many Indian leaders have often given the impression that official language planning implies essentially a technical assignment. Even the Official Language Commission declared that language is only "the garb and it is the garb which must be tailored to the requirements of the body politic, not the body politic amputated to the requirements of the garb."[1] The majority of the members of the commission were convinced that the success of language planning could be assured if only the political authority of the state were to exert its maximum efforts to achieve the objectives set forth by the commission. As for the objectives, the commission was certain that they represented the interest of the nation. Behind this certainty one could detect a clear assumption that language planning is like any other rational form of planning. It involves a rational order of priorities. Once these priorities have been settled, efficient administrative action should put the plans into practice. In this process of administrative action, political conflicts are irrelevant, if not outright reactionary. This technocratic conviction underlies the propensity of many Indian leaders to disparage political action that tends to disrupt the smooth im-

[1] *Report of the Official Language Commission,* 1956 (New Delhi, 1957), p. 262.

plementation of official language policies. It is not surprising, therefore, that language politics has occasionally been viewed by the official policy-makers as a menace that needs to be eradicated rather than as a political issue which demands political solution. It was in this context that the Official Language Commission urged the Union government to attain the constitutional objectives regarding language as quickly as possible, "so as to reduce to the minimum the manifestly unsatisfactory period of transition."[2] The Union government, accordingly, stepped up its administrative efforts to meet the fifteen-year deadline.

By 1959, however, it was apparent that the fifteen-year period was not adequate for the proposed changeover to Hindi. In September 1959, the Union home minister declared in Parliament that English could not be replaced completely until 1965. The leaders of the Hindi associations thought that such a statement was a confession of surrender to the pressures of the non-Hindi groups. On the other hand, Nehru declared in Parliament that it was the overenthusiasm of the leaders of the Hindi groups which came in the way of the spread of Hindi.[3] He urged a flexible policy and stated that he did not like any rigidity regarding specific dates concerning the linguistic changeover. The efforts of the Hindi language planners to rush the coinage of new terms and the production of volumes of "so-called translations" failed to persuade him. Mentioning specifically the excessive enthusiasm of two leaders of Hindi associations, Raghuvira and Govind Das, he warned that artificial efforts would not win confidence from any quarter.[4] Nehru did not wish to minimize the importance of the reactions and the fears of the non-Hindi speech communities. In this connection the assurance that he gave in Parliament to the non-Hindi states is worth noting:

English will continue as an associate language to the official language

---

[2] *Ibid.*, p. 262.

[3] See *Jawaharlal Nehru's Speeches*, IV, 60.

[4] See *ibid.*, pp. 57–60. He said: "The business of some kind of slot-machine turning out Hindi words and Hindi phrases is artificial, unreal, absurd, fantastic, and laughable. We cannot have that kind of approach to a language" (p. 60).

Hindi, and the question as to how long English should continue as an associate language will be determined only by the non-Hindi speaking people. . . . There will be no bar or handicap imposed on the non-Hindi speaking people in the matter of recruitment to services. While I would certainly welcome a man who does not know Hindi to learn it, I would like all feelings of disability to vanish. . . . I do not wish to impose Hindi compulsorily on any state which does not want it.[5]

The assurance of Nehru that Hindi would not be imposed had no formal sanction behind it, however. Hence, the scepticism of the non-Hindi areas persisted. The leaders of the non-Hindi associations were not prepared to be satisfied by personal assurances alone. They wanted more positive guarantees embodied in institutional compromises and formal legislation by the Union Parliament.

### Compromise and Political Parties

In addition to Parliament, a major arena of conflict between the language groups also existed inside the Congress party. The general principles regarding the language policy of the Congress party were laid down, said a Congress resolution in 1958, "not only in the Constitution, but in a number of resolutions passed by the Working Committee on May 17, 1953, and April 5, 1954, and in the A.I.C.C. resolution of June 3, 1956."[6] In 1958, speaking on the language resolution at the meeting of the subjects committees of the Congress session of Pragjyotishpur, Nehru maintained that "the use of any of the fourteen national languages in India, even for official All India purposes, was not ruled out even though it might be a little inconvenient."[7] G. B. Pant declared, at about the same time, that the regional languages should be supreme in their own areas, not only in the

---

[5] Speech in the Lok Sabha on September 5, 1959, reproduced in the *Survey of the Dakshina Bharat Hindi Prachar Sabha*, (New Delhi: Dakshina Bharat Hindi Prachar Sabha, 1964), p. 13 (mimeo). See also *Hindustan Times*, September 5, 1959, and *Jawaharlal Nehru's Speeches*, 4:59.

[6] *National Herald*, January 17, 1958.

[7] *Ibid.*, January 17, 1958.

administrative sphere but also in the spheres of commerce, law, and education.[8] The softer tones of Pant and Nehru stood in sharp contrast to that of Govind Das, who insisted on the inviolability of the deadline for changing over to Hindi. He accused the government of deliberately slowing down the process of the changeover and maintained that if the proper steps had been taken, no difficulty would have arisen and the deadline of 1965 could have been attained. He firmly pleaded for a proper scheme for a phased introduction of Hindi to be drawn up "without a moment's delay."[9] In his campaign against any compromise on the deadline, Govind Das found a major ally in a conservative faction within the Congress, led by Morarji Desai. Though hailing from a non-Hindi state, Desai and his faction formed a coalition with the Hindi faction due to a convergence of interests not limited to the language issue. The impatience and sense of hurry displayed by this coalition tended to unite most of the factions from the non-Hindi areas against the move to treat the deadline as a rigid one. The urge to compromise, on the basis of treating the non-Hindi factions' grievances as real, was revealed in a tendency on the part of the dominant leadership to find a consensual decision on the language question. Expressing this urge, Nehru reiterated in the Pragjyotishpur session that there should be no majority decisions imposed on a minority. He said that they were dealing with a very delicate and living thing and that decisions on this issue must be arrived at by general consensus of opinion.[10] This position was in marked contrast to the Hindi leaders' approach and also to the technocratic assumptions of the Official Language Commission.

The compromising tone set by the Pragjyotishpur formulations of the Congress party was welcomed by the Communist party of India. Its leader, Ajoy Ghosh, agreed with the view that Hindi should be introduced gradually and with mutual consent. However, like the Congress party, the Communist party was divided in its views on the introduction of Hindi. The con-

[8] See *ibid.*, January 10, 1958.
[9] *Ibid.*, January 18, 1958.
[10] *Ibid.*, January 17 and 18, 1958.

centration of the strength of the Communist party in the non-Hindi areas placed it in a different situation from that of the Congress party, which draws organizational support from all areas in India. For the Communist party, therefore, it is easier to advocate a policy that tends to conform to the interests of the non-Hindi areas. However, in Uttar Pradesh, the followers of the Communist party were already bitterly divided amongst themselves on the question of Hindi. Thus, Rahul Sankritayan in the Hindi Sahitya Sammelan led a group of Communist intellectuals to work with the traditionalist leaders of the Sammelan, and the Marxist faction of the Nagari Pracharani Sabha was deeply committed to a policy of immediate introduction of Hindi. The Muslim intellectuals in the Communist movement in Uttar Pradesh were at the same time engaged in fighting the "revivalist elements of Hindi." Ali Sardar Jafri, a leading Communist Urdu writer, resented the compulsion and coercion in the linguistic atmosphere, and in 1960 he accused the official publication concern of the Communist party of India of playing "straight into the hands of reaction and [helping] the revivalist and decadent elements of Hindi to mutilate a highly evolved language, popularly known as Hindi, Urdu or Hindustani."[11] This reaction is worth noting, especially because a resolution of the central committee of the Communist party had declared in 1957 that "the case of Urdu should . . . be especially considered for giving it a suitable place in the educational and administrative spheres" in the Urdu areas.[12]

For the Communist party the question of language policy is essentially dependent on the question of recruitment of mass support for the party. In trying to rationalize the mobilizational need of the party, many Communist leaders attempted to derive a coherent language policy from the ideological statements of Stalin. Stalin's theory of the close relation between language

[11] A. Sardar Jafri, "Mass Communication," *Seminar*, July 1960, p. 26.

[12] See *Asian Recorder*, October 12–18, 1957. In the Rajya Sabha debates on the report of the Official Language Commission, Abdur Rezzak Khan of the Communist party declared that Hindustani, and not Hindi, should be the official language of India. See *Hindustan Times*, September 10, 1959.

and nationality, and his idea that a Marxist cannot regard language as a superstructure, gave rise to an unending debate among the Communist leaders both in India and abroad.[13] In the course of this debate, Communist leaders admitted the need to describe India as a multinational area, but they were sure neither of the criteria for determining nation and nationality, nor of their boundaries. At times they suggested that language is the determining criterion, but in supporting the Pakistan movement they adopted the criterion of religion. In this confusing debate only one thing was clear—that the criteria suggested by the Communist leaders depended less on ideology and more on the pragmatic concern to use language and religion as convenient issues for deriving mass support for the party. But it was not easy to utilize all particularist mass movements to the benefit of the party's goal, because to support the claim of one particular group inevitably meant the alienation of the others.[14]

On the specific question of Hindi, the Communist leaders in India have never been able to find a coherent solution. Even the Hindi-speaking leaders of the Communist party could not arrive at an agreed formulation on the Hindi question. Rahul Sankritayan, as we have seen before, at one time thought that even the speech communities based on the dialects of Hindi should be recognized as nationalities. But his own activities in the Hindi Sahitya Sammelan showed that he had no doubt about Hindi as the unifying language for all Indians. Ram Bilas Sharma at that time thought that Rahul Sankritayan's advocacy of Hindi was a concession to chauvinism.[15] He suggested that the entire Hindi speech community is a single nationality and that Hindi

[13] For Stalin's theory, see his *Marxism and the National Question*, 1942; *Marxism and Linguistics*, 1951; and *The National Question in Leninism*, 1951 (New York: International Publishers).

[14] For an account of the shifting positions of the party on the issues of language and religion, see Gene D. Overstreet and Marshall Windmiller, *Communism in India* (Berkeley and Los Angeles: University of California Press, 1959), pp. 490–507.

[15] See *ibid.*, p. 501. Ram Bilas Sharma, one of the most sophisticated authors in the Communist party, has written extensively on the language problem. See his *Bhasha Aur Samaj* for an elaborate discussion of his ideas on the national language issue, especially chaps. 10–15 (in Hindi).

can be treated only as the language of this particular national-ity.[16] To suggest that Hindi can be the national language of India, Sharma added, would be to play into the hands of Indian big business, which is dominated by Hindi-speaking business-men.

By 1958, the Communist party veered around to a moderate support for Hindi as the official language of India. But, due to the Hindi-Urdu conflict within the Communist party, the lead-ership could not unite on a definition of Hindi. The ambiguity of the Communist party and the tenuous unity of the various language factions within the party were brought more sharply to the surface after the division of the party into two separate Communist parties.[17] The Left Communist party demanded that the use of Hindi as an All-India language should not be obliga-tory. The Right Communist party preferred to stick to the policy of accepting Hindi as the official language. This time some Hindi leaders of this group maintained that "the demands of the people inhabiting the different regions of the country must be subordinated to the central task of consolidating na-tional unity."[18] It is doubtful whether the entire leadership of the party agreed with this formulation. In practice, meanwhile, the regional leaders of both the Right and the Left Communist parties have found it expedient to identify themselves with mu-tually conflicting language demands wherever such identifica-tion has served the basic purpose of recruiting popular support.

The attitude of the Praja Socialist party (PSP) to the official language question was a product of factional compromise. The PSP draws its support from different regions of India, and it has been reluctant to follow any rigid position in respect of of-

[16] See "On the Formation of the Hindustani Nationality and the Prob-lems of its National Language," *Indian Literature*, no. 1, 1953 (Bombay). See also S. S. Narula, *Scientific History of the Hindi Language*, p. 113.

[17] On the background of this split, see John B. Wood, "Observations on the Indian Communist Party's Split" in *Pacific Affairs* 38, no. 1 (Spring 1965): 47–63.

[18] See R. B. Sharma, "Hindi and National Unity," *New Age* 1, no. 5 (new series, September 1964): 67; and for a discussion of the Left-Right debate on language in the Communist party of India, see *ibid.*, pp. 47–72.

ficial language policy. Officially, it recognizes Hindi as "the common language of India."[19] But regionally, its leaders have identified themselves with the politics of the dominant language groups. As we have seen before, Acharya Narendra Deva was one of the most active leaders of the Nagari Pracharani Sabha. But neither he nor the other Hindi leaders within the PSP could pull the party as a whole decisively toward any single language cause. When the PSP and the Socialist party (SP) merged—temporarily in 1964—in the Samyukta Socialist party (SSP), one of the major strains in the unity was caused by conflict over Hindi policy. This merger broke down in 1965, and on this occasion the reconstituted PSP accused the SP of heavily weighting their language policy in favor of Hindi extremism. Such a policy, the PSP thought, "might severely strain the unity of a multi-lingual country like India."[20]

Unlike the PSP, the SSP draws its support mainly from the Hindi areas. Most of its important leaders are actively involved in Hindi politics. These leaders, inspired by the ideas of Dr. Ram Monohar Lohia, believe that the proper national language policy should be one of an immediate removal of English from all sectors of life. A gradualist policy is no policy at all. Moreover, it is useless to depend on the Congress government to remove English. Lohia wrote in 1959 that what the Congress government has so far done regarding official language was to deliberately deceive the people.[21] His view was that popular struggles must force the political authorities to replace English with Hindi immediately.

The views of the SSP and especially of Lohia were different,

---

[19] See the *Report of the National Conference of the P.S.P.* (Bangalore), November 25–28, 1956 (New Delhi: Praja Socialist Party, 1957), p. 218. Similarly the Swatantra party has attempted to stay moderate on the language issue though some of its notables are strongly pro-English. For details see H. L. Erdman, *The Swatantra Party and Indian Conservatism*, pp. 202–204.

[20] See *Hindustan Times*, February 2, 1965.

[21] See Ram Monohar Lohia, "English and the People's Languages in India," in *Mankind*, December 1959, p. 15. Dr. Lohia died on October 12, 1967.

however, from those of the major Hindi language associations. Unlike the latter, they had little faith in the efforts to gradually work through the established legislative, administrative, and advisory bodies. The question of language planning with the aid of professional experts was of no concern to them. As Lohia put it, "once English goes, other things will be alright in ten or twenty years."[22] For him the primary concern was the immediate removal of English, and he was sure that Hindi at the Union level and the regional languages at the state level would be able to perform all the tasks that English had so far done. In order for English to be removed, the intellectuals have to be compelled by mass agitations. As he explained this course of action, "In order to get good work done by the educated people, illiterate people must ride on them."[23] It was on this premise that he and his associates launched, in 1957, the most militant anti-English agitation, called the Banish English movement. This movement gained attention only in North India, and one of the major tactics initially employed was an extensive campaign to deface English shop-signs and billboards.[24] This movement continued for about two years; after 1959 it tended to recur intermittently, and the Socialist leaders have remained firm in their conviction that English must be replaced without delay.[25] The only time these leaders came close to some moderation was when the SP and PSP merger efforts had broken down and some PSP leaders had stayed on in the reconstituted SSP. Many of these PSP leaders were drawn from non-Hindi states, and to induce their loyalty, the new SSP conceded that "English may be used for Union purposes by the people of the non-Hindi states, if they so desire."[26]

[22] *Ibid.*, p. 28.

[23] *Ibid.*, p. 21.

[24] For details concerning this movement, see *Mankind*, December 1959, pp. 46–50.

[25] Till 1964, Lohia's party was known as the Socialist party, since then it has been reconstituted into the Samyukta Socialist party.

[26] See the draft statement of the interim conference of the SSP held in Benaras in *Hindustan Times*, February 3, 1965. This conference took place after the major sections of the PSP had broken away from the SSP. For de-

Even this vestige of compromise was absent in the Hindi extremism that was initially pursued by the Jana Sangh. This party derives its support almost entirely from the Hindu population of the Hindi-speaking areas. This limited support structure and the revivalist orientation made it easier for the Jana Sangh to pursue a policy of uncompromising Hindi extremism.[27] Both in Punjab and in Uttar Pradesh the Jana Sangh leaders have taken an active role in the Hindi movement. Its Hindi leadership was strengthened in 1961 when Dr. Raghuvira resigned from the Congress party and joined the Jana Sangh.[28] Like the Jana Sangh in North India, in the South the Dravida Munnetra Kazagham (DMK) is based on an exclusively unilingual support structure. This has enabled the DMK to carry on an apparently uncompromising opposition to Hindi.[29]

## Violence and Compromise

The third general elections of 1962 brought about several important changes which affected the subsequent course of language politics in India. It was already apparent that the influence of the Hindi groups on the Union government was not enough to cause the latter to rush with a program to replace English with Hindi. After the third general elections the composition of the Congress Parliamentary party revealed a loss of strength of its Hindi components. While the Congress parliamentary representation from the non-Hindi states of Gujarat, West Bengal, Orissa, Madras, and Maharashtra rose from 100 to 124, the Congress parliamentary representation from the Hindi region dropped from 186 to 150. In addition, the opposition

---

tails, see Benjamin N. Shoenfeld, "The Birth of India's Samyukta Socialist Party," *Pacific Affairs* 38, nos. 3 and 4 (Fall and Winter 1965–66): 252. The entire article (pp. 245–268) is useful for this purpose.

[27] For details concerning the organization and operation of the Jana Sangh, see Craig Baxter, "The Jana Sangh: A Brief History," in *South Asian Politics and Religion*, ed. D. E. Smith (Princeton, N.J.: Princeton University Press), pp. 74–101.

[28] He enrolled himself as a primary member of the Jana Sangh in December 1961. He had resigned from the Congress party on the China issue of that time. See *Organizer*, January 1, 1962.

[29] See Robert L. Hardgrave, Jr., *The Dravidian Movement*, pp. 45 ff.

inside the Hindi states registered larger gains, so that the Hindi region was in a way "threatened with the possibility of five years of uncertain . . . government."[30] The Congress leadership in the Hindi areas faced an increasing challenge from the Hindu communalist political parties. As a result, the Congress monopoly of Hindi politics was being undermined, and a corresponding increase in a more direct identification between the Hindi and the Hindu platforms followed.[31] At about the same time, P. D. Tandon disappeared from the political scene,[32] and Lal Bahadur Shastri replaced G. B. Pant as the minister of home affairs.[33] Meanwhile, the increasing control of the Union government over the Hindi Sahitya Sammelan, through the new legislative provisions concerning that organization, tended to weaken the Sammelan for a while as a channel of public pressure on the Union government. The non-Hindi groups noted in these developments a possibility of decline of the effectiveness of the pressure from the Hindi groups.[34]

[30] Myron Weiner, "India's Third General Elections," *Asian Survey* 2, no. 3 (May 1962): 5. The data concerning this election cited above are from the same article.

[31] One commentator has observed, "The problem of Hindu Communalism is peculiar to the Hindi-speaking areas; Hindu communal parties have succeeded in making headway only in these areas." The same commentator asks, "Is it only coincidence that the Jan Sangh increased its representation in the U.P. Assembly from 17 (in the Second Assembly) to 49 (in the new Assembly) and its vote from 9.84 percent in 1957 to 16.79 in 1962?" He adds, "In Madhya Pradesh . . . the Sangh's representation in the Assembly increased from 10 to 41 and its vote from 9.89 percent to 16.69 percent; the Hindu (Maha) Sabha and Ram Rajya Parishad were not represented in the former Assembly but in the new Assembly they were able to get six and ten seats respectively" (*Link*, June 3, 1962, p. 11). See also Mayadhar Mansinh, "National Integration," *Illustrated Weekly of India*, July 1, 1962, p. 17, for similar comments on communalism in Hindi areas.

[32] P. T. Tandon (U.P.), former president of the Indian National Congress, was a member of the first Lok Sabha. He did not contest in the second general elections. He was later nominated to the Rajya Sabha. He resigned from Parliament in January 1960. He died on July 1, 1962. See *Amrita Bazar Patrika*, July 2, 1962.

[33] Though both Pant and Shastri were from Uttar Pradesh, Pant was supposed to be more capable of offsetting Nehru's influence than Shastri. See *Statesman Overseas Weekly*, August 24, 1962.

[34] See C. Rajagopalachari, "Good News on the Language Issue," *Swarajya*, June 9, 1962.

The Official Languages Act of 1963 provided for the retention of English as an associate language for official purposes of the Union and for use in Parliament. Section 3 of this act stipulated that "notwithstanding the expiration of the period of fifteen years from the commencement of the Constitution, the English language *may*, as from the appointed day, continue to be used, in addition to Hindi, (a) for all the official purposes of the Union . . . ; and (b) for the transaction of business in Parliament."[35] The object of the act, Nehru declared during the discussion on the Official Language Bill, "is to remove a restriction which had been placed by the Constitution on the use of English after . . . 1965."[36] The form of the act itself, however, failed to satisfy the non-Hindi groups. They concentrated their criticism on Section 3 of this act, which provides that English "may" be used, not that English "shall" be used. The non-Hindi associations interpreted the use of the term "may" as a concession to the Hindi pressures and as an evasion of responsibility on the part of the government to translate Nehru's earlier informal assurances into positive legal terms.

The dissatisfactions concerning the Official Languages Act of 1963 were only partially mitigated by Nehru's personal assurances to the South that whatever vagueness might exist in the language of the law, no injustice would be done to the South. With the death of Nehru in 1964, the source of this assurance was removed. The new prime minister, Lal Bahadur Shastri, did not show any conspicuous willingness to put any of Nehru's assurances to the South into new legislation. Meanwhile, there was only one more year to go before the expiry of the deadline. The Hindi leaders were growing more impatient. Several Union ministries became unusually hasty in preparing their departments for the linguistic changeover in the coming year. Instructions were given to the effect that the Union government's correspondence with the states would be in Hindi, and that in the case of the non-Hindi states, English translation would accompany. The

[35] *The Official Languages Act, 1963* (New Delhi: Law Ministry, Government of India, May 10, 1963), pp. 1–2 (emphasis added).

[36] *Jawaharlal Nehru's Speeches*, 4:64.

Information and Broadcasting Ministry notified that all routine circulars after January 26, 1965, would be in Hindi. This ministry also instructed its officers and staff to use Hindi as far as possible in meetings and discussions.[37] To the non-Hindi-speaking officials and politicians, all these appeared to be ominous indications of things to come. Everywhere the idea gained ground that from January 26, 1965, Hindi was going to be the sole official language of India.

Voices of resentment were raised in different parts of India. But it was in Madras that the resentment was most intense. The Congress government in Madras and the Congress legislators in Parliament from Madras took no initiative in channeling this protest into adequate institutional forms. The leadership of the protest thus passed to the non-Congress political forces. These leaders organized the Madras State Anti-Hindi Conference on January 17, 1965.[38] The participants in this conference included a mixed crowd led by the DMK and C. Rajagopalachari. It severely attacked the Hindi policy of the Union government and declared the determination of the Tamil people to resist Hindi. The conference designated January 26, 1965, as a day of mourning. The Congress party and government in Madras refused to take these overtures seriously, except that the government made it clear that no agitation would be tolerated on January 26, which happened to be Republic Day. On January 25, the students of Madras challenged the attitude of the government and took the initiative in mobilizing popular resentment, using signs and posters that dramatically declared, "Hindi never, English ever." The following day the students organized widespread agitation in Madras and Madurai. They demanded that the position of English be protected by a constitutional amendment. On January

[37] These and other instructions are discussed in S. Mohan Kumaramangalam, *India's Language Crisis*, pp. 82–84, and Michael Brecher, *Nehru's Mantle* (New York: Praeger, 1966), p. 155.

[38] For details, see Duncan B. Forrester, "The Madras Anti-Hindi Agitation, 1965," *Pacific Affairs* 39, nos. 1 and 2 (Spring-Summer, 1966): 19–36. See also Robert L. Hardgrave, Jr., "The Riots in Tamilnad: Problems and Prospects of India's Language Crisis," *Asian Survey* 5, no. 8 (August 1965): 399–407; and S. Mohan Kumaramangalam, chap. 8.

26, most of the DMK leaders, including C. N. Annadurai, were arrested. The agitation was now entirely in the form of spontaneous action by the students. A wave of repression was let loose on the students and this inflamed the general people. Two workers of the DMK publicly burned themselves to death, thus importing a Vietnam style of action in the Madras agitation. A cumulative intensification of mass violence and violent repression followed. The agitation continued for about two months. In all, sixty-six people were killed during this agitation.

Even at the height of this agitation, which had succeeded in gaining widespread mass support, the Congress leaders underestimated the popular basis of the anti-Hindi movement and refused to negotiate with the students. The government of Madras relied exclusively on repression and declared that the agitation was nothing more than mob rioting. But behind these public declarations, there was a gradual tendency to recognize the popular basis of the agitation as the government increasingly found out that repression alone could not stop the agitation. Perhaps the Congress leaders were expecting that the Union government would come forward with some positive solutions. But when the prime minister belatedly recognized the gravity of the situation, he offered nothing more than a set of vague assurances. By the second week of February, the situation was completely out of control, and two ministers from Madras resigned from the Union ministry.[39] The Congress leadership in Madras was now publicly divided, and both the Madras and the Union governments eventually realized that they had completely misunderstood the popular nature of the agitation. Ultimately, the major demands of the agitation were partially conceded, if not in immediate measures, at least in principle, and by the middle of February the agitation was suspended.

Both in the initiation of the agitation and in the restoration of normalcy,[40] it was the students' organization, called the Tamilnad Students' Anti-Hindi Agitation Council, which assumed the most salient role. Some of these student leaders were con-

[39] Subsequently, they withdrew their resignations.
[40] See "The Language Crisis," *Link*, February 21, 1965, pp. 11–14.

nected with the DMK, but most of them were drawn from a variety of forces. The only common link among these student leaders was a common resentment against Hindi and a concern for the retention of English for the purposes of official transaction. These leaders not only succeeded in rapidly organizing such a widespread agitation, but they also succeeded at the same time in rallying many student groups from outside Madras in the All-India Students' Anti-Hindi Agitation Council.[41] In order to make sure that the Anti-Hindi cause struck its roots deeper, the leaders of these two councils devised a long-term program and urged students to work for the defeat of the Congress party in the fourth general elections.[42]

The Madras agitations indicated a severe incapacity of the ruling Congress party to measure public feelings concerning a vital issue like official language. It also revealed a generational gap. It was clear that the older Congress leaders had little appreciation of the fact that the new generation of young men did not share the emotional commitment of the Congress leaders against English. The question of English is of great import to the students, especially because of their concern for their careers. The students of Madras have been the most successful contenders for Administrative Service jobs. In 1965 the representation of Madras in the All-India Administrative Service was 18 percent, while the population of Madras was 8 percent of that of India.[43] The students of Madras believed that this lead was due to their better control over English.[44] The Congress leaders were not unaware of this question, but they failed to make an adequate institutional representation of the students' problems to the decision-makers in the Union government. Neither did the latter reveal any particular sensitiveness to the popular grievances in

[41] See Duncan B. Forrester, "Madras Anti-Hindi Agitation," p. 35.

[42] Especially in Madras, this decision turned out to be of serious consequence. In the 1967 elections the DMK won a thumping victory. In fact, one of the leaders of the Madras students' agitation challenged the Congress president, Kamaraj Nadar, in his own constituency and defeated him in this election.

[43] See *Statesman*, April 1, 1965.

[44] Whether this is actually so is beside the point.

the South. At both the Union and the state levels, the Congress leaders at first denied the reason of the grievances and then refused to negotiate with the leaders of the agitation; finally, and only after the situation went out of their control, they came around to conceding a compromise.

As in many Indian agitations, the Madras agitation made visible what the official leaders had consistently refused to see. Violence brought into the open what was seething underneath and thereby opened a way to the seeking of a solution of the problem. In this sense it performed an important political function. The manifest function of this violence was to help construct a bridge of communication between the leaders in power, who lacked sensitivity, and the sensitive people, who lacked power. Its latent contribution was to give a unique confidence to a body of young leaders, who found a new sense of importance in the structure of politics and who were successful in organizing the generally apathetic masses for a psychologically satisfying cause.[45] This is not to say that the Madras agitation was entirely based on violence. In fact, the magnitude of violence in the initial stage was minimal, and the acts of violence were largely products of the ruling authority's failure to establish communication with the people who had intense feelings concerning the language issue. The effect of violence was to initiate this communication and to open up the subsequent opportunities for compromise.

But the compromise itself proceeded along a tortuous path, for it was not easy for the government to prepare a decisive policy that could satisfy the Hindi and the non-Hindi groups equally. Immediately after the initial phases of the anti-Hindi agitations, the dominant leader of the Hindi Sahitya Sammelan warned "against any amendment of the Constitution to end the anti-Hindi agitation of the South."[46] The Delhi Provincial Hindi Sahitya Sammelan urged the government in a conference on

---

[45] For a general discussion of the functional role of violence, see Lewis A. Coser, "Some Social Functions of Violence," *Annals of the American Academy of Political and Social Science* 364 (March 1966): 8–18.

[46] See the statement of C. B. Rao in *Hindustan Times*, February 15, 1965. For his attitude toward the southern agitation, see his "Bhasha Samashya ko Uljhaya Kisne," *Dharmayug*, May 2, 1965, pp. 9 and 48 (in Hindi).

January 28, 1965, to move forward with the policy of introducing Hindi.[47] In this conference, the Union deputy education minister, Bhakt Darshan, announced that the Union Public Service Commission would allow candidates to use Hindi for competitive examinations from September 1965. The mood of the conference was to ignore the pressures from the South. The same mood was reflected in a joint statement issued by fifty-five members of Parliament belonging to the Congress Hindi faction, who opposed any move to amend the constitution.[48] This move was matched by thirty-four members of Parliament belonging to the opposition parties, who demanded an amendment to the constitution to provide safeguards for the non-Hindi-speaking people.[49] The most vocal leader of the Hindi faction of the Congress party in Parliament, Govind Das, stated that "no power can impose English on the . . . country."[50] He criticized the moves for moderation as being reactionary. He directed his attack against the chief ministers' conferences because it seemed to him that they were usurping the role of Parliament in the policy-making process concerning the language of the Union.

The reaction of the Hindi groups was not confined to persuading the legislators and the masses. The more extreme pro-Hindi political parties staged mass demonstrations against the Union government in the Hindi-speaking areas. The Jana Sangh and the Samyukta Socialist party took an active role in organizing these demonstrations. However, the scale of these demonstrations usually remained too small to perturb the Union government.[51]

[47] For a report of this conference, see *Hindustan Times*, January 29, 1965.

[48] See *Hindustan Times*, February 17, 1965.

[49] See *ibid.* It may be noted that this group included members from the Communist party, Swatantra party, DMK, Revolutionary Socialist party, etc. In another statement issued by thirty members of the pro-Hindi opposition parties, such as the Jana Sangh and the SSP, it was urged that the chief ministers should not be allowed to have an upper hand in the decision-making process concerning language policy. This group also included one of the most important independent advocates of Hindi, Prakash Vir Shastri. See *ibid.*

[50] For his views, see *Hindustan Times*, February 17, 1965. Das was then the president of the Hindi Sahitya Sammelan.

[51] For reports of such demonstrations, see *Hindustan Times*, February 21 and 22, 1965.

An important feature of these demonstrations as well as of the Hindi leaders' campaigns was the greater energy that was expended in attacking English than in defending Hindi as the official language. Anyone opposed to the claim of Hindi as the only official language was branded immediately as a defender of English and hence as unpatriotic. The southern cry of "Hindi imperialism" was now matched by the Hindi groups' cry of "English imperialism." This was a relatively new strategy, and henceforth the Hindi leaders appealed to the non-Hindi leaders to focus a common attention on the task of first pushing out English. In order to induce the non-Hindi leaders, they were now prepared to be more generous toward the claims of the regional languages in some spheres, the foremost of which were examinations for public services. The Hindi leaders hoped that once the combined support of all the language groups achieved the elimination of English, the resulting confusion of languages in those spheres would automatically lead to the non-Hindi groups' accepting the case for Hindi. But the non-Hindi leaders were not enthusiastic about this move. And caught between the Hindi and the non-Hindi pressures, the political decision-makers were groping for various measures of compromise.

## Adjustment and Decision-Making

In order to appreciate the specific measures of compromise, it is necessary to note the nature of the decision-making process which handled the problems of reconciling the conflicting language interests at the institutional level. In formal terms the problem of official language is supposed to be handled primarily by the Union government. But the formal powers of the Union government have usually attracted an exaggerated attention. This has been due to a widespread belief that the unitary elements of the Constitution of India largely overwhelmed the federal provisions.[52] The partial supremacy of the constitution, the

[52] For discussions on Indian federalism, see R. L. Watts, *New Federations, Experiments in the Commonwealth* (London: Oxford University Press, 1966), pp. 17–20 and *passim*. See also D. D. Basu, *Commentary on the Constitution of India*, vol. 1, and his *Introduction to the Constitution of India*;

relatively limited scope of the judicial review, the vast range as well as the superordinate nature of the powers of the Union Parliament, the potentially sweeping powers of the president of the Union, the unified administrative service, and the actual responsibility of the Union government to direct economic planning—all these have apparently lent support to the view that the political structure of India is essentially quasi-federal.[53] On the basis of this view, many observers have concluded that the most important decisions for the nation are formulated exclusively by the Union government.

These observers tend to underestimate the growing importance of the politics conducted at the state level, and they fail to take into account the increasingly important role that the state governments have been assuming in national politics. Since the reorganization of the states in India, regional consciousness and pride have found an organized institutional representation through the new role of the chief ministers. This role implies that the chief ministers are not merely state leaders but have also become important participants in national policy-making through a common forum of all the chief ministers. In the particular field of policy-making concerned with official language specifically, the role of the Chief Ministers' Conference has been of considerable importance.

One conference of the chief ministers, held in August 1961, welcomed the declaration made on behalf of the Union government that English would continue to be used as an associate language for all-India official purposes even after Hindi becomes the

M. V. Pylee, *Constitutional Government in India* (Bombay: Asia Publishing House, 1965); K. Santhanam, *Union-State Relations in India* (Bombay: Asia Publishing House, 1960); and S. P. Aiyar and U. Mehta, eds., *Essays on Indian Federalism* (Bombay: Allied Publishers, 1965).

[53] This is the view of K. C. Wheare in his *Federal Government* (London: Oxford University Press, 1951), p. 28. Among those who have attempted to refute this view, see C. H. Alexandrowicz, *Constitutional Developments in India* (London: Oxford University Press, 1957) pp. 157–170; and D. D. Basu, *Commentary on the Constitution of India*, 1:20. See also N. C. Roy, *Federalism and Linguistic States* (Calcutta: Firma K. L. Mukhopadhyay, 1962).

all-India official language.[54] It was noted by this conference that although an official language is meant to be used largely for official business and for communication with the politically concerned public, the great majority of the public should be able to understand the major communications. In order to facilitate the process of communication, the chief ministers urged the acceptance of a three-language formula for adoption at the secondary stage of education for teaching language subjects. The formula suggested the teaching of the following languages:[55] (*a*) the regional language and mother tongue when the latter is different from the regional language: (*b*) Hindi or, in Hindi-speaking areas, another Indian language; and (*c*) English or any other modern European language.[56]

It is obvious that the idea behind this formula was one of ensuring equality among all the language communities of India in respect of the distribution of the burden of language learning. The suggestions of the chief ministers were aimed at the political conciliation of the non-Hindi speakers by assuring them that the adoption of Hindi as the official language would not mean a lighter burden for the Hindi speakers in language learning. The three-language formula immediately evoked interest among the leaders of various language groups, and it was accepted in a conference of all important political parties in October 1961.[57] In practice, however, this formula was "misapplied in several ways by the various state governments."[58] In general, it has not so far attained the desired success. Among the reasons for this lack of success are the general reluctance to incur the heavy cost of providing for the teaching of the second and the third languages for

[54] See the memorandum agreed to by the chief ministers of India meeting on August 11 and 12), 1961 at New Delhi, in *Vital Speeches and Documents of the Day* 1, no. 20, (September 1, 1961): 545–46.

[55] See *ibid.*

[56] The three-language formula was initially suggested by the Central Advisory Board of Education in 1956.

[57] This refers to the National Integration Conference. For a statement of the conference, see *Report of the Committee on Emotional Integration*, pp. 223–224.

[58] *Ibid.*, p. 53.

five to six years in the school curriculum, defective planning of
the entire enterprise, and above all, "the lack of motivation for
the study of an additional modern Indian language in the Hindi
areas as well as the resistance to the study of Hindi in some non-
Hindi areas."[59] The three-language formula, despite its initial
failure was strongly upheld by the Report of the Education Commission in 1966, though the commission recommended a different form of the formula.[60]

The entry of the Chief Ministers' Conference into the national
policy-making process indicated a new channel of compromise
for the language issue. The legitimacy of this channel was difficult to challenge. Despite the protest of some of the Hindi leaders, the importance of the Chief Ministers' Conference as a
compromise-initiating body could not be denied. The non-Hindi
leaders, especially, found in this conference an acceptable authoritative source, mostly because in the Chief Ministers' Conference the number of chief ministers from Hindi states could
never overwhelm their counterparts from other states. Moreover,
after the death of Nehru, both in the succession procedures for
the choice of the prime minister and in other nationally important issues, the Chief Ministers' Conference was firmly asserting
its importance.

At about the same time the Congress Working Committee was
fast becoming a crucial component of the national decision-
making process. Especially after Nehru's death, the Congress
president, Kamaraj Nadar, and the Working Committee had
attained a new status in the political leadership of the country.[61]
Himself a leader from Tamilnad, Kamaraj had a difficult time

[59] India, Ministry of Education, *Report of the Education Commission,
1964–66, Education and National Development* (New Delhi, 1966), p. 191.

[60] The modified formula of the Commission includes (1) the mother
tongue or the regional language, (2) the official language of the Union or
the associate official language of the Union, and (3) a modern Indian or
foreign language, not covered under (1) and (2) and other than that used as
the medium of instruction. *Ibid.*, p. 192.

[61] For an extensive treatment of this aspect, see Michael Brecher, *Nehru's
Mantle* (n.37 above), esp. pp. 132 ff. See also W. H. Morris-Jones, "India
Under New Management," *Asian Survey* 5 no. 2 (February 1965): 63–73.

in working out a compromise between the Hindi and the non-Hindi factions of the Congress party.[62] After some hesitation, the Congress Working Committee recommended that Nehru's assurances on the continued use of English should be incorporated in an amendment to the Official Languages Act.[63] Expressing regret over the lack of implementation of the three-language formula in some of the states, the Working Committee recommended that the introduction of the three-language formula in the educational curriculum should be obligatory for all states, the Hindi states being required to introduce as a compulsory subject a non-Hindi language, preferably a southern language. The Working Committee urged that the Union Public Service Commission examinations should be conducted in English, Hindi, and the regional languages.[64] The candidates would be required to learn Hindi and English, or in the case of a candidate choosing Hindi as the medium of examination, one non-Hindi regional language. The other recommendations were concerned with raising the status of the regional languages as the medium of administration and of instruction at the university level in each state, raising the standard of Hindi in schools, and

[62] For the background of Kamaraj's political career, see V. K. Narasimhan, *Kamaraj, a Study* (Bombay: Manaktalas, 1967), and R. P. Kapur, *Kamaraj, The Iron Man* (New Delhi: Deepak Associates, 1966), esp. chaps. 8, 13, 14, and 19.

[63] For the Working Committee's resolution adopted after discussions with Union ministers, chief ministers of fourteen states, and the governor of Kerala, see "Language: Accord or Uneasy Compromise?" *Link*, February 28, 1965, pp. 6–7.

[64] To conduct the Union Public Service Commission examinations in fifteen languages will obviously create a variety of problems, one of the most important of them being the task of fair evaluation of the candidates. Immediately after the southern agitation, there was a revival of discussions on a possible quota system for each state. But the quota system is likely to create more problems than it would solve. For an earlier discussion of the quota system, see *R.O.L.C.*, pp. 465–467. For a discussion of the new system, see G. C. Chatterjee, "Dangers of Three Language Formula," *Statesman Overseas Weekly*, August 7, 1965; and S. K. Gupta, "English Vital for Unity of Central Services," *Statesman Overseas Weekly*, August 21, 1965; and B. K. R. Kabad, "A Leap in the Dark?" in *Times of India*, Bombay, February 1, 1969.

continuing English as an important language. The compromise plan advocated by the Working Committee was based on a consensus between the chief ministers and the members of the Working Committee, and the basic assumption of both these bodies was that a working solution for the language problem should be built upon the premise of equal distribution of burdens rather than upon the premise of favoring either a numerical majority or an established language.

Meanwhile, similar trends were gaining ground inside the leadership of the Union government and the Congress Parliamentary party. But Prime Minister Shastri did not seem to be eager to force a radical solution. A decision was made to amend the Official Languages Act to incorporate the basic elements of compromise as suggested by the Congress leaders through the Chief Ministers' Conference and by the Working Committee. But there was no unanimity on the exact form of this proposed amendment. Several proposals were tried, but fortunately for Shastri, no immediate decision had to be taken, because of the pressure of the unexpected international developments of 1965. As the government got involved in the Indo-Pakistan war, the nation was eager to forget the linguistic rivalry and to rally round the government during the emergency. It was an indication that no amount of language rivalry could make the rivals forget that their conflict was essentially one that concerned the internal affairs of the nation and that the defense of the nation demanded a clear primacy over everything else.

But the war did not solve the language problem; it only deferred the attempt of the decision-makers to find a solution. The aftermath of the war saw some notable changes. Shastri died in 1966, and Indira Gandhi became the prime minister. Though hailing from Uttar Pradesh, Indira Gandhi was capable of evoking a more sympathetic response from the South for many reasons, one of which was that, of all the nationally eminent leaders, it was she who had dashed to Madras during the height of the anti-Hindi agitation and had since established herself in the South as a leader who could be trusted. It was widely believed that after coming to power, she would be capable of and sincerely interested in evolving a language solution that would be acceptable to the non-Hindi areas.

However, the official language question assumed a renewed salience after the fourth general elections of 1967. This election introduced several unexpected changes in the composition of the decision-making authority in India. As a result of this election, the overwhelming dominance of the Congress party was drastically curtailed. Though the decline of the Congress vote was not spectacular, the loss of Congress seats was almost catastrophic.[65] The Congress party, of course, retained a workable majority in the Lok Sabha, but it lost control over more than half of the states.[66] In the Hindi area, usually supposed to be a Congress stronghold, it was able to secure precarious control over Rajasthan but lost Uttar Pradesh, Bihar, Haryana, and Madhya Pradesh.[67] In the Lok Sabha the representation from the Hindi areas in the Congress Assembly party continued the trend of decline which had started in 1962. Out of a total of 211 seats in the Hindi areas, the Congress won only 120 seats in 1967. Meanwhile, the rest of the seats were captured mostly by the radical Hindi extremists belonging to Jana Sangh and SSP. The Jana Sangh increased its seats from 11 to 32, the SSP from 3 to 15. So far as the non-Hindi areas were concerned, in Madras the landslide victory of the DMK over the Congress is worth noting. The DMK increased its Lok Sabha seats from 8 in 1962 to 25 in 1967, against the corresponding Congress decline from 31 to 3. In the Madras State Assembly, similarly, the DMK increased

[65] In the Lok Sabha, as compared to 1962, the Congress vote declined by 3.7 percent; similarly in the state assemblies the corresponding decline was 4.3 percent. For details concerning the 1967 elections, see *Report on the Fourth General Elections in India 1967* (New Delhi: Election Commission, India, 1967), vol. 2, part 1; "Election Outcome," *Seminar*, no. 94 (June 1967), especially pp. 10–22; and Norman D. Palmer, "India's Fourth General Elections," in *Asian Survey* 7, no. 5 (May 1967): 275–291.

[66] Initially the loss was of eight states. In July 1967 one more state was lost to Congress.

[67] Due to factional struggles, the state government of Madhya Pradesh fell in July 1967. For details, see Ranajit Roy "Is Democracy in Peril?" in *Hindustan Standard*, Overseas Weekly Edition, August 5, 1967.

its seats from 53 to 142; whereas the Congress seats declined from 139 to 49. However, outside Madras, Kerala, and West Bengal, the performance of the Congress party in the non-Hindi areas in respect of state assemblies was relatively better as compared to the Hindi areas. In fact, major non-Hindi states like Andhra Pradesh, Mysore, Maharashtra, and Gujarat gained a new significance in the Congress support structure.

After the 1967 elections it was evident that the non-Hindi forces, both inside the Congress Assembly party and outside it in the Lok Sabha, assumed a relatively greater importance than was possible before. Among the Congress chief ministers the non-Hindi component gained an overwhelming importance. Within the Congress organization the non-Hindi components similarly improved their status, owing mainly to the uniformly unsuccessful performance of the Congress party in the major Hindi states, both during elections and afterwards. In this context it was not surprising that when the language issue came up before Parliament, the configuration of actors active in the language front was bound to change.

Immediately after the election, C. N. Annadurai, the DMK leader, declared that his party was going to "press for a constitutional amendment for immediate recognition of official status for all the 14 languages and for keeping English as link in the meantime."[68] This was clearly a continuation of the demand of the Madras agitation of 1965, but this time it had the added assurance of the freshly won DMK parliamentary strength to back it, both in Madras and in the Union Parliament. Annadurai, however, was a much mellowed leader after his party's electoral triumph, and he couched his demands in a considerably softer language than he used before. The newly formed Union government, depending on a slender majority, was more sensitive to the language demands of the opposition and of its own constituents than before. Within two weeks of the meeting of the new Parliament, the Union Home Ministry made it clear that it was committed to the introduction of new legislation incorporating

---

[68] The *Hindu Weekly Review*, March 6, 1967. For a background, see K. S. Ramanujam, *The Big Change*, esp. chaps. 11–15.

the assurances given to the South in 1965, in the form of an amendment to the Official Languages Act of 1963, but that there would be no constitutional amendment for this purpose.[69] At about the same time, stormy scenes were witnessed in the Lok Sabha when a member from Mysore insisted on and got recognition of his right to speak in Kannada without offering an advance translation of his speech in Hindi or English. This recognition, breaking with past practice, gave rise to a disorderly protest in the course of which a leader of Jana Sangh reminded the Lok Sabha that the above concession was a violation of the constitution and a deliberate affront to its language provisions.[70]

### Rising Importance of Regional Languages

One of the most important developments in the language policy-making process after the 1967 elections was the unusual importance accorded to the regional languages. Until 1967 most of the debates concerning the official language policies centered around the question of English or Hindi. Even in the constitution, the primary attention was focused on the official language of the Union. It should be noted in this connection that though the constitution contains an imperative provision concerning the official language of the Union, it is merely permissive in providing that the legislature of a state may by law adopt any one or more of the languages in use in the state, or Hindi, for official transactions.[71] Moreover, no deadline was suggested for adoption of such regional language for official purposes. In practice the adoption of regional language and the replacement of English in the states for official purposes was considerably delayed. One reason for this delay was that the redistribution of the states on

[69] See *Hindu Weekly Review*, April 3, 1967.

[70] See *ibid.* It should be noted that the member from Mysore was a leader of the SSP. This incident brings out the basic difference between the SSP and the Jana Sangh on the question of the relation between Hindi and the regional languages. The SSP believes in a status of equality, but the Jana Sangh believes in the primacy of Hindi over all other languages.

[71] Compare, for instance, the provisions of Art. 343 with Art. 345 of the Constitution of India.

a linguistic basis took place several years after the effective date of the constitution. Another reason is that though there are elaborate provisions in the constitution for periodic reviews of the progress of Hindi as the official language, there are no comparable provisions for reviewing the progress in introducing regional languages for official purposes of the states. Above all, there was no coordination of actions on this front. It was only in the Hindi states that there was a general effort to push forward the role of Hindi as the official language at the state level. Even in Madras, under the Congress government the progress of Tamil as official language was more nominal than substantial. There was no effort to introduce it systematically either in the administrative transactions or in the educational spheres.[72]

It was only after the DMK came into power in Madras that extensive efforts were made to introduce Tamil for official purposes in substantive measures. Elsewhere, too, such efforts were strengthened.[73] But the greatest boost received by the regional languages was from the recommendations of the Report of the Education Commission, 1966, and the attention given to these by the Union and the state governments. This report suggested that in order to develop national education it is essential to "move energetically in the direction of adopting the regional languages as media of education at the university stage."[74] In July 1967, the Union government agreed in principle that the Indian languages would become the media of education at all stages and in all subjects, including agriculture, engineering, law, medicine, and technology. In announcing this decision, the Union minister for education declared that the government was convinced that this was the only way to mobilize the creative

[72] This aspect has been considered in detail in S. Mohan Kumaramangalam, *India's Language Crisis*, pp. 59–71.

[73] For details concerning the efforts to force the pace of Kannada in Mysore, see "Kannada Medium in Varsities and Government Offices," *Hindu Weekly Review*, June 12, 1967.

[74] *Report of the Education Commission, 1964–1966*, p. 291. This idea was earlier advocated by both the Committee on Emotional Integration and the National Integration Council. See *ibid.*, pp. 13–14.

energies of the people, to raising the standards of education, and to bridge the wide gulf that separated the elite from the masses in India.[75]

The Union minister of education made it clear that "the program of change-over to regional languages as media of education will have to vary from university to university, from subject to subject, and even from institution to institution, in the same university. The criteria in each case should be that the change-over helps, at every stage, to raise standards. Moreover, the case of the central universities or of those in the metropolitan cities will need special consideration and safeguards, on merits or in view of prior commitments."[76] He also reiterated the need for a special safeguard for the minorities and a general flexibility in the entire enterprise of the changeover.

By 1967, thirty-five universities in the country already allowed a regional language as a medium of examination. In nearly fifteen universities the large majority of the students opted for regional languages as the media of instruction. About an equal number of universities provided facilities for graduate instruction in regional languages. The enthusiasm of the Union minister of education supported by that of the Education Commission seemed to be well warranted by the existing drift of events. Transformation of this drift into a planned policy was sought. Any such plan necessarily raises the question of a deadline. Some experts suggested a time limit of five years, but the Education Commission and the education minister preferred a period of ten years.[77] It was thought that such a change would facilitate higher education and at the same time the adoption of Hindi as a link language. To expedite these processes, there were indica-

[75] Dr. Triguna Sen's statement in the Lok Sabha. See *Hindu Weekly Review*, July 24, 1967.

[76] Dr. Triguna Sen, *Vice Chancellors' Conference, Address*, 11–13 September, 1967 (New Delhi: University Grants Commission, 1967), p. 9. For a background account, see "English, Hindi and the Medium of Instruction, II," *Minerva* 6, no. 2 (Winter 1968): 287–300, and A. B. Shah, ed., *The Great Debate* (Bombay: Lalvani, 1968).

[77] Dr. Sen denied that he ever proposed a five-year deadline. See *Address*, p. 10.

tions of some efforts to make Hindi the medium of instruction in the all-India institutes of higher learning. These experiments obviously envisaged a lesser role for English than what was current in India, but the utility of English for educational function was stressed repeatedly.[78] The Union Ministry of Education proposed a substantial investment for preparing text books in Indian languages and for the general development of these languages.[79] (See table 19.) Meanwhile, the Union Public Service Commission expressed its hopes of conducting its examinations in the regional languages as well as in English from 1968—a deadline which was later moved to 1969.

TABLE 19

FINANCIAL ASSISTANCE TO REGIONAL LANGUAGES: UNION MINISTRY
OF EDUCATION, 1967–1969

|  | 1967–1968 Revised estimates | 1968–1969 Budget estimates |
|---|---|---|
|  | (in hundred thousand rupees) | |
| Voluntary associations for regional languages | 4.76 | 5.00 |
| Assistance to specified voluntary organizations | 0.58 | 0.58 |
| State governments for regional languages | 1.00 | . . |
| NEW PROJECT | | |
| Regional languages media adoption: university level | 50.00 | 100.00 |
| Totals | 56.34 | 105.58 |

SOURCE: India, Ministry of Education, *Report*, 1967–1968 (New Delhi, 1968), p. 123.

[78] According to Dr. Sen, "it is only a close cooperation and collaboration between English and regional languages that can raise standards" (*ibid*, p. 11).

[79] In 1967, the Union government sanctioned a sum of 180 million rupees for this program (*ibid.*, p. 11). In 1968 the Union government considered giving assistance to the states for production of books in regional languages under a centrally sponsored plan on the basis of 75 percent of the approved expenditure. From the initial investments in this production, it was expected that a revolving fund would be created from the proceeds of the sale so that the entire program might become self-sustaining after a period of six years. See India, Ministry of Education, *Report, 1967–1968*, pp. 118–119.

The trend was clear. The Union education minister made it explicit that once the regional languages assumed the dominant role in education the problem of official language would finally be solved. The replacement of English by the regional languages as dominant in education would satisfy the pride of all the major language communities of India, and eventually Hindi would be accepted as a link language by virtue of necessity, without forcing it at the moment. At the same time it was stated that English would remain mostly as a library language.[80] The study of English would continue. Elaborating on the idea of the role of English as a library language, the Report of the Education Commission stated:

No student should be considered as qualified for a degree, in particular a Master's Degree, unless he has acquired a reasonably proficiency in English (or in some other library language). The implications of this are two-fold: all teachers in higher education should be essentially bilingual in the sense that they would be able to teach in the regional language and in English, and all students (and particularly post-graduate students) should be able to follow lectures . . . in the regional language, as well as in English.[81]

What was not so clear was to what extent the importance of the library language would actually be emphasized. As long as it was substantially emphasized, how would Hindi assert its place as a link language? The Education Commission, and also the Union education minister, had no doubt about Hindi as the only acceptable link language of the people. But with the regional languages as the media of education and with English as the library language, it was difficult to assume that Hindi would in fact develop as a link language either for the intelligentsia or for the masses. Even if Hindi became the official language of the Union, the masses would rarely have the motivation to learn a language

[80] The future of English in the context of the introduction of regional languages for education is discussed in details in India, Ministry of Education, *The Study of English in India*, Report of a Study Group appointed by the Ministry of Education (New Delhi, 1967), esp. chaps. 7 and 8. This report was submitted to the Education Commission in 1965.

[81] *Report of the Education Commission, 1964–1966*, p. 292.

that would be of little concern for their daily life. Of course, the intelligentsia might be motivated to learn it if Hindi became the only official language of the Union. But this is precisely the point which could not be taken for granted at this stage.

### Amendment Act, 1967

It is here that the question of the amendment of the Official Languages Act of 1963 comes in. During the first budget session of the new Parliament, a draft bill for this purpose was circulated by the Union government to all the states. This bill proposed to provide for the continued use of English on a compulsory basis for certain categories of official correspondence. It affirmed that the status of English as an associate language would continue as long as the non-Hindi states wanted it.[82] In discussing this bill in a meeting of the Congress Parliamentary Party Executive Committee, Indira Gandhi, the prime minister, stated that this bill was drafted in a way that would leave no room for suspicion or apprehension in the minds of the non-Hindi-speaking people. In this meeting the Hindi Sahitya Sammelan leader, Govind Das, maintained that there was no need for such a bill, because the question has been settled in favor of Hindi once and for all.[83] The Hindi leaders were afraid of the veto power that this draft evidently reserved for any state. On the other hand, the leaders of Madras, understandably, defended this veto. Outside this meeting, both these groups attempted to mobilize forces for the coming battle in the Union parliament.[84]

---

[82] For details of the features of this bill, see *Hindu Weekly Review*, July 17 and August 14, 1967.

[83] See *ibid.*, July 17, 1967.

[84] The Hindi group circulated a petition signed by 200 members of Parliament belonging to the Congress party, urging a time limit for the retention of English, after which Hindi would be the sole official language. Fifty members from the opposition parties led by the Jana Sangh and the SSP submitted a petition stating that no state should be given the veto over English. The DMK continued to demand an amendment to the constitution. Some left-wing opposition leaders initiated a campaign for signatures favoring the safeguarding of the interest of the non-Hindi people. This campaign was led by the Left Communist party. See *Hindu Weekly Review*, July 31, 1967.

The pattern of mobilization was bound to be affected by the altered configuration of power which existed in the states and at the Union level. The depleted strength of the Hindi leaders inside the Congress party and the lack of a stable Congress government in any major Hindi state meant that the role of Congress as the dominant decision-maker could not be depended upon. As a result, the Congress Hindi leaders had to place equal importance on the mobilization of support from the Jana Sangh, the SSP, and the dissident Congress leaders who were in charge of the major Hindi state governments. The latter, however, remained in such a state of disarray that the support derived from them could hardly provide an organized, single-minded direction. The recent emphasis on the importance of the regional languages divided them further. On the other hand, the Union government badly needed general support from the non-Hindi Congress states as well as from the stable non-Congress state governments. The latter required a good deal of adjustment with the Communist government in Kerala and specially the DMK government in Madras in general terms. The DMK government, from the very beginning, pursued a policy of minimum embarrassment to the center and, in fact, seemed to be more cooperative with the leadership of Indira Gandhi than many factions working within the Congress party. Given this situation, it was clear that the very political survival of the Union government depended to a large extent on a heterogeneous potential support structure, which it could ignore only at its peril. All these developments augured well for a generally acceptable compromise on the language question, involving a continued role of Hindi and English at the Union level, a three-language formula for language learning, and a general equality of the major regional languages wherever the questions of comparative advantage in competitive services, higher education, and regional status were concerned.

The determination of the Union government to reach a compromise on the question of official language led to the introduction of a bill in the Lok Sabha providing for the continued use of English in accordance with Nehru's earlier assurance to the

South. Before the introduction of this bill on November 27, 1967, there was some anxiety concerning the hostility of the Hindi leaders to the idea of amending the Official Languages Act of 1963. The actual voting in the Lok Sabha on the question of giving leave to Chavan, the home minister, to introduce the bill, revealed, however, that there was an overwhelming support for this bill. The majority for Chavan was 181 against the opposing vote of 25.[85]

As was expected, the Hindi extremist leadership within the Congress organization led by Govind Das opposed the bill. But it was characteristic of the political situation following the 1967 general elections that the center of the Hindi political forces could not rely on exerting pressures within the Congress organization alone. In fact, the most vocal resistance to the bill generated by the Hindi leadership was expressed through the Jana Sangh and the SSP. These two parties used their office in the ruling coalition in the Uttar Pradesh and Bihar governments to augment opposition to the bill. From late November to the middle of December 1967, the Hindi militants of the Jana Sangh and the SSP staged a series of agitations in the Hindi areas, which often assumed violent forms. The most militant participants in these agitations were led more by the SSP than by the Jana Sangh. In fact, the Jana Sangh gradually softened its demands and often succeeded in providing a corrective to the extreme strategy of the SSP.

The national organization of the Jana Sangh was aware of its prospect of extending the Hindi-area support-base to the other areas of India. It was interested in maintaining its relation with the Akalis in Punjab, and the party had been making some headway in a southern state like Kerala. An endorsement of extremism for Hindi was obviously against its organizational interest as defined by its national leaders of this time.[86] The compromising mood of the Jana Sangh was thus understandable, and this was later embodied in a three-point plan which stressed that

[85] See *Statesman*, November 28, 1967.

[86] See Dilip Mukerjee, "Consensus Emerging out of Conflict on Language," *Statesman*, December 8, 1967.

Hindi must grow through voluntary acceptance and not by imposition.[87] Similarly, other non-Congress organizations revealed
an equal sense of moderation—even the SSP was less extremist at
its national level than its unit in Uttar Pradesh.[88] At the state
level, on the other hand, most non-Congress parties chose to remain silent spectators to the militant agitations led by the SSP
against the bill. In many cases their local workers joined these
agitations when their national organizations were busy working
out compromise strategies in order to satisfy the DMK.

The DMK had its own share of problems raised by the bill.
The younger generation within the DMK was dissatisfied with
the compromise provisions and started agitations for more radical amendments.[89] The leaders of the DMK, however, wanted
to utilize the broad Congress and non-Congress support for the
continuance of English and generally lent support to the bill.
This strategy proved successful in the end. After a series of
sporadic demonstrations of Hindi militancy both inside and outside Parliament, the Hindi agitations calmed down. With the
solitary exception of the Uttar Pradesh unit of the SSP, all the
national parties gradually moved toward the basic compromise
incorporated in the bill, and the ground was soon cleared for its
parliamentary acceptance.

On December 16, 1967, the Lok Sabha adopted the Official
Languages (Amendment) Bill by a margin of 205 to 41 votes.[90]
This body also adopted the Policy Resolution on language which
set the guidelines for the Union government on official languages. The Official Languages (Amendment) Act, 1967, legal-
ized assurances on the continuance of the use of English, in addition to Hindi, for all the official purposes of the Union and for
the transaction of business in Parliament and for communication

[87] This plan emerged in the 14th annual conference of the Jana Sangh
held in Calicut. See *Statesman*, December 31, 1967.

[88] In the SSP, the former PSP leaders operating mainly at the national
level (like S. M. Joshi) and in Bihar (like Karpuri Thakur) proved to be
more moderate than the Uttar Pradesh leaders (like Raj Narain).

[89] For evidence of the DMK leaders' embarrassment, see the reports of the
anti-Hindi agitation in Madras in *Statesman*, December 23 and 24.

[90] See *ibid.*, December 17, 1967.

between the Union and "a State which has not adopted Hindi as its official language."[91] It also provided that rules would be made to ensure that persons having proficiency either in Hindi or in English and serving in connection with the affairs of the Union, could function effectively. The idea was that the knowledge of either language would be deemed sufficient and there would be no penalization for not knowing Hindi. In general, the new act and the resolution represented a broad reconciliation of the current conflicting demands regarding the official language policy of the Union, and the resulting product can be challenged effectively only when all the states resolve to discontinue the use of English for official transactions. In this way, the amended Act of 1967 established a two-language policy for official transactions while the accompanying resolution authorized a three-language policy for the school-system and a regional language policy for Union public service examinations with a requirement in addition of a knowledge of Hindi or English.[92]

## *Division, Cohesion, and Political Development*

Given the nature of the Indian language situation, it is hard to imagine a more acceptable solution than this compromise. The critics of this compromise usually fail to appreciate the value of such a language policy in the context of national consolidation and democratic development. In two decades, the newly constituted democratic political authority of India has been able to approximate realistic solutions for two of the most important problems of language politics in India. The problems of official language policy and linguistic redistribution in the states have, at times, generated considerable tension, agitation, and sporadic

---

[91] *The Gazette of India*, extraordinary, part 2, sec. 1, January 8, 1968.

[92] The original text of the Resolution, as moved by the home minister, appears in *Lok Sabha Debates*, 4th Series, vol. 10, no. 18, cols. 5419–5421. For the amendment inserted at the last moment see *Statesman*, December 17, 1967. Chavan admitted that an unequal burden would be placed by the amended text requiring Hindi or English in addition to regional languages for Union public service examinations. He stated that the U.P.S.C. would soon conduct all its tests in regional languages and that this would mitigate the inequality of the burden in some way. *Ibid.*

violence. Eventually, however, negotiations have led to viable solutions. It is true that there are still some language problems waiting for solution—for example, the problem of minority languages within each state. Given the kind of language diversity that prevails in India, the very complicated nature of the distribution of the linguistic minorities in each state is bound to leave some loose ends even after the major contours of the problems have been realistically tackled. Again, language problems in the educational sphere raise many complex issues. Although these issues do not directly concern the present work, it may be mentioned here that these secondary problems can be handled more efficiently after the basic national issues concerning official language and linguistic reorganization in the states have been taken care of.

The achievements of the national decision-makers in solving the basic national issues have been considerably underestimated. The Indian and the international prophets of despair usually nurse a notion of elegant monistic solutions in this regard. They are impatient of untidy compromises yielding good-enough pluralistic solutions. Thus one can understand why many Indian leaders and intellectuals find a convenient scapegoat in "linguism."[93] The urge to blame the democratic political system may also be appreciated in this particular context.[94] These patterns of thought are products, no doubt, of a set of assumptions and inferences derived from a fundamentally authoritarian model of integration and development which we have discussed earlier.[95]

Such a model is based on the conviction that the only decision-system that is appropriate for the initial task of national integration follows the rule of amalgamation.[96] The idea of amalgama-

---

[93] See for example, Prabhu Datta Sharma, "Linguism and Regionalism—Challenges to Democracy," in S. P. Aiyar and R. Srinivasan, *Studies in Indian Democracy* (Bombay: Allied Publishers, 1965), pp. 429–447.

[94] See for example, Selig S. Harrison, *India: The Most Dangerous Decades*, esp. p. 10.

[95] These assumptions are explicitly or implicitly found in many works, notably those of Selig Harrison, Rupert Emerson, Claude Ake. These are cited elsewhere.

[96] The amalgamative and the pluralistic models are discussed in Karl W.

tion is appealing to the rationalistic modernizers because it puts a premium on the imposition of the modernizers' ideology of social homogenization and elite control. Basically, this implies a pyramidal structure of authority where the men at the top are assumed to have advance knowledge of what the people below actually need and how to satisfy these needs.[97] It also implies that the processes of representation must be controlled by the guiding elite, so that the factors of strain can be eliminated by suppression.

These ideas are by no means novel. Throughout the history of political theory these ideas have persuaded many theorists that the haphazard behaviors of the social units must be subjected to a specialized discipline of the ruling group, which can create and maintain political order. The element of discipline has been sought in the amalgamation of the units of random aggressiveness into a smooth solidary system. It is no wonder that these ideas still constitute the core values in forming the major models of integration, especially the prescriptive models advanced for the new states based on uncertain integrative foundations.

In this sense, the democratic system is widely perceived as a postintegrational system and not as a developmental system which can initiate and promote integration in a new state. This is more a sign of a lack of confidence in appreciating the developmental capability of the democratic system than a reflection of its genuine appreciation. A better appreciation can be had if one assumes that democracy can provide an alternative model of integration based on a pluralistic decision-system. Under this system the responsibility of coordination is not delegated or left to an agency which is external to the components of this system. Rather, this responsibility is located in the components of the

Deutsch, "Communication Theory and Political Integration" in *The Integration of Political Communities*, ed. P. E. Jacob and J. V. Toscano (Philadelphia: Lippincott, 1964), pp. 58–61 (paperback).

[97] For a discussion of this point, see S. N. Eisenstadt, "The Problems of Emerging Bureaucracies in Developing Areas and New States" in *Industrialization and Society*, ed. B. F. Hoselitz and W. Moore (Paris: UNESCO, 1963), esp. p. 168.

system by the avoidance of the function of an amalgamating agency. The responsibility of decision-making is thus widely dispersed over the system. This dispersal facilitates the development of the communications equipment as well as the capability of the units of the system and thereby increases the chance of political coordination through voluntary representation. It provides for the development of the art of making demands, for the formation of a coalition of the demand groups for their own interest, for support to aggregating institutions, and ultimately for the art of negotiating these interests for the optimum payoff from the interaction of diverse interests. Such a pluralistic decision-system requires a preliminary normative legitimation to start with, and evidence that the system, in fact, is capable of optimizing at least the core demands of the actors involved.

Given this context, one may ask if, in the specific case of India, the democratic system has been useful for institutionalizing such a pluralistic decision-system. In this connection it should be noted that the elements of preliminary normative legitimation of this system were evolved in India from the very beginning of the national movement. The norms of a democratic decision-system were instilled in the participants in the national movement long before they were used to applying these norms through formal political authority. Even in the case of the latter, the experience of partial representative mechanisms during the later phase of British rule tended to reinforce this norm and generated confidence in its feasibility.

It is true that the penetration of these norms in the society as a whole was limited by the very nature of the situation. Even after the adoption of the democratic system the degree of penetration fell far short of the ideal expectations. This raises the question about the discrepancy that exists in India between the traditional social structure and the normative orientation of the politically relevant actors engaged in the democratic process. Political observers have often pointed out that the infinite segmentation of the Indian society and the primordial attachments that inevitably accompany such segmentations are enough to negate the democratic norms as well as the representative institutions. This assumes that social cleavages invariably determine political cleavages and that the nature of the cleavages remains unaffected by the political institutions. But these seem to be unwarranted assumptions.

For one thing, the pattern of social segmentation does not remain constant. In the case of India these segmentations have always been relatively fluid. But, especially as a result of social mobilization initiated by the processes of modernization, the traditional basis of segmentation has gradually been eroded. However, the erosion of old relations is no indication of the direction the pattern of the new relations is following.[98] It is here that the question of the impact of political change on social direction assumes a crucial importance. Political change itself has been one of the most important agents of social change, but perhaps its greater importance lies in the organized direction that it impresses on the process and the result of social changes.[99] The impact of the rising political consciousness during the nineteenth century on the structure of caste, and the role of democratic representation in the formation of secularized, political caste associations have been noted in many recent studies.[100] The common point of most of these studies is that by facilitating the entry of new participants in politics, representative institutions tend to detach people from their traditional loyalties and initiate a process of grouping in secondary associations based on wider and civil loyalties. In this way, representative politics opens up a series of adaptive possibilities for the social structures, and the democratic political institutions largely determine the pattern of

[98] For a general discussion of social change in India, see for example, M. N. Srinivas, *Social Change in Modern India* (Berkeley and Los Angeles: University of California Press, 1966), esp. chaps. 1–4.

[99] For a case study explicating this point, see John G. Leonard, "Politics and Social Change in South India: A Study of the Andhra Movement," *Journal of Commonwealth Political Studies* 5, no. 1 (March 1967): pp. 60–77.

[100] For a discussion of this trend, see L. I. and S. H. Rudolph, *The Modernity of Tradition*, part I; F. G. Bailey, *Politics and Social Change, Orissa in 1959* (Berkeley: University of California Press, 1963), esp. pp. 127–134; and C. Von Furer-Haimendorf, "Caste and Politics in South Asia," in *Politics and Society in India*, ed. C. H. Philips (New York: Praeger, 1962), pp. 52–70. The other relevant works have been cited previously.

the realization of those possibilities. As long as the system remains open and political support can be used as a relatively liquid exchange-resource for the realization of the interests of the newly formed secondary associations, more and more people become convinced of the potential payoff of the newly extended loyalties. Given this possibility, the utilization of such resource generates its own momentum in favor of institutionalization of the new groups and their relation with other groups. Two decades of democratic experience in India has strengthened this trend and has given a new political confidence to the actors involved in such processes.

Forms are often deceptive in the realm of politics. They are all the more so in the transitional politics of the developing areas. Thus, what look like primordial groups may actually be mobilizational agencies seeking a transitional resource in apparently irrational symbols. As in the case of the caste associations, they use traditional symbols, but in fact they perform a crucially needed representational function forging a linkage between the remote centers of power and the immediate peripheries of existence of the newly politicized masses.[101]

The transformational effect of politics is clearly evident in the sphere of language rivalry. As we have seen in our study, language diversity has always been a feature of India. But language consciousness articulated in political terms is relatively recent. Social mobilization is responsible in part for this growth. But it does not explain the differential pattern of political mobilization of the language communities even when they operate in the context of similar social development. The major Hindi states, for example, are fairly comparable in terms of the usually suggested indexes of social mobilization. But the intensity of the Hindi movement that one finds in Uttar Pradesh, for example, has no parallel in any other part of what is called the *Hindi sansar*, the Hindi community. Again, the question remains why

[101] See, for example, Lloyd I. Rudolph, "The Modernity of Tradition: The Democratic Incarnation of Caste," in *American Political Science Review* 59, no. 4 (December 1965): 975–989; and Andre Beteille, *Caste, Class and Power* (Berkeley and Los Angeles: University of California Press, 1966).

the very definition of Hindi interest has varied so widely during the course of the Hindi movement. We have seen that the majority in the Hindi movement has not only defended the interest of Hindi but also created a new form of Hindi and popularized it as the only legitimate form. They have not behaved as traditional actors defending a given primordial cause; they have, in fact, formulated the cause, defined it, and gained legitimation for it in the Hindi area, and have sought to establish Hindi as the official language for the entire nation. It is worth noting that the cause of Hindi has been taken up by a large number of leaders and intellectuals from outside the Hindi areas. In fact, without their crucial support, Hindi could never have attained the political status that it has so far gained.

As in the case of Hindi, so the interest of the non-Hindi language communities cannot be understood simply by looking at the linguistic landscape of India. It is often said that the South represents the most intense opposition to Hindi. But the question remains, why in the South this opposition has varied from intense hostility in Madras to almost invisible resentment in Kerala.

These and other questions indicate the complexity of the political motivation that underlies the mobilization of language groups to gain clearly political objectives. In this sense, language functions more as a political role-sign for mobilization than as a symbol of primordial loyalty.[102] Hence, neither the political role nor the political demands of the language communities can be derived from the natural properties of the structure of linguistic divisions in a country like India. Linguistic cleavage is politically generated cleavage, and the kind of conflict and the outcome of the conflict generated by these cleavages can be understood only in the context of the use of language loyalty as a valuable resource by the modernized political strata in these communities.

The pattern in which this resource is used is largely determined by the political expectations of those who use it. These

[102] This is somewhat similar to the treatment of race as a role-sign. See Michael Banton, "Race as a Social Category," in *Race* 8, no. 1 (July 1966): 7–8.

expectations have been shaped by the calculation of possibility that is congruent with the normative and the institutional structure of modern Indian politics. The language associations of modern India grew up as a part of the institutional representation of modern political consciousness. In their initial period of growth these associations came to realize the functional efficiency of institutionalized protest and promotion. This knowledge was facilitated by the fact that the political leaders, acting through these associations, were not merely organizing for protest; they were also engaged in their constructive role of literary and linguistic modernization. Language, for them, provided a way of binding people drawn from narrower group loyalties into wider regional frameworks, which sometimes even transcended regional and communal boundaries. It was, therefore, a way of extending loyalty to wider networks.

But, more than that, language politics offered a way to diversify the structure of the political movements through autonomous, modernized, interest associations. Like trade unions and peasant associations, these associations operated as centers for recruitment of new participants and year-round organizational activities during the national movement. After independence, language associations found it profitable to continue and develop their organizational gain. Because of their special situation, the Hindi organizations found greater opportunities. But with the increasingly wider recognition of all the major regional languages, the distribution of opportunities has also favored the development of other associations. It is because of these associations that language planning in India was not completely concentrated under bureaucratic authority. To be sure, the administrative structures have utilized the services of these associations, but they were also considerably influenced by these associations.

But the more spectacular success of these associations has been achieved in their attempts to influence the legislative structures through the Congress party as long as the latter enjoyed overwhelming dominance, and later through other parties as well. By influencing these parties they succeeded in exerting significant pressures on the policy-making process through both the legislative and the executive channels.

In the process of using their influence these associations were impressed by the need to form coalitions. The Congress party is itself a flexible coalition of various factions. No single faction can assure any association or any cause a complete victory. The competitive system within the Congress party, and the balance of factions, thus compel the advocates of any particular cause to seek adjustment and compromise. Thus, the Hindi leaders working through Congress find it hard to display total hostility to the non-Hindi leaders. This compulsion to compromise stands in a sharp contrast to the consistent Hindi extremism that has been found to be permissible in the smaller political parties which operate with a regional base of support.[103] At times the necessity of the leaders to compromise may become embarrassing for their careers. In 1964, at the very height of the Hindi leaders' campaign against English, they themselves had to back down from an extreme stand, even in a state like Uttar Pradesh. On this occasion the Congress leaders in Uttar Pradesh, following the directive of the national organization, introduced a bill in the legislature seeking to provide for the continued use of English in the transaction of legislative business. Many newspapers in Uttar Pradesh condemned this bill as a betrayal of Hindi. But the leading Hindi associations issued only mild statements of protest or mild threats of agitation. On the other hand, the Jana Sangh and the SSP violently opposed this bill and attacked both the Uttar Pradesh Congress and language association leaders as puppets of the Union government.[104] But the leaders of the

[103] Duverger indicates how it becomes easier for a small party, having a majority in certain limited areas of a country, to become autonomist or secessionist. See M. Duverger, *Political Parties* (London: Methuen, 1954), p. 294.

[104] The bill concerned was the Uttar Pradesh Language (Transaction of Business in Legislature) bill of 1964. See *National Herald*, August 20, 1964. On this occasion both the Nagari Pracharani Sabha and the Hindi Sahitya Sammelan were under heavy fire. See, for example, *Aj*, August 22, 1964 (in Hindi). The nature of the extreme opposition to English organized by the non-Congress critics can be estimated with reference to the description of

major Hindi associations could not pursue such an extreme course because of their relations with the Congress party and the Union government.

In Madras most of the leaders of the DMK were once associated with the demand for a homeland for the Dravidians. But as soon as they discovered that they too were capable of winning the elections and capturing the political authority of the state, they gave up their secessionist associations. The willingness of the DMK to adapt to the institutional demands of representative democracy, and its cooperation with the central authority, show that the transition from an agitational mode of politics to normal forms of politics is not difficult. It was due in a large measure to the language agitations that the DMK succeeded in gaining support from wider sections of the people.[105] The ability of the DMK to adapt itself to the new role also means a simultaneous linkage of these people to the general political system.

The important contribution of language politics in general, and of the language associations in particular, has been the initiation of large numbers of people in organizational modes of participation. Attempts to absorb the new recruits into structured associations have been successful. They have been trained to love their regional community, but in the process of working for their demands, they have been increasingly socialized into the values of the wider political community. This aspect is undoubtedly prominent in the language politics operating on the national level, though it may be less apparent in the strictly regional lin-

English used during this week. One article referred to English as a language related to a literature which describes "only suicide, murder and promiscuity." Such a language, it was said, obviously "defiles" Hindi spoken in the "sacred land of Ganges." See *Aj*, August 24, 1964 (in Hindi). As for the attitude of the major language associations, see for example, L. K. Verma, ed., *Hindi Andolan* (Allahabad: Hindi Sahitya Sammelan, 1964), part 4 (in Hindi).

105 From an anti-Brahmin movement the DMK gradually extended its role to the advocacy of Tamil regionalism, and later it attempted to relate the Tamil cause to the wider national cause. For the development of the DMK's attitudes, see for example, Robert L. Hardgrave, Jr., "The D.M.K. and the Politics of Tamil Nationalism," *Pacific Affairs* 37, no. 4 (Winter 1964–65): 336–411.

guistic movements.[106] One important lesson the participants in language politics ultimately learn is that given the nature of the language situation in India, no single language community can overwhelm all the rest. The success of any demand concerning national language invariably requires coalition and compromise. Often these are arrived at through conflict, but none of these conflicts have proved to be threats to the national political community as a whole.[107] These conflicts, more often than not, have proved to be the schools of bargaining and negotiation. Very often they lead to a convergence of interests, which could not have been possible without the mediating conflicts. Often, as well, in the process of mediation, the definition of the interests undergo modifications. Perhaps the very nature of language politics permits a special degree of flexibility. Unlike socioeconomic interests, the cultural and linguistic interests admit of greater subjective definition and, therefore, a greater possibility of political manipulation and negotiation, especially in a situation of plural groups where the very nature of segmentation imposes a limit on the possible dominance of a group.

On the basis of the above contributions one can appreciate the relation of language politics to the problems of political development in India.[108] We have seen how language politics has given a new meaning to the political community in India. It has indicated that a viable political community can be built in India on

[106] Though it is not necessarily so, some of these movements are integrally related with wider nationalism. See for example, Robert W. Stern, "Maharashtrian Linguistic Provincialism and Indian Nationalism," *Pacific Affairs* 37, no. 1 (Spring 1964): 37–49.

[107] Various aspects of this point have been discussed in, for example, Richard D. Lambert, "Some Consequences of Segmentation in India," in *Economic Development and Cultural Change* 12, no. 4 (July 1964), esp. pp. 418–419. See also David H. Bailey, "The Pedagogy of Democracy: Coercive Public Protest in India," *American Political Science Review* 51, no. 3 (September 1962): 663 ff.; and Myron Weiner, *The Politics of Scarcity*, esp. pp. 207 ff.

[108] It may be pertinent to remember that the basic categories used here follow the definitions suggested earlier. These definitions have been abstracted from, among others, the theoretical works of Karl Deutsch, David Easton, Samuel Huntington, and H. Eckstein. Their relevant works have been cited earlier.

the basis of the recognition of the separate yet related language communities. The process of asserting distinct linguistic pride has at the same time been related to a system of coordinated community based on the convergence of interests rather than on amalgamative integration. Meanwhile, the interaction of such interests has given rise to a developing structure of organizational representation which has created new institutional settings that strengthen the pluralistic decision-system. Both in respect of building the national community and furthering the representational institutions, language politics in general, and the language associations in particular, have provided crucial support. How much of this support has been consciously intended and how much of it is due to the unintended consequences of their actions are, for our purpose, unimportant questions. The more important point is that language politics has proved to be one of the most important positive democratic channels for pursuing political integration as well as political development.

# *Appendix*

THE OFFICIAL LANGUAGES (AMENDMENT)
ACT, 1967
No. 1 of 1968

[*8th January*, 1968]

An Act to amend the Official Languages Act, 1963.

Be it enacted by Parliament in the Eighteenth Year of the Republic of India as follows:—

1. This Act may be called the Official Languages (Amendment) Act, 1967.

2. For section 3 of the Official Languages Act, 1963 (hereinafter referred to as the principal Act), the following section shall be substituted, namely:—

"3. (*1*) Notwithstanding the expiration of the period of fifteen years from the commencement of the Constitution, the English language may, as from the appointed day, continue to be used, in addition to Hindi,—

(*a*) for all the official purposes of the Union for which it was being used immediately before that day; and

(*b*) for the transaction of business in Parliament:

Provided that the English language shall be used for purposes of communication between the Union and a State which has not adopted Hindi as its official language:

Provided further that where Hindi is used for purposes of communication between one State which has adopted Hindi as its official language and another State which has not adopted Hindi as its official language, such communication in Hindi shall be accompanied by a translation of the same in the English language:

Provided also that nothing in this sub-section shall be construed as preventing a State which has not adopted Hindi as its official language from using Hindi for purposes of communication with the Union or with a State which has adopted Hindi as its official language, or by agreement with any other State, and in such a case, it shall not be obligatory to use the English language for purposes of communication with that State.

(2) Notwithstanding anything contained in sub-section (*1*), where Hindi or the English language is used for purposes of communication—

(*i*) between one Ministry or Department or office of the Central Government and another;

(*ii*) between one Ministry or Department or office of the Central Government or by any office of such corporation or controlled by the Central Government of any office thereof;

(*iii*) between any corporation or company owned or controlled by the Central Government or any office thereof and another, a translation of such communication in the English language or, as the case may be, in Hindi shall also be provided till such date as the staff of the concerned Ministry, Department, office or corporation or company aforesaid have acquired a working knowledge of Hindi.

(3) Notwithstanding anything contained in sub-section (*1*), both Hindi and the English language shall be used for—

(*i*) resolutions, general orders, rules, notifications, administrative or other reports or press communiques issued or made by the Central Government or by a Ministry, Department or office thereof or by a corporation or company owned or controlled by the Central Government or by any office of such corporation or company;

(*ii*) administrative and other reports and official papers laid before a House or the Houses of Parliament;

(*iii*) contracts and agreements executed, and licences, permits, notices and forms of tender issued, by or on behalf of the Central Government or any Ministry, Department or office thereof or by a corporation or company owned or controlled by the Central Government or by any office of such corporation or company.

(*4*) Without prejudice to the provisions of sub-section (*1*) or sub-section (*2*) or sub-section (*3*), the Central Government may, by rules made under section 8, provide for the language or languages to be used for the official purpose of the Union, including the working of any Ministry, Department, section or office, and in making such rules, due consideration shall be given to the quick and efficient disposal of the official business and the interests of the general public and in particular, the rules so made shall ensure that persons serving in connection with the affairs of the Union and having proficiency either in Hindi or in the English language may function effectively and that they are not placed at a disadvantage on the ground that they do not have proficiency in both the languages.

(*5*) The provisions of clause (*a*) of sub-section (*1*), and the provisions of sub-section (*2*), sub-section (*3*) and sub-section (*4*) shall remain in force until resolutions for the discontinuance of the use of the English language for the purposes mentioned therein have been passed by the Legislatures of all the States which have not adopted Hindi as their official language and until after considering the resolutions aforesaid, a resolution for such discontinuance has been passed by each House of Parliament."

3. To sub-section (*4*) of section 4 of the principal Act, the following proviso shall be added, namely:—

"Provided that the directions so issued shall not be inconsistent with the provisions of section 3."

# Selected Bibliography

## DOCUMENTS

India, Government
  *Census of India, 1961.* Vol. 1.
  *Census of India.* Paper No. 1 of 1954.
  *Census of India.* Paper No. 1 of 1962.
  Commissioner for Linguistic Minorities. *Reports.* 1959–1963.
  Committee of Parliament on Official Language. *Report.* 1958.
  *Constituent Assembly Debates.* Vols. 1–12. 1946–1950.
  *Constitution of India* (as modified up to 1965).
  *Directory of Educational, Scientific, Literary and Cultural Organizations in India.* 1948.
  Education Commission. *Report, 1964–1966: Education and National Development.*
  *India, a Reference Manual.* 1967.
  Ministry of Education:
    *Annual Reports*: 1962–1968.
    Committee on Emotional Integration. *Report.* 1962.
    *Educational Activities of the Government of India.* 1963.
    *Education in India.* 1961–1962. Vol. 1.
    *Kendriya Hindi Nirdeshalaya ki Barshik Report.* 1969 (in Hindi).
    *Programme for the Development and Propagation of Hindi.* 1960.
    *Study of English in India*: Report of a Study Group Appointed by the Ministry of Education. 1967.
  Ministry of Home Affairs:
    *Annual Reports*: 1962–1968.
  Ministry of Information and Broadcasting:
    *Press in India, 1967.* Eleventh Annual Report. Parts 1 and 2.
    *Radio and Television*: Report of the Committee on Broadcasting and Information Media. 1966.
  Official Language Commission. *Report.* 1956.
  Punjab Boundary Commission. *Report.* 1966.

Sanskrit Commission. *Report.* 1958.
Secondary Education Commission. *Report.* 1953.
*Selections from Educational Records of the Government of India.*
    Vol. 1 (1960); vol. 2 (1963).
States Reorganization Commission. *Report.* 1955.
University Education Commission. *Report.* Vol. 1, 1949.
India, State Governments
Gujarat. *Report of the Official Languages Committee.* 1960.
Uttar Pradesh. *Report of the Uttar Pradesh Language Committee.* 1962.
Uttar Pradesh. *Uttar Pradesh me Hindi.* 1959 (in Hindi).
Uttar Pradesh. *White Paper on Language Policy.* 1961.
India, University Grants Commission
*Medium of Instruction: Report.* 1961.
*Report on Standards of University Education.* 1965.
*Report of the English Review Committee.* 1965.
*Report of Seminar on National Integration.* 1961.
National Council of Educational Research and Training
*Indian Yearbook of Education.* 1961, 1964.
*Recommendations on Secondary Education.* 1966.
Voluntary Associations: Reports
Association for the Advancement of the National Languages of India.
    *Modern India Rejects Hindi* (Report) 1958.
*Bihar Rashtrabhasha Parishad ka Barshik Karyabibaran.* 1960 (in Hindi).
Bihar Rashtrabhasha Parishad. *Rashtrabhasha Hindi: Samasyaen Aur
    Samadhan.* 1962 (in Hindi).
Hindi Sahitya Sammelan. *Barshik Bibaran.* 1950–1967 (in Hindi).
Jamia Millia Islamia. *Report.* 1954–1955.
Nagari Pracharani Sabha. *Barshik Bibaran.* 1950–1967 (in Hindi).

SECONDARY SOURCES

Group Process: General
Almond, Gabriel A., and Coleman, James S. *The Politics of The Develop-
    ing Areas.* Princeton, N.J.: Princeton University Press, 1960.
Almond, Gabriel A., and Powell, Bingham G. *Comparative Politics, A
    Developmental Approach.* Boston: Little, Brown, 1966.
Almond, Gabriel A., and Verba, Sidney. *The Civic Culture.* Princeton,
    N.J.: Princeton University Press, 1963.
Banton, Michael, ed. *Political Systems and the Distribution of Power.*
    New York: Praeger, 1965.
Bendix, Reinhardt. *Nation-Building and Citizenship.* New York: Wiley,
    1964.
Bentley, Arthur F. *The Process of Government.* Evanston, Ill.: Principia
    Press, 1949. First published in 1908.
Charlesworth, James G. *Contemporary Political Analysis.* New York:
    Free Press, 1967.
Coser, Lewis. *The Functions of Social Conflict.* New York: Free Press,
    1964.
Dahl, Robert A. *Who Governs?* New Haven: Yale University Press, 1961.

Dahrendorf, Ralf. *Class and Class Conflict in Industrial Society*. Stanford: Stanford University Press, 1965.

Deutsch, Karl W. *The Nerves of Government*. New York: Free Press, 1966.

Easton, David. *A Framework for Political Analysis*. Englewood Cliffs, N.J.: Prentice-Hall, 1965.

———. *The Political System*. New York: Knopf, 1953.

———. *A Systems Analysis of Political Life*. New York: Wiley, 1965.

———, ed. *Varieties of Political Theory*. Englewood Cliffs, N.J.: Prentice-Hall, 1966.

Eckstein, Harry. *Division and Cohesion in Democracy: A Study of Norway*. Princeton, N.J.: Princeton University Press, 1966.

———. *Pressure Group Politics*. Stanford: Stanford University Press, 1960.

Eckstein, Harry, and Apter, David E. *Comparative Politics*. Glencoe, Ill.: Free Press, 1963.

Ehrmann, Henry W., ed. *Interest Groups on Four Continents*. Pittsburgh: Pittsburgh University Press, 1964.

Eisenstadt, S. N. *Modernization: Protest and Change*. Englewood Cliffs, N.J.: Prentice-Hall, 1966.

Etzioni, Amitai, ed. *Complex Organizations*. New York: Holt, 1962.

———. *Modern Organizations*. Englewood Cliffs, N.J.: Prentice-Hall, 1964.

Finkle, Jason L., and Gable, Richard W., eds. *Political Development and Social Change*. New York: Wiley, 1966.

Gerth, H. H., and Mills, C. Wright. *From Max Weber*. New York: Oxford University Press, 1958.

Huntington, Samuel P. *Political Order in Changing Societies*. New Haven: Yale University Press, 1968.

Key, V. O. *Politics, Parties and Pressure Groups*. New York: Crowell, 1964.

La Palombara, Joseph. *Interest Groups in Italian Politics*. Princeton, N.J.: Princeton University Press, 1964.

Levy, Marion J. *Modernization and the Structure of Societies*. 2 vols. Princeton, N.J.: Princeton University Press, 1966.

Lipset, Seymour M. *Political Man*. New York: Doubleday, 1963.

———, and Rokkan, Stein. *Party Systems and Voter Alignments*. New York: Free Press, 1967.

Macridis, Roy C., and Brown, Bernard E. *Comparative Politics*. Homewood, Ill.: Dorsey, 1965.

Montgomery, J. D., and Siffin, W. J. *Approaches to Development, Politics Administration and Change*. New York: McGraw-Hill, 1966.

Myrdal, Gunnar. *Asian Drama*. Vols. 1 and 2. New York: Pantheon, 1968.

Narain, I. *State Politics in India*. Meerut: Meenakshi, 1967.

Nettl, J. P. *Political Mobilization*. New York: Basic Books, 1967.

Parsons, Talcott. *Structure and Process in Modern Societies*. Glencoe, Ill.: Free Press, 1960.

Pye, Lucian W. *Aspects of Political Development*. Boston: Little, Brown, 1966.

———, ed. *Communications and Political Development*. Princeton, N.J.: Princeton University Press, 1963.

Pye, Lucian W., and Verba, Sidney, eds. *Political Culture and Political*

*Development*. Princeton, N.J.: Princeton University Press, 1965.

Riggs, Fred W. *Administration in Developing Countries*. Boston: Houghton Mifflin, 1964.

Rudolph, Lloyd I. and Susanne H. *The Modernity of Tradition*. Chicago: University of Chicago Press, 1967.

Simmel, Georg. *Conflict and the Web of Group Affiliations*. New York: Free Press, 1964.

Truman, David B. *The Governmental Process*. New York: Knopf, 1964.

Weiner, Myron. *The Politics of Scarcity*. Chicago: University of Chicago Press, 1962.

——, ed. *State Politics in India*. Princeton, N.J.: Princeton University Press, 1968.

Wolin, Sheldon S. *Politics and Vision*. Boston: Little Brown, 1960.

Zeigler, Harmon. *Interest Groups in American Society*. Englewood Cliffs, N.J.: Prentice-Hall, 1964.

Language and National Development: General

Alisjahbana, Takdir S. *Indonesian Language and Literature: Two Essays*. New Haven: Yale University, South East Asia Studies, 1962.

Aucamp, A. J. *Bilingual Education and Nationalism with Special Reference to South Africa*. Pretoria: Van Schaik, 1926.

Bright, William, ed. *Sociolinguistics*. The Hague: Mouton, 1966.

Callard, Keith. *Pakistan*. New York: Macmillan, 1957.

Dakin, J., Tiffen, B., and Widdowson, H. G. *Language in Education*. London: Oxford University Press, 1968.

De Francis, John. *Nationalism and Language Reform in China*. Princeton: Princeton University Press, 1950.

Deutsch, Karl W. *Nationalism and Social Communication*. New York: Wiley, 1966.

Deutsch, Karl W., and Foltz, W. J., eds. *Nation-Building*. New York: Atherton Press, 1963.

Dominian, L. *The Frontiers of Language and Nationality in Europe*. New York: Holt, 1917.

Emerson, Rupert. *From Empire to Nation*. Cambridge, Mass.: Harvard University Press, 1960.

Farmer, B. H. *Ceylon, A Divided Nation*. London: Oxford University Press, 1963.

Ferguson, Charles A., and Gumperz, John J. *Linguistic Diversity in South Asia*. Bloomington: International Journal of American Linguistics, 1960.

Fishman, Joshua A., ed. *Readings in the Sociology of Language*. The Hague: Mouton, 1968.

Fishman, Joshua A., Ferguson, Charles A., and Das Gupta, Jyotirindra, eds. *Language Problems of Developing Nations*. New York: Wiley, 1968.

Geertz, Clifford, ed. *Old Societies and New States*. Glencoe: Free Press, 1963.

Gumperz, John J., and Hymes, Dell H., eds. *The Ethnography of Communication*. Washington, D.C.: American Anthropological Association, 1964.

Harrison, Selig S., ed. *The Most Dangerous Decades: An Introduction to the Comparative Study of Language Policy in Multi-Lingual States.* New York: Language and Communication Research Center, Columbia University, 1957.

Haugen, Einar. *Language Conflict and Language Planning.* Cambridge, Mass.: Harvard University Press, 1966.

Hayes, Carlton J. H. *Essays on Nationalism.* New York: Macmillan, 1926.

Heyd, Uriel. *Language Reform in Modern Turkey.* Jerusalem: Israel Oriental Society, 1954.

Hymes, Dell H. *Language in Culture and Society.* New York: Harper, 1964.

Jespersen, Otto. *Mankind, Nation and Individual from a Linguistic Point of View.* Bloomington: Indiana University Press, 1964.

Kann, R. A. *The Multinational Empire.* 2 vols. New York: Octagon Books, 1964.

Kohn, Hans. *The Idea of Nationalism.* New York: Macmillan, 1944.

Kurman, G. *The Development of Written Estonian.* The Hague: Mouton, 1968.

Le Page, R. B. *The National Language Question.* London: Oxford University Press, 1964.

Noss, R. *Higher Education and Development in South-East Asia.* Vol. 3, no. 2, Language Policy. Paris: UNESCO, 1967.

Rice, F. A., ed. *Study of the Role of Second Languages in Asia, Africa and Latin America.* Washington, D.C.: Center for Applied Linguistics, 1962.

*Royal Commission on Bilingualism and Biculturalism, A Preliminary Report* (Canada). Ottawa: Queen's Printer, 1965.

Rundle, S. *Language as a Social and Political Factor in Europe.* London: Faber, 1946.

Sayeed, Khalid B. *The Political System of Pakistan.* Boston: Houghton Mifflin, 1967.

Shafer, Boyd C. *Nationalism: Myth and Reality.* New York: Harcourt, Brace, 1955.

Silvert, Kalman H., ed. *Expectant Peoples.* New York: Random House, 1963.

Spencer, J., ed. *Language in Africa.* Cambridge: Cambridge University Press, 1963.

Stalin, J. V. *Marxism and Linguistics.* New York: International Publishers, 1951.

———. *Marxism and the National Question.* New York: International Publishers, 1942.

Tauli, Valter. *Introduction to a Theory of Language Planning.* Uppsala: Acta Universitatis Upsaliensis, 1968.

UNESCO. *The Use of Vernacular Languages in Education.* Paris: UNESCO, 1953.

Weinrich, U. *Languages in Contact.* New York: Linguistic Circle, 1953.

Woolner, A. C. *Languages in History and Politics.* London: Oxford University Press, 1938.

Wriggins, W. H. *Ceylon: Dilemmas of a New Nation.* Princeton: Princeton University Press, 1960.

Znaniecki, Florian, *Modern Nationalities: A Sociological Study.* Urbana, Ill.: University of Illinois Press, 1952.
Language Politics: India
Ahmad, Aziz. *Studies in Islamic Culture in the Indian Environment.* London: Oxford University Press, 1964.
Ahmad, Z. A., ed. *National Language for India.* Allahabad: Kitabistan, 1941.
Airan, J. W., et al., eds. *Climbing A Wall of Glass.* Bombay: Manaktalas, 1965.
Aiyar, S. P., ed. *The Politics of Mass Violence in India.* Bombay: Manaktals, 1967.
Asrani, U. A. *What Shall We Do About English?* Ahmedabad: Navajivan, 1964.
Awasthy, G. C. *Broadcasting in India.* Bombay: Allied Publishers, 1965.
Basu, D. D. *Commentary on the Constitution of India.* 5th ed. rev. 5 vols. Calcutta: S. C. Sarkar, 1964.
———. *An Introduction to the Constitution of India.* 3d ed. Calcutta: S. C. Sarkar, 1964.
Bhave, Vinoba. *Language Problem.* Benaras: Sarva Seva Sangh, 1965.
Bondurant, Joan V. *Regionalism Versus Provincialism: A Study in Problems of Indian National Unity.* Berkeley: Indian Press Digests, 1958.
Chatterjee, Suniti K. *Indo-Aryan and Hindi.* Calcutta: Firma K. L. Mukhopadhyay, 1960.
———. *Languages and the Linguistic Problem.* London: Oxford University Press, 1945.
———. *Languages and Literatures of Modern India.* Calcutta: Bengal Publishers, 1963.
Chaudhuri, Nirad C. *The Autobiography of an Unknown Indian.* Berkeley and Los Angeles: University of California Press, 1968.
Desai, M. P. *The Hindi Prachar Movement.* Ahmedabad: Navajivan, 1957.
———. *Our Language Problem.* Ahmedabad: Navajivan, 1956.
———. *The Problem of English.* Ahmedabad: Navajivan, 1964.
Erdman, H. L. *The Swatantra Party and Indian Conservatism.* Cambridge: Cambridge University Press, 1967.
Faruqi, Z. H. *The Deoband School and the Demand for Pakistan.* Bombay: Asia Publishing House, 1963.
Gandhi, M. K. *Thoughts on National Language.* Ahmedabad: Navajivan, 1956.
Gokak, V. K. *English in India.* Bombay: Asia Publishing House, 1964.
Gopal, Madan. *This Hindi and Dev Nagri.* Delhi: Metropolitan Book, 1953.
Gopal, Ram. *Indian Muslims.* Bombay: Asia Publishing House, 1959.
———. *Linguistic Affairs of India.* Bombay: Asia Publishing House, 1966.
———. *Swatantrata-Purva Hindi Ke Sangharsh Ka Itihas.* Prayag: Hindi Sahitya Sammelan, Saka 1886 (in Hindi).
Gorekar, N. S. *Glimpses of Urdu Literature.* Bombay: Jaico, 1961. (See R. Zakaria's foreword.)

Govind Das, Seth. *Atma-Nirikshan.* 4 vols. Delhi: Bharatiya Biswa Prakashan, 1958. Vol. III (in Hindi).

Hardgrave, Robert L., Jr. *The Dravidian Movement.* Bombay: Popular
Prakashan, 1965.

Harrison, Selig S. *India: The Most Dangerous Decades.* Madras: Oxford
University Press, 1960.

Heimsath, Charles H. *Indian Nationalism and Hindu Social Reform.*
Princeton: Princeton University Press, 1964.

*Hirak Jayanti Granth.* Benaras: Nagari Pracharani Sabha, Sambat 2011
(in Hindi).

Husain, S. A. *The Destiny of Indian Muslims.* Bombay: Asia Publishing
House, 1965.

Husain, Y., ed. *Selected Documents from the Aligarh Archives.* Bombay:
Asia Publishing House, 1967.

Iqbal, A., ed. *Select Writings and Speeches of Maulana Mohamed Ali.*
Lahore: Ashraf, 1963. Vol. 1 (for a discussion of "the Lingua franca
of India").

Kabir, Humayun. *Muslim Politics (1906–1942).* Calcutta: Gupta, Rahman,
Gupta, 1943.

Kanungo, G. B. *The Language Controversy in Indian Education.* Chicago: Comparative Education Center, University of Chicago, 1961.

Kaul, J. M. *Problems of National Integration.* New Delhi: People's Publishing House, 1963.

Kochanek, Stanley A. *The Congress Party of India.* Princeton, N.J.:
Princeton University Press, 1968.

Kumaramangalam, S. M. *India's Language Crisis.* Madras: New Century
Book House, 1965.

Majumdar, A. K. *Problem of Hindi.* Bombay: Bharatiya Vidya Bhavan,
1965.

Majumdar, R. C. *History of Freedom Movement in India.* Calcutta:
Firma K. L. Mukhopadhyay. Vols. 1–3, 1961–1963.

Malik, H. *Moslem Nationalism in India and Pakistan.* Washington, D.C.:
Public Affairs Press, 1963.

Malvia, K. B. *Hindi: The National Language.* New Delhi: Malvia, 1958.

McCully, Bruce T. *English Education and the Origins of Indian Nationalism.* New York: Columbia University Press, 1940.

Misra, B. B. *The Indian Middle Classes.* London: Oxford University
Press, 1961.

Mukherjee, H. and U. *The Growth of Nationalism in India (1857–1905).*
Calcutta: Firma K. L. Mukhopadhyay, 1957.

Mujeeb, M. *Indian Muslims.* London: Allen & Unwin, 1967.

Narasimhan, V. K., et al. *The Languages of India.* Madras: Our India
Directories, 1958.

Narula, S. S. *Scientific History of the Hindi Language.* New Delhi: Hindi
Academy, 1955.

Natarajan, S. *A Century of Social Reform in India.* Bombay: Asia Publishing House, 1962.

Nayar, B. R. *Minority Politics in the Punjab*. Princeton, N.J.: Princeton University Press, 1966.

Nehru, Jawaharlal. *Jawaharlal Nehru's Speeches*. Delhi: Publications Division, Government of India. Vol. 4, 1964.

———. *The Unity of India*. London: Lindsay Drummond, 1941.

Nurullah, S., and Naik, J. P. *A Student's History of Education in India, 1800–1965*. Bombay: Macmillan, 1964.

Pandeya, C. B. *Sasan Me Nagari*. Allahabad: Hindi Sahitya Sammelan, 1948 (in Hindi).

Prasad, R. *India Divided*. Bombay: Hind Kitab, 1947.

Rai, Satya M. *Partition of the Punjab*. Bombay: Asia Publishing House, 1965.

Rajagopalachari, C. *The Question of English*. Madras: Bharathan Publications, 1962. A collection of most of his important writings on language politics.

*Rajat Jayanti Granth*. Bombay: Hindi Vidyapith, 1963 (in Hindi).

*Rajat Jayanti Granth*. Wardha: Rastrabhasha Prachar Samiti, 1962 (in Hindi).

Ramanathan, G. *Educational Planning and National Integration*. Bombay: Asia Publishing House, 1965.

Ramanujam, K. S. *The Big Change*. Madras: Higginbothams, 1967.

Ray, P. S. *Language Standardization*. The Hague: Mouton, 1963.

Richey, J. A., ed. *Selections From Educational Records*. Part 2, 1840–1859. New Delhi: National Archives, 1965.

Satyanarayana, M., et al. *Affinity of Indian Languages*. Delhi: Publications Division, Government of India, 1959.

Saxena, R. B. *A History of Urdu Literature*. Allahabad: R. N. Lal, 1927.

Seal, A. *The Emergence of Indian Nationalism*. Cambridge: Cambridge University Press, 1968.

Shah, A. B., ed. *The Great Debate*. Bombay: Lalvani, 1968.

Sharma, D. N. *Rashtrabhasa Hindi Samasyae aur Samadhan*. Delhi: Rajkamal, 1965 (in Hindi).

Sharma, R. B. *Bhasha Aur Samaj*. New Delhi: People's Publishing House, 1961 (in Hindi).

Sharp, H. *Selections from Educational Records*. Part 1, 1781–1839. New Delhi: National Archives, 1965.

Shastri, B. B. *Kashi Nagari Pracharani Sabha ka Ardhashatabdi-Itihas*. Benaras: Nagari Pracharani Sabha, Sambat 2000 (in Hindi).

Shastri, Lal Bahadur, et al. *Rajarshi Abhinandan Granth*. Delhi: Delhi Pradeshik Hindi Sahitya Sammelan, n.d. (in Hindi). A volume presented in honor of P. D. Tandon.

Shukla, R. S. *Lingua Franca for Hindustan and the Hindustani Movement*. Lucknow. Oudh Publishing House, 1947.

Singh, K. *A History of the Sikhs*. 2 vols. Princeton, N.J.: Princeton University Press, 1966. Vol. 2.

Thirtha, N. B. *National Integration*. Delhi: University Publishers, 1964.

Tinker, Hugh. *India and Pakistan*. New York: Praeger, 1962.

Unnithan, T. K. N., et al., eds. *Towards a Sociology of Culture in India*.

New Delhi: Prentice-Hall of India, 1965.

Wadia, A. R. *The Future of English in India*. Bombay: Asia Publishing House, 1954.

Yadav, R. K. *The Indian Language Problem*. Delhi: National Publishing House, 1966.

Indian Newspapers

*Aj* (Benaras) (in Hindi).

*Hindu* (Madras).

*Hindu Weekly Review* (Madras).

*Hindustan Standard Overseas Weekly* (Calcutta).

*Hindustan Times* (New Delhi).

*Leader* (Allahabad).

*National Herald* (Lucknow).

*Statesman* (Calcutta).

*Statesman Weekly* (Calcutta).

*Times of India* (Bombay).

Indian Periodicals

*Bhasha* (New Delhi) (in Hindi).

*Economic and Political Weekly* (Bombay) (formerly *Economic Weekly*).

*Link* (New Delhi).

*Madhyam* (Allahabad) (in Hindi).

*Mainstream* (New Delhi).

*Mankind* (New Delhi).

*Modern Review* (Calcutta).

*New Age* (New Delhi).

*Organiser* (New Delhi).

*Seminar* (New Delhi).

*Swarajya* (Madras).

Other Journals: General

*American Journal of Sociology*.

*American Political Science Review*.

*Asian Survey*.

*British Journal of Sociology*.

*Daedalus*.

*Indian Journal of Political Science*.

*Journal of Asian Studies*.

*Journal of Commonwealth Political Studies*.

*Journal of Politics*.

*Journal of Social Issues*.

*Minerva*.

*Sociological Inquiry*.

*World Politics*.

Note: All of the journal articles used in the text have their full citations in the notes.

# Index

www.ingramcontent.com/pod-product-compliance
Lightning Source LLC
Chambersburg PA
CBHW031408270326
41929CB00010BA/1372